When
Families
Feud

When Families Feud

Understanding and Resolving Family Conflicts

IRA HEILVEIL, PH.D.

A PERIGEE BOOK

A Perigee Book
Published by The Berkley Publishing Group
A member of Penguin Putnam Inc.
375 Hudson Street
New York, NY 10014

Copyright © 1998 by Ira Heilveil, Ph.D.
Book design by Tiffany Kukec
Cover design by Joe Lanni
Cover art by Charles Björklund and Joe Lanni
Kennedy genograms from *Genograms in Family Assessment*
by Monica McGoldrick and Randy Gerson.
Copyright © 1985 by Monica McGoldrick and Randy Gerson.
Reprinted by permission of W. W. Norton & Company, Inc.

First edition: October 1998

Published simultaneously in Canada.

The Penguin Putnam Inc. World Wide Web site address is
http://www.penguinputnam.com

Library of Congress Cataloging-in-Publication Data

Heilveil, Ira.
    When families feud : understanding and resolving family conflicts
/ Ira Heilveil.
        p.   cm.
    Includes index.
    ISBN 0-399-52440-1
    1. Communication in the family.   2. Family—Psychological
aspects.   3. Interpersonal conflict.   4. Reconciliation.   I. Title.
HQ734.H467   1998
306.87—dc21   97-52661
                                                                     CIP

Printed in the United States of America

10   9   8   7   6   5   4   3   2   1

Contents

Acknowledgments   vii

Introduction   1

PART ONE

Why Family Feuds Erupt: Your Psychological Legacy   7

1   Unlocking the Mystery of Family Feuds   9
2   Too Close for Comfort   23
3   Three's a Crowd   43
4   Wounds That Time Won't Heal   77
5   Family Myths and Secrets   95
6   Great Expectations   127

PART TWO

From Feud to Reconciliation   153

7   How to Create a Genogram   157
8   From Blame to Responsibility   175
9   Forgiving the Family Tree   203
10   The Courage to Confront   225
11   Creating the Climate for Change   253
12   Acceptance and Letting Go   271

Index   285

Acknowledgments

LAURA GOLDEN BELLOTTI HAS BEEN AS CLOSE TO PERFECT AS AN EDITOR CAN BE. SHE MIXES ENCOURAGEMENT AND CRITICISM WITH THE acumen of a well-seasoned psychologist. I am also appreciative of my agents, Betsy Amster and Angela Miller; their tenacity and patience is the ultimate reason this book has made it to your hands. My friend Barbara Dalton-Taylor introduced me to Betsy, and she and her husband made their home available to me as a shelter from distraction. I thank them for their support and friendship.

The idea that we are products of repetitive patterns through the generations was fully developed by the family therapy pioneer Murray Bowen. Just as he predicted patterns of behavior repeat from one generation to the next, his ideas have already influenced generations of family therapists who came after him.

Other well-known names and people in the family therapy field have contributed to the ideas presented in this book. In particular, the work of Monica McGoldrick, Cloe Madanes, and Salvador Minuchin undergird the contents of this book. Terry Hargrave's work on forgiveness has been helpful to me as well. The late Carl Whitaker has been a model for me in my own work, and I am grateful to him for inspiring me and moving me so often. On a more personal level, I learned how to do family therapy in large part from Dr. Irv Borstein, director of the Los Angeles Family Institute. Along with Dr. Whitaker, Dr. Borstein's work has given me courage, as well as the technical know-how. He has taught me how to "confront with an arm around" my patients, and I thank him for that.

My clients and students have been my best teachers. One of those students, Martine Van Milder, took me aside after a class I taught at Harbor-UCLA Medical School one day, and asked me if I was interested in writing a book about families. Her question reminded me of the same question I had once asked a professor of mine whose work I admired when I was a graduate student. That professor responded to me humbly, saying that he really had nothing new to say, so why write a book? When I gave Martine the same answer, unlike me, she persisted. "It's not whether you say something new that matters. It's how well you put together what you know." I thank her for her encouragement; it was that response that reacquainted me with writing—my first love.

When I was growing up, my family rarely celebrated. My mother was superstitious, and she believed that celebrating tempted "the evil eye." My wife, on the other hand, believed in celebrating birthdays and holidays, and she brought these rituals to our family. Last Christmas, my sister, brother, mother, and father, along with my wife and children, sat around a beautifully decorated table for Christmas dinner. My mother, frail and suffering from a chronic illness and a serious fall she had taken the day before, sat contentedly, as did my father. My brother, whose troubled past cast a large shadow over much of our family history, sat next to his son.

Each of us at the table had our own memories, our own private pain, yet we shared much of the same history. We sat together with many miles traveled and many years between us. There were years in which one family member refused to speak with another. There were times it seemed as though the more miles that existed between us, the better. Yet each of us worked hard, slowly and in our own ways, to repair the damage that had been done in our earliest years. My siblings and I struggled to understand how our parents worked to overcome the legacy of their own childhoods. My parents accomplished what many of us cannot—they fought and they changed. As the now-grown children sat around the table, we were all deeply grateful and indebted to our parents for giving not only the best years of their lives, but nearly all the years of their lives, to their children. I learned in large part from my family how patience, combined with working hard to understand others' lives, can heal families.

After so many years of conflict, the most remarkable aspect of that Christmas dinner was the resounding peace. There was a contentment we all felt that the conflicts that tore us apart were no longer weighing us down or burdening us too heavily. And there was a gratitude that after all of it we remained together, still able to occasionally comfort and support one another, able to annoy each other and fight in a way that wasn't likely to tear us apart. As I did that night, I thank my parents for waiting around for their adult children to grow up, and for continuing their struggle to become better parents. They succeeded immensely.

There is no healing more profound than that provided by a nurturing family. My own family has given my life meaning and depth beyond words. They have been patient and supportive with me. My children, Benjamin and Lillian, are gifts that I struggle to be worthy of having received. They are magic. I love them deeply, I am proud of them, and I respect them.

My wife, Marsha McKeon, is my companion in every respect. She has been my mentor, my friend, my therapist, my editor, and the best clinical supervisor I could ever ask for. I was once told that a marriage works best when you decide anew every day whether or not you want to be married to your spouse. Every day I choose to be married, I find myself falling deeper in love. She has taught me more about love, commitment, and children than I ever imagined. Thank you, Marsha, for being my partner and my inspiration.

Introduction

As a young teenager, I lived on the thirteenth floor of a twenty-three-story apartment building in Brooklyn. Directly across a courtyard stood another building, a mirror image of the one that was my home. As I dreamily peered out through my windowpane, I faced what looked to me like a huge, concrete beehive, filled with mysterious people determinedly buzzing through their secret lives. From time to time, I would stare at the half-closed curtains and balconies, and think to myself with amazement that behind each window lived a family whose lives told a story. Hundreds of stories, filled with passion, anger or confusion, were just a stone's throw away. Some, I wondered, might be similar to mine, others a world apart. They were stories that I yearned to hear, but thought that I would never know.

This book is filled with stories undoubtedly like the ones from across the courtyard. They are real stories about real people whose families failed them, stories about grown children who could no longer bear talking to their siblings, or who remained so frightened of their parents' recrimination that they constructed lives completely separate from any reminders of their childhood. And they are also success stories, about turning family ties that were once binding into ties that are nurturing and fulfilling. They are stories about how one courageous family member, with the right tools, can transform her family from a cauldron of animosity into a safe harbor.

Whatever curiosity propelled me to want to know these stories as a teenager may have taken me down the road that eventually led to my becoming a family therapist. My interest in children began as an undergraduate in college, when I worked part-time in both a local preschool and elementary school. I found myself making deep connections with the children, many of whom had serious emotional problems. I became acutely aware of the pain in their lives—pain that caused some children to hide in corners, others to wantonly lash out at other children. Some couldn't stop playing, while others were afraid of the playground. Many of them were too frightened to sit still long enough to draw a picture. I could learn little about their families in my position, but the little I learned fueled my interest in psychology. They were innocents, I thought, victims of forces I couldn't yet understand.

When I began my formal training as a psychologist, the specialty of family therapy was less than two decades old. It was still working out its late adolescent struggle for an identity, and very few professionals identified themselves as family therapists. After graduate school, nine years since I had worked at that preschool, I began working full-time as a psychologist at a child guidance clinic. There, I spent many hours sitting on the floor of therapy rooms trying to decipher children's messages encoded in their play. I became frustrated with the painstaking progress that was continually undermined by families whose stability appeared threatened by their child's improvement. My one-hour-a-week attempt to create a safe and nurturing environment with a particular child was often countered or undone as soon as the child left my office and went back into the world of his or her family.

It became clear to me that for many children it was the child's family that held the keys to how well that child would cope with life's pressures. When the family worked well, the child often blossomed. When the family faltered, failing to provide either the attention, acceptance, or loving discipline so desperately needed, the child faltered.

As soon as a child leaves the safe world of her mother's uterus, she enters the world of her family. She must quickly learn to deal with the complexities and potential dangers of family life—a jealous sibling poking his finger (or pencil) into her abdomen, or a zealous father tossing her playfully (and frighteningly) toward the ceiling. Even her mother's degree of comfort and success in holding and nursing her is often determined by the support the mother receives from the rest of the family members. Even more important, in what may seem like a mysterious, intangible passing of an emotional torch from one generation to the next, each parent's ability to care for his children is laced with the deeply embedded memories of his own experiences with his mother and father. In that very important sense, every child is born not only into her immediate family, but also into the generations of family that came before.

Given the profound influence of the family on the children (and the adults) I was seeing, it seemed odd to focus so intensely on the individual child. It felt as though I was attempting to do something akin to heart surgery with only a heart in front of me, and little knowledge or awareness of how the vital organs worked together, or how one diseased organ might infect another.

Though at that time I had little formal training in family therapy, I began to see whole families together. I was well aware of the claims family therapists had been making that they offered a quicker, more lasting solution than traditional one-on-one approaches, but I knew well to take any claims of quick and easy solutions with skepticism. What I did discover when I began to do family therapy was a new world of hope. In my family therapy sessions, I began to feel as though I was finally playing cards with a full deck. Though I knew a child's history, it was a different thing to see it acted out in front of me. I could empathize with a child's suffering when I heard his father deride him or give him a threatening look to a much greater extent than if I had seen the child draw a picture of an angry father scolding a son. But I could also feel for the father, who could describe his pain and torment, and his struggles to harness his own anger when dealing with his children.

It seemed to me that if a family was powerful enough to do severe damage, it must also be powerful enough to do great good. Now, having seen scores of families in the last two decades, I'm more convinced than ever before that the most powerful kind of healing comes when people are able to compassionately confront the source of their conflicts. Sometimes it's a matter of simply getting the warring factions together in a room, facing each other for the first time in a neutral environment, that leads to the ability to get past rough spots in their lives.

At other times, family therapy becomes a more complex undertaking, a chess game in which strategic maneuvering is used by each person to gain his or her own sense of integrity, power or safety.

When fighting in a family turns into the chronic, deep divisions of a feud, everyone in the family suffers. The more coherently a family functions, the more likely each individual will come away from the family with a sense of integrity and wholeness. Likewise, schisms in the family become schisms within each individual. Silent wars with parents or siblings become unresolved internal struggles, conflicts that end up polluting future relationships.

When you do something to heal the family you are in, you are also helping to heal the families of the following generations, the families of your children and their children's children. In this sense, when you heal the wounds in your own family, you not only create a better life for yourself, but you end up doing your part in healing the world as well.

When I first began working with families, I wasn't aware of how prevalent family feuds were, how deeply ingrained they were in our society, and how destructive they could be. The longer I worked with families, the more clearly I came to understand how family feuds also reflect societal concerns.

Family feuds are to be found in the opening chapters of two of the most ubiquitous and influential religious documents of our time. In the story of the very first family in the Judeo-Christian Bible, Cain, the first child born to the first parents, murders his brother Abel in a classic case of extreme sibling rivalry. And the Bhagavad Gita, one of the central texts in Hinduism, opens with the indefatigable Arjuna, standing on the battlefield of Kurukshetra, poised to do battle against his own cousins and seeking the guidance of his blind charioteer Krishna (an incarnation of God). Arjuna, "his mind overwhelmed with grief," casts aside his bow and arrows and plaintively asks Krishna how he could possibly wage war against members of his own family.

Throughout history, countries were governed by monarchies of one fashion or another, the rulers typically assigned by virtue of their positions within their family. Such high stakes magnifies family discord, creating a dangerous mix of family schism with a lust for power. The fabric of history is no doubt indelibly colored with the bloodstained strands of family feuds.

Family feuds reverberate through all tiers of our culture. They are often the subject matter of addictive soap operas. And as the headlines of the tabloids will attest, few things sell more newspapers than the feuds of celebrity families, or the internal family wars of the British and other royalty.

Nearly all the people I know have in one way or another been affected by a feud in their families. If they aren't involved directly, they usually know someone who continuously has a problem with someone else that goes beyond everyday family conflict, or they know someone who has stopped talking to someone else. Many family members find themselves caught between two warring factions, having to do a careful dance of diplomacy in order not to alienate one or another family member.

Family feuds are as unique as the families who have them, yet there are patterns that link them together. I distinguish family feuds from family fights, because I believe they are two different things and are based on two distinct phenomena. I can point to many families whose members don't fight, yet there are feuds that divide them deeply. And more commonly, many healthy families fight, but most fights don't end up in feuds.

I believe the distinction between the two is primarily historical. Family feuds almost always seem to have their roots in a long, multigenerational history of patterns that repeat themselves, while fights are usually responses to current crises or conflicts. Because they are rooted so deeply in a long family history, feuds are often difficult to resolve. Family fights, on the other hand, often work themselves out with minimal effort.

As it goes in baseball, we humans struggle against the odds to leave home. Once we break free, we seek home again, wishing to arrive at a familiar place with the exuberance of having succeeded at leaving and having seen some of the world. Sometimes the home we seek is the familiar home we came from, and sometimes we seek to create a new home, one in which we strive to retain the good that came from our own upbringing while erasing the damage we suffered at the hands of imperfect parents. For many people, family feuds are desperate attempts to leave home and to break free of the influence of a family that hurt them.

One of the many paradoxes of human nature is that we are all comforted by familiarity, even when what's familiar is uncomfortable. Wayward Catholics, passionately disagreeing with the decrees of the Vatican, talk about feeling empty and alone without the rituals of Catholicism in their lives. Methodists, disturbed by notions of heaven and hell, go back to the church because the familiar hymns fill their souls in a way little else can. Orthodox Jews, troubled by the dogmatic and judgmental teachings of the rabbis, seek the familiar sounds of Hebrew chanting, even when they don't understand the words.

This book is about coming home again, to a familiar place, but a place irrevocably altered by time and experience. It's about creating a new, restructured family, one in which nurturance, support, and mutuality is possible. It's about learning what happened in your family that actually caused the feud, about learning how to see your family in a new light. It's about transcending the role of victim, and gaining a deeper understanding that will allow you to see, in one sense, all of your family members as victims of something larger than themselves. And it's about learning how to heal the wounds of a family that is deeply divided, for the sake not only of yourselves, but for the sake of your children and the generations to come. They are the ones who will suffer most, because they are the recipients of the unspoken, divisive patterns that are brought to them. Many of us choose to believe that our children will not see or be affected by the dust of our shattered families that we carefully sweep beneath the carpet. But, in fact, the home we leave them with is the home they will inherit.

Throughout this book you will read stories about families. They are true stories, although the names have been changed in order to respect their privacy and confidentiality. Most of the stories are about families with whom I have worked professionally, and others are stories based on interviews conducted for this book. In some cases, they are stories of families I saw many years ago, so I may have merged two families or even remembered a detail inaccurately. I trust that none of my errors change significantly the messages and lessons the family members have given me.

Why Family Feuds Erupt:
Your Psychological Legacy

Unlocking the Mystery of Family Feuds

The son dishonoreth the father, the daughter
riseth up against her mother, the daughter-in-law
against her mother-in-law; a man's enemies are
the men of his own family.

—MICAH

MARGARET, A FORTY-ONE-YEAR-OLD COLLEGE PROFESSOR, STOPPED
TALKING TO HER MOTHER NINE YEARS AGO, WHEN MARGARET'S FATHER
was lying on his deathbed. The feud began when Margaret's mother
wedged her small frame between Margaret and the door to Margaret's
father's hospital room. Margaret's mother was abandoning her husband
of nearly fifty years in his final hours, leaving him to die alone. Margaret knew that the physician and nurses would soon disconnect the
respirator that kept her father's cancer-ridden body alive, and she knew
that for some reason her mother couldn't tolerate anyone in the room
with him as he took his last breaths. Margaret looked at her mother in
disbelief, and even attempted to push her way into the room against
her mother's body, only to be held back by her older brother, whose
sharp gaze pierced Margaret as he announced, "Mother wants it this
way."

Margaret turned away, bowing to their wishes as though she were
still a five-year-old girl in pigtails, a girl who never dared to talk back,
argue or disobey. She couldn't fathom that her father, whom she revered

as a decent, handsome, devoted man, could be left to die alone. As the days turned into weeks, she found her bewilderment eating at her. At first she felt isolated, and then she felt angry. She tried to confide in her husband, who accompanied her on the two-thousand-mile journey to be with her family as her father's death drew near, but Margaret was so overwhelmed with grief and rage that all she could do was detach and hold the feelings inside.

Before the feud, she had spoken with her mother on the phone several times a week, sharing recipes, cheerfully revealing their daily victories, gossiping about the people back home. Margaret's mother offered moral support when Margaret had difficulties with her children, bought Margaret's children gifts, and sent greeting cards for every family occasion. As Margaret's grief and rage festered, all contact ceased. She could not bring herself to call her mother on the phone or write. Margaret's mother responded with an equal measure of resounding silence. Margaret chatted with her brothers on the phone only when they telephoned her, and then only superficially.

As a family therapist for two decades, I've seen many families shattered by family feuds. Some of the most devastating emotional injuries are those inflicted by family members upon each other. In fact, struggles within a family can lead to feuds that may irrevocably tear families apart. Yet, I've also witnessed and facilitated the awe-inspiring process of healing among family members who had for a time considered each other enemies. In this process, wives have insisted beforehand that nothing short of a miracle will make their ex-husbands understand the needs of their children, and husbands have assured me that their wives or ex-wives are incapable of ever understanding their needs. Through a mixture of gentle coaching and provocative prodding, using the basic principles described in these pages, bitter enmity can be transformed into accepting, tolerant, and occasionally even warm, caring relationships.

Even for clients who come to me with other issues, deep conflicts with family members are usually at the root of their pain. For many of them, unresolved family struggles profoundly influence their current emotional dilemmas.

FAMILY FIGHTS, FAMILY FEUDS

Family feuds are not family fights. Normal, healthy families fight. In fact, when I hear of a family whose members "never fight," I worry. Some of the worst feuds I have witnessed were silent ones. A family fight happens when one member disturbs the family's equilibrium. Perhaps a family rule is broken—Jed takes the car without asking, or Lisa is caught smoking. A fight with their parents follows, and sometimes family members team up against each other. Eventually, a punishment is dealt out, an understanding reached, and the family moves on. Such fights are necessary in families if couples are to mature through the many stages of marriage and if children are to grow up asserting their individuality.

Spouses fight between themselves for innumerable reasons; marriage without the spice of an occasional argument would be tedious. "Healthy fighting" helps to establish a sense of independence and a respect for the dignity and integrity of both partners. Fighting between marital partners often follows predictable patterns, almost like symphonic arrangements with beginnings, middles and ends. What makes fights healthy is the fact that they are eventually resolved, often ending with both partners enjoying a greater understanding of one another.

While normal families fight, normal families can also feud. But where fighting is healthy, feuding is not. In healthy families, fighting leads to some sort of resolution; in all families, feuding leads to more divisiveness and separateness. Wounds don't heal; they grow insidiously like a cancer, until the vital organs of the family break down.

In a family feud, people don't get angry at each other, they become enraged. People don't feel hurt; they feel mortally wounded. And because of such deep wounds, the resulting injuries seem nearly impossible to heal. If they heal at all, they heal slowly. Usually, the wound is left to fester and combine with other wounds, until the family is so torn apart that members become cut off from one another. Feuds become tenacious; each person involved feels as though change is impossible. Family members dig their heels in so deeply that their heels might as well be imbedded in concrete. There is simply no place to go, nowhere to move. It's more than a matter of mere pride; it's a matter of survival. People find themselves making vows to never let themselves be hurt again: "Why talk to someone who's undoubtedly going to hurt me again? I just can't take it anymore."

Feuds with family members often take on a spiritual dimension. People sometimes talk about their feuds as based on damage done to themselves on the deepest level. You hear them say things such as: "My spirit has been crushed," or "I can't allow myself to become entangled in a relationship that wears away at my soul."

Margaret's break with her family has many characteristics of the typical family feud. While seemingly triggered by specific events or behaviors, most feuds are rarely about those events or behaviors at all. Rather, they were spawned long ago—the culmination of unconscious historical factors, which ultimately ignite into a full-blown war. This is why many people whose break with a family member was touched off by less dramatic events than those described in Margaret's story will tell you their feud makes no sense even to them. Although Margaret's family feud was sparked by a major milestone—her father's death—it could easily have been started by a much less traumatic incident: how to decorate Mom and Dad's fiftieth anniversary cake, not receiving a thank-you note, or a discussion about whether or not to invite an ex-husband to a wedding.

So why is it that, given the same circumstances, one family fights and another family feuds? Why is it that the same family may fight one day, and another day the same set of circumstances causes a rift so deep that the family members stop talking to one another? What is at the heart of such bitter alienation? What is the hidden yet powerful force that has the ability to destroy strong family ties?

There are two keys to understanding and resolving family feuds. The first is to comprehend how family conflicts become so intense, and the second is to understand the time and distance the feud has traveled to get where it is today. With both keys firmly in hand, there are very few family feuds that cannot be put to rest.

THE FIRST KEY: EMOTIONAL INTENSITY

By the time a family feud erupts, the stage has been set by a series of past events and struggles. Margaret had a long history of minor conflicts between her and her mother, and also between her and her brothers, which were never completely resolved. Gestalt psychology teaches us that people have an innate need to resolve emotional conflicts. Whenever something emotional is left unfinished, the result is a sense of incompleteness that is experienced as anxiety or tension. What we often do to alleviate such tension is to rationalize for ourselves the aspect of the conflict that we either don't understand or cannot resolve. People feel restless and upset during an argument or a disagreement, and if they walk away from the disagreement without a conclusion, the upset feelings tend to increase. On the other hand, when an argument or disagreement is settled, there is a sense of relief, calm, and completion.

Family feuds arise when the tension that accompanies unresolved conflicts continues to mount, resulting in a volcano of feeling. This kind of emotional intensity is so strong that it's palpable; I literally *feel* it when I'm with a family whose interpersonal tension is extremely severe. With such a strong feeling of incompleteness comes an urgent need to bring hidden issues to a climax.

Such intensity is always present in a family feud. When small clashes don't get resolved, and resentments become stronger and more entrenched, the people involved are left with deep emotional wounds that leave them in a state of "suspended tension." Their lingering hurt or anger has the potential to erupt at any moment, under nearly any circumstance. When the moment arises, this emotional intensity shoots to the surface, causing either a complete severing of communication, or an endless stream of malicious innuendos expressed among family members. One "side" of the feud must always be on the lookout for the other—listening for hostile remarks or watching for disapproving expressions, fearful that the tension will erupt at any moment, preparing to defensively jump on the smallest remark or raised eyebrow. Family gatherings are avoided, for fear that something will happen to catalyze another explosive reaction.

The kind of intensity that underlies a family feud is often apparent to me in a client's initial phone call. For example, a divorced mother might be seeking therapy for her child. When I ask about bringing her ex-husband to the first session, she responds that she wants to avoid the kind of scene that would occur if they were all to come together in the same room. Although little more might be said, I can feel her intensity, her fear of the unresolved anger and sadness that might spill out if she and her child were to face her ex-husband together. When I'm aware of such intensity, I know that a family's problems have escalated to the level of a feud.

Intensity is the lifeblood of family feuds. Without it, a feud can neither erupt nor be sustained.

THE SECOND KEY: FAMILY HISTORY

Psychological theories that ultimately have profound effects on the way society thinks and acts are often ahead of their time and not easy to accept. It took years to understand that Freud's contributions to our understanding of human behavior went further than "the application of old Greek myths to one's private parts," as Vladimir Nabokov once said. Now, most people accept the notion that our early childhood experiences affect the way our personalities eventually develop. In the 1950's the founders of the family therapy movement went further and asserted that people are not just the product of their early family lives, but that their families are also the product of the generations of family that came before them. Thus, if I'm the product of my early experiences with my parents, and they are the products of their early experiences with their parents, and so on, we are all inextricably linked to our own multigenerational family, a group of people most of us know little about. Yet, just as our early childhood is often the breeding ground for own individual anxieties, it is this multigenerational family history that is the breeding ground for unresolved conflicts that may unconsciously spiral into family feuds.

One dramatic example of how past generations of family can transmit emotional intensity presented itself to me when I was only nineteen. A fellow patient in group therapy, Charles, revealed in a slow, trembling voice that his grandfather, on his fortieth birthday, committed suicide by placing a shotgun to his head and pulling the trigger. Likewise, Charles's own father, in exactly the same way, on his fortieth birthday, also killed himself. Charles, with less than a decade to go before his fortieth birthday, had begun to feel the terror welling up inside him, the same ineffable fear that had taken the lives of his father and grandfather.

While I never did find out what happened to Charles, as a family therapist I have learned just how powerful one's ancestral history can be. Every one of us contains in us the patterns of our forebears. If we think of only our physical selves, we can easily accept that physical like-nesses can be traced back to certain ancestors or projected onto the next generations of grandchildren or great-grandchildren. We can attribute our height, hair or eye color, complexion, and build to the DNA cod-ing on our chromosomes. But what about behavioral patterns? Is there a code that explains a facial expression your husband says reminds him of your mother? Is there a gene for being a chronic worrier or for suf-fering from an anxiety disorder? Does your daughter's flaring temper travel the generational chromosome line from your father? While the jury remains out on whether emotional intensity can be passed from one generation to another through our genetic encoding, we have identified other specific processes through which we know it is carried. These processes allow us to understand the very essence of how fam-ily feuds develop, and they are also the keys to resolving them.

Margaret couldn't begin to resolve her feud with her mother and brother until she understood her parents' life stories. Even in the midst of the feud, Margaret was able to reconstruct the information she needed to break through her "stuckness" by using some simple tools discussed in this book. She created diagrams of her family relationships, wrote histories of what she knew about her family, and looked for pat-terns that repeated themselves from one generation to the next. In doing so, she learned that the pattern of emotional abandonment dur-ing times of great need did not begin at her father's deathbed. Her fam-ily history revealed that on her mother's side there was a strong tendency for women to be isolated and alone. Margaret's mother Jane, an only child, lived in constant conflict with her mother, a conflict that was mostly unspoken but deeply felt. Jane's mother Edith abandoned her husband when Jane was very young. Jane grew up enraged at her mother for depriving her of a father. She witnessed as well her mother's habit of cutting off emotionally from those with whom she experi-enced even the slightest conflict.

Margaret's mother married Oliver and devoted her life to him. She attempted to make up for her lack of a family life by creating a "model" family of her own. She cleaned her home, cooked delicious meals, and raised three respectable children. But as she was growing up, Margaret sensed that while her mother could care for her family's external needs, her ability to be involved with them emotionally was very limited. While Margaret assumed that because her parents didn't argue and acted civilly toward each other, their relationship was close, there was also a detectable coldness between them. Margaret could not recall her parents ever holding hands, embracing each other, or expressing any form of affection.

Understanding Margaret's father's side of the family presented a greater challenge. The twin brother of a diffident, kind sister, Margaret's father was raised by a gruff Irish fireman and a reserved Protestant mother. Margaret remembered her grandfather, the colorful fireman, as a kindhearted man who often played with her and read her stories, but she also recalled that he was alleged to be a stern father to her own father, and prone to alcoholic binges. Margaret remembered her father as a gentle man, but her brothers saw him differently, as a strict, authoritarian disciplinarian. Margaret mused that her father must have treated her brothers more like his stern father had treated him, and that he treated her with the sort of kindness his father reserved for women.

One of the more difficult aspects for Margaret to accept, despite knowing how her brothers perceived their father, was how they could side with their mother in letting their father die alone. Only as Margaret studied the family relationships could she see that her brothers had not been cherished as she had been. She was her father's prized daughter, an object of acceptance and affection. Margaret achieved whatever power she had in the family by pleasing her father. Her brothers, conversely, were the recipients of a strong disciplinary hand. Resentful of the positive attention Margaret got from their father, the brothers joined with their mother.

At the moment of the father's death, every member of the family played out their historical roles. Jane, the mother, unable to be an emotional nurturer, avoided the pain of her husband's death by withdrawing from the event. Not being able to tolerate Margaret's attempts at nurturing him, she blocked access to him, just as she herself had been deprived of a father by her own mother. Margaret's brothers continued in their long-established alliance with their mother, siding with her wishes, and also her need to avoid pain, by leaving when the father's respirator was being disconnected. Margaret was separated out from this triangle, abandoned, like her father, to isolation and powerlessness.

The profound insights Margaret came to did not lead immediately to forgiving her mother and brothers. But understanding the family's emotional history did make it possible for her to feel some measure of compassion and begin to consider how to melt the icy walls that had been constructed during the feud. Just as important, it led Margaret to think about her relationship with her own daughter and to question whether she was inadvertently blocking her daughter's access to her husband the way her mother had with her, and her mother's mother before her. In allowing herself to feel the potent emotions associated with these unconscious predilections, Margaret experienced a kinship with both her mother and her daughter, as well as a strong motivation to avoid passing on this unwanted legacy. She decided to make amends.

Most family feuds appear at first glance to be complex, but a little bit of structured homework can yield a lot of valuable information. Once the patterns are identified, complex family feuds become simple to grasp, and the route that needs to be traveled to free oneself from the feud becomes clear.

Let's say you and your sister no longer speak with one another. You think this is because you always felt resentful that your mother paid more attention to your sister than to you. Over the years since your mother died, the two of you "grew apart" from each other. Now the thought of calling your sister repulses you. Something about making the first move infuriates you, yet you can't say exactly why. You know in your heart that your mother paying more attention to your sister couldn't have been enough to have created the feud that developed. But you aren't exactly sure what happened to account for your feelings.

By looking at certain specific aspects of your family history, you can begin to understand the root causes of your feud with your sister. These are the questions to ask:

- What was going on in your family when you were born?

- What was going on in your family when the rift between you and your sister began?

- In exploring your family's past, what patterns seem to echo from one generation to the next that might unwittingly be affecting your feelings about your sister?

You could be in for some surprises. In answering the first question, you might discover that just before your birth, your father had an affair, and when your mother found out about it, your parents separated. Your father was uninvolved in your birth, and questioned whether or not he would stay married to your mother. After you were born, he came back. Your mother accepted him, but continued to feel resentful and angry with him. Her resentment and anger at best made it difficult for her to focus her love and attention on you, and at worst made her take out her anger on you, the new baby. Your mother may have even blamed the pregnancy—and you—for your father's affair.

Knowing this, you would understandably feel angry and resentful toward your mother for not giving you the same kind of love and affection that your sister received. But now let's turn to the second question. What was going on for you in your family at the time your troubles with your sister began? You might discover, for example, that your problems with your sister escalated when you entered high school; let's say when you were fifteen and your sister was twelve. In exploring your family history, you discover that both your parents felt that education was the key to success, even though neither of them had graduated high school. Your mother became pregnant when she was seventeen, and had to leave high school prematurely. Your father had to leave high school to get a job to support his new family. So for both of your parents, high school represented a particularly troublesome time.

Your entering high school, because of *their* history, made *them* nervous. While they were careful not to share their fears with you, you sensed those fears in little things they said and did. You knew they were worried about you, although you didn't know quite why. You also knew that they didn't seem so terribly worried about your sister (she wasn't entering high school at the time), so once again you felt singled out and resentful. Thus, an even greater burden was placed on your relationship with your sister.

These two multigenerational patterns could be enough to cause a deep rift between you and your sister, but for many people there is yet a third set of circumstances that enter into the picture. Patterns that repeat from one generation to the next without regard for who the particular players are—such as *enmeshment* (when two people's identities merge into one), *triangulation* (when one person gets closer to another as a way of avoiding a third person), *family myths* and *secrets, birth order, anniversary dates,* and others—often lie at the very core of family feuds and are invisible unless you look deeper and more carefully into your family's unique history.

This last question concerning patterns that have existed in your family for generations is the trickiest one to answer; one needs to become a bit of a family detective.

Birth Order

Were you born with a heavier mantle of responsibility than your siblings? If you look at your family's relationships over the generations, you might discover that the eldest child in every generation was expected to be the star—the great success story of the family. This is a very common pattern. So, in a sense, just by virtue of your position in the family, you were born with one strike against you, or if you're able to make the best of it, one strike in your favor. If nothing else, the fact of your being the firstborn adds a certain amount of intensity to your presence in the family. Now your sister comes along, and she feels less of a burden. She may resent that lower expectations are placed on her, feeling as though your parents view her as less capable. Similarly, you too may resent that lower expectations are placed on her, feeling that she gets more of a break and doesn't have to work as hard to accomplish great feats. So you can see how your relationship with your sister is burdened by an inherited intensity, having nothing to do with your actual personalities or how the two of you get along. This, of course, is just one example of how birth order may play a key part in transmitting emotional intensity from one generation to the next.

Anniversary Dates

Often, family patterns run like an underground stream from one generation to the next, unbeknownst to the family members themselves. Such is the case with anniversary dates. JoAnne's feud with her sister Catherine is a vivid example of how hidden anniversaries can culminate in a feud.

JoAnne and Catherine stopped talking to each other when JoAnne turned eighteen. That was fifteen years ago, and now neither of them manages to pick up the phone and call the other. It may seem absurd, but JoAnne's feud with her sister may have actually started twenty years before either of them were born.

JoAnne recounted how one day her father called her and asked her to accompany him to the cemetery to visit his long-deceased parents. JoAnne remembered her grandparents from her childhood, and she wanted to see where they were buried, pay her respects, and support her father. In addition, her father told her that because she was the trusted and responsible one in the family, she was to be the executor of his estate, and since he had just purchased a lot for himself next to his parents, he wanted JoAnne to know where it was.

At the cemetery, JoAnne noticed a headstone near those of her grandparents engraved with the name of a girl who died at age seventeen and who had the same last name as hers. After inquiring, JoAnne was told by her father that he had a sister, two years younger than he, who died of rheumatic fever at the age of seventeen. He apologetically told JoAnne that, because the loss of his sister was the most painful thing in his life, he could never bring himself to talk about it.

JoAnne's father innocently believed that his "secret" would not affect his family and, if anything, would protect them from unnecessary pain and worry. JoAnne felt a bit angry at not being told about this important piece of family history, although she struggled successfully to understand and be empathic with her father.

What JoAnne didn't realize at the time was the subtle but powerful connection between her father's secret and her feud with her sister. When JoAnne turned seventeen, her father was flooded with images of his sister dying, images that he could share with no one. This turned into very intense feelings of worry about JoAnne and her health, worries that her father knew were excessive, so he struggled hard to hold them in. Instead, what came out were a lot of intense, overprotective feelings, feelings of not wanting to let go of JoAnne, not wanting to lose her the way he lost his sister. Although he tried to fight these feelings, his relationship with JoAnne took on a thick tension, a powerful connection, a focused intensity. JoAnne felt burdened by this tension.

Because JoAnne's father lost a sibling two years younger than he, it became no accident that in his overprotectiveness, his haunting memories orchestrated a family struggle that culminated in JoAnne also "losing" a sibling two years younger. JoAnne didn't know why; all she knew was that she found yourself growing more and more distant from her sister as she played out a drama that repeated itself from her father's generation to her own.

Normally, JoAnne's fights with her sister Catherine were met with encouragement from their parents to get in there and "work it out." Usually, one of their parents would intervene and offer himself or herself as a mediator. But because their father was suffering from the invisible pangs of grief over the loss of his sister at age seventeen, a loss he had buried until JoAnne reached her seventeenth birthday, he felt unable to mediate any longer. Even though he had always hoped his children would share the same kind of closeness he had with his sister, he found himself either impotent as a mediator, or too involved and intense, so he again backed off. He may have even felt oddly comforted by the replaying of the family drama, as though by repeating it he might somehow have been able to work his way through his own terrible pain.

FROM FEUD TO RECONCILIATION

Understanding the answers to the three questions presented earlier is often all you need to begin healing deep family wounds. Sometimes discovering the seeds of your family feud provides the motivation for doing things differently in your family, for renewing contacts with a different understanding. For some, understanding provides the grounds for forgiveness and the resolving of differences.

Just as every family is unique, every family feud is unique as well, and consequently, the pathway from feud to reconciliation will be different for each family and family member. Yet, just as there are patterns that are shared by almost all families, there are certain crucial steps in untangling feuds. Understanding how a family feud came about, especially the underlying patterns of relationships that reverberate through a family's history, is the first step in the healing process. While some feuds can be mended by sheer determination and the courage to do things differently, unless you comprehend your unique family history, the feud will likely repeat itself.

Margaret's feud was the result of several ingrained family patterns, among them "women abandoning men" and "intense conflicts between mothers and daughters." Charles, whose forefathers committed suicide on their fortieth birthdays, and JoAnne, whose father was overly sensitive when his daughter reached the same age his sister was when she died, suffered from the multigenerational intensity that followed the pattern called "anniversary dates," in which particular times of the year or of one's life are associated with traumatic historical events.

Recognizing hidden patterns that run through a family's multigenerational history is an essential key to understanding the bitter confrontations that alienate and separate us from mothers, fathers, sisters, brothers, even our own children.

Too Close for Comfort

Did sea define the land or land the sea?

—Seamus Heaney

A BITTER FEUD ERUPTED BETWEEN PEPPI AND HER FATHER AFTER A BRIEF VISIT IN WHICH HER FATHER MADE THE "INNOCENT" COMMENT that Peppi could be doing more to help her mother recover from hip replacement surgery. Peppi told her father in no uncertain terms that she was fed up with the "years of unhappiness" he had given her over how good a daughter she was, and that she wanted to have nothing more to do with him. Peppi's astonished father turned away defiantly. His pride was hurt, and he made up his mind that he would not come back and beg for Peppi's forgiveness. She would have to apologize to him. They had always been close, and the pain of her rejection was too much to bear. They shut each other out, and haven't spoken in almost five years.

Dawn, a thirty-three-year-old teacher and part-time salesperson, and Ron, a thirty-five-year-old teacher, had been married for over fifteen years. They were each other's first and only loves. Holding back tears, Dawn told me that she could not conceive of ever loving anyone as much as she loved Ron. She devoted her life to him, thought of him constantly, and did everything she could to meet all his needs. She knew their relationship wasn't as romantic as it once had been, but she still felt passionately that he was the only one for her. There could never be another man she could love. When Dawn discovered that Ron was seeing another woman at the school where he worked, she couldn't understand it. Ron had always told Dawn that he was madly in love with her. They never fought, and they did everything together. Theirs was a marriage made in heaven, and it was inconceivable to Dawn that Ron could be doing anything behind her back. The only option, she felt, was to leave the relationship or kill herself. She left the relationship, and she hasn't seen or spoken to Ron in two years.

Rhonda was the apple of her mother's eye. While there were three children in the family, everyone knew that spunky Rhonda was her mother's favorite. Rhonda's mother Grace made no bones about it; there was "something special" about Rhonda. Maybe it was the fact that Rhonda had the same sparkle in her eye as Grace's mother— Rhonda's grandmother. Grace grew so attached to her daughter that for several years they were inseparable. When Rhonda became a teenager and began to go out on dates, Grace insisted that she go along, not as a chaperone, but more as a "teenage friend." Grace thought that she could help Rhonda cope with the challenges of adolescence by joining her on her teenage adventures, so Grace went roller-skating with Rhonda, and took Rhonda to the movies. Rhonda never objected to her mother's company. She was so used to her mother's companionship throughout her life that she felt comforted by her mother's presence. It wasn't until Rhonda became seriously interested in boys that all hell broke loose. Rhonda panicked at the thought of being alone with a boy, but knew she wanted to do what the other teenage girls were doing. She became frozen in fear at the thought of venturing out into the world on her own, and her mother subtly reinforced this fear. For Rhonda, there were only two choices she could make: stay a child forever and be constantly comforted by her mother, or break away completely. She decided to break away completely, and fell deeply into the "comfort" of drugs and strangers. Grace felt as though she had been an ultimate failure, although she insisted that she had done everything right.

• • •

In all of these situations, the two people involved began their relationship with each other feeling extremely close. In fact, Rhonda and Grace, Dawn and Ron, and Peppi and her father might all be described as being "too close for comfort." Family therapists call this kind of extreme closeness *enmeshment*. It's one of those psychological jargon words that actually means exactly what it implies; when two people are enmeshed, they can't be torn apart without doing extreme damage to both. They become so intertwined with each other's feelings that they forget exactly who they are as individuals.

Enmeshed relationships can take many forms. As with Dawn and Ron, the enmeshed relationship can occur between husband and wife. It can just as easily occur between siblings, and sometimes even between friends. But in the case of Peppi and her father, or Rhonda and her mother, enmeshment can stretch across the generations between parent and child. This cross-generational enmeshment is usually the foundation for other types of future enmeshment.

PARENT-CHILD ENMESHMENT

Parents who foster a sense of enmeshment between themselves and their children do so by becoming extremely overattentive to their children. They tend not to let their children grow up, and do many things with or for their older children that are only appropriate for a much younger child. They may tie the child's shoe, even though the child is able to do it for himself or herself. They may answer difficult questions for their children, or talk for them in public, as though their children had no voice of their own. A child may start a sentence, only to find the parent completing it, "stealing" the child's voice.

Certain families are wellsprings for enmeshment. These households have few rules designed to foster responsibility. A child who can be responsible will grow up and eventually leave home, and this is threatening for a parent who needs to feel enmeshed with a child. Parents will make life easy at home—children who become enmeshed often don't have to do chores around the house; instead of having to clean their bedrooms, their parents will do it for them.

Families where enmeshment is fostered typically lack a sense of separateness or privacy. Bathroom doors are not closed or locked. Children are discouraged from leaving their own doors closed, or from using their bedrooms as a place of respite. They are often encouraged to sleep in their parents' beds, regardless of their age or wishes. Breast-feeding mothers will push their children to nurse long after their children desire or need to.

But this overly dependent relationship truly takes two, and children who are enmeshed with their parents eventually become very willing participants. In fact, children who may have unique needs due to childhood illness, birth defects, or other reasons may be singled out for this type of treatment. Often not knowing any other way of being in a relationship than to be completely dependent, some children learn that the only comfort they can feel is from another. Self-reliance is not an option, because such children have had no encouragement to develop a separate sense of themselves.

When a parent and child are involved in an enmeshed relationship, the stage is set for that child to choose an enmeshed relationship with another when he or she "grows up." The words "grow up" must be placed in quotation marks, because children who are in enmeshed relationships with a parent have great difficulty actually growing up. More often than not, they physically leave home without emotionally doing so. They carry their views, expectations, and feelings about being in a relationship directly from their home into the world, and as a result will insist on creating a relationship with someone just as equally unable to "grow up," and the couple will repeat the cycle all over again.

ENMESHMENT WITHIN A GENERATION

Dave and Nancy were one of the most difficult couples I ever met. Their relationship was not only enmeshed, but Dave had a well-thought-out, almost Talmudic rationale for his enmeshment. Usually, it's not terribly difficult convincing a couple that their overly fused, enmeshed relationship is the source of their conflicts. By simply connecting the enmeshed feelings of being smothered, feeling trapped, losing one's identity, and having no choices with their current struggles, most couples begin to understand and accept that their enmeshment is at the root of their problems. But in Dave and Nancy's case, Dave was so entrenched in his fused relationship that he developed a rationale, no matter how irrational, to defend his belief that this was the only way to be married.

In essence, Dave believed this because he knew that the pain of losing his wife would be so intolerable to him, he would die without her. Unfortunately, he wasn't referring only to his wife's possible demise, but also of any dissatisfaction she might have with him as a spouse. If Nancy seemed the slightest bit interested in another man, or if her passionate attachment toward him waned, that would indicate that she didn't love him enough and that he might as well kill himself. If she had too many interests of her own, that would also mean he wasn't good enough. He wanted to be a perfect husband, and in a perfect marriage, his wife would never be dissatisfied with him.

What Dave couldn't see at all was how his overdependence and his enmeshment with his wife was tantamount to holding her hostage. She felt absolutely trapped by Dave's insistence on a perfect marriage. She felt she was not entitled to have any feelings that didn't somehow reflect the intense love between them. She could never be angry or disappointed with Dave, because if she felt any of those things, he would kill himself. Because the threat of Dave's suicide always lurked in the background, any disenchanted feelings that Nancy might have would ultimately turn her into a murderer.

This dramatic example represents an extreme form of enmeshment, but sadly, one that I have seen many times. Even as I write these words, I was telephoned today by a hospital telling me a client of mine had been admitted because he had cut his throat with a razor after a fight with his wife in which she told him she didn't know if she loved him anymore. Other forms of enmeshment between couples are more subtle but can be devastating to a family in the long run. The husband who gives up his friendships because he believes that his wife should be his best *and only* friend, and the wife who gives up her own aspirations and centers her whole life around pleasing her husband, are examples of how couples sometimes behave when there is an underlying enmeshment. Regardless of how it looks on the surface, underlying an enmeshed relationship is the feeling of one person that life would be utterly meaningless without the other. Without one's partner, there would be an unfathomable loneliness or empty feeling, a feeling that some people describe as "vanishing" or "disappearing."

After many years of a loving relationship, anyone who goes through a divorce or the loss of a spouse through death is likely to feel these feelings of emptiness. The difference between a healthy intimate relationship and an enmeshed one is that in the enmeshed relationship, with the loss of the spouse or partner there is also a loss of one's individual identity. Life was meaningful *only* because of the relationship. When a spouse dies, *or even threatens to leave because of problems in the marriage,* the enmeshed partner feels as though he or she must die as well. Life cannot go on after the loss, or threatened loss, of the spouse.

ENMESHED RAGE

The reason feelings of enmeshment can lead to feuds is that when people feel as though they are losing their identity (i.e., their partner), they will fight like wounded animals for their very survival. This puts the enmeshed husband and wife, father and son, or sister and brother at risk for a feud.

There is a tricky conundrum at work that fans the flames of an enmeshed feud. People who are in an enmeshed relationship unconsciously *insist* on a loss of their own identity, because this is what they know and what they are comfortable with. If one person in the relationship makes efforts toward becoming emotionally healthier, the relationship becomes destabilized. One person's move toward independence threatens the other, and both people fall into a deeply troubling, panic state. Going backward would restabilize the relationship, by allowing both partners to settle back into a comfortable, fused relationship, with little identity of their own. But going backward becomes threatening to the individual trying to grow up. So the person who makes moves toward independence feels trapped in a no-win situation—either I grow up and become independent and have to suffer the loss of this comfortable, fused relationship, or I go backward, seeking the comfort of my relationship and losing my budding sense of an individual, unique identity.

It may seem odd that being "too close" can cause the kind of rage or detachment that undergirds a family feud. But this is exactly what happens. Being "too close" to someone leads to a feeling of being smothered, or of drowning. It leads a person to feel as if he or she has no choices in life. The only "choice" is to follow the rules dictated by the relationship, which require remaining continuously closely attached. A person who is enmeshed with another feels as though she is slipping away, losing her identity. This sets off a feeling of panic and, like the panic of a drowning person, leads to a flailing struggle for survival in which careful, reasoned compassion for another person is impossible.

Losing oneself in another person and being enraged at him or her are two sides of the same coin. It is similar to the notion that people who are suicidal are actually enraged at others. The feeling of outrage at being threatened underlies both the suicidal and the murderous person. I remember the time that two Burbank police officers arrived at my office with Charlie—one of my patients—in tow. The police were called to the factory where Charlie worked because he had brutally beaten up a coworker. Both the coworker and the coworker's mother, who also worked at the factory, refused to press charges against Charlie, because they knew Charlie as a sensitive, kind, and shy person, who had finally reached his limit and exploded. The police, who were used to taking in violent criminals, had the perspicacity to ask Charlie if he was feeling suicidal. Charlie said he was, and instead of taking Charlie to jail they brought him to my office.

These police officers knew what psychologists have known for years, that the impulse to hurt oneself is often the same impulse that drives one to hurt others. Similarly, the feeling of needing to join completely with another person is driven by the same panic that drives the rageful explosions in an enmeshed feud: the panic of not having one's own identity.

The rage that erupted between Nicole and Frank is typical of what arises in a feud caused by an enmeshed relationship. Frank is a ruggedly handsome, sixty-two-year-old sportswriter, let go from his previous employer "to make room for a younger crop." Semiretired, he now works as a part-time freelancer. His European-born wife Nicole, ten years younger, has never worked out of the home. The feud between Frank and Nicole began, according to Nicole, when Frank "suddenly" moved out and filed for custody of their two young children. He successfully gained custody by claiming that Nicole was an unfit mother.

Frank's version of the story, as was always the case in matters that concerned the two of them, was different. He claims that the feud between him and Nicole began long ago, shortly after they were married and Nicole "tricked him" into having children. He discovered that Nicole had a very different personality than he had been led to believe; she was manipulative, vindictive, and insulting, and constantly tried to undermine his parenting of their children.

Their feud was not unlike many other marital feuds I have seen over the years. When I got the two of them together in the same room, there was nothing one spouse could say that the other could agree with. Every statement, whether positive or negative, whether loving or angry, was viewed by the other as a vicious allegation. The content of the statement seemed relevant to the other parent only as far as it could be used for fuel to fire the animosity between them.

The venom between Nicole and Frank was so poisonous that any interaction between them sparked a rageful fight. Just being in the same room together was enough to set up the conditions for the kind of defensiveness that guaranteed an eventual outburst. Nicole's rage was so intense that even when she wasn't around Frank, she plotted schemes to sabotage his parenting of the children, and spoke about him cruelly to the children. Verbal injunctions by mental health professionals, as well as legal injunctions by the court, to not speak disparagingly in front of the children about the other parent had no impact. Neither spouse could fathom the depth to which their venom toward each other tore their children in half.

How could two people, both of whom apparently love their children, be so blind as not to see how harmful their rage toward each other was to their children? One answer is simply that rage is blind. When people become enraged, they're only able to think about themselves and their own survival. Sadly, they will grab at anything to hurl at the perceived source of danger in order to protect themselves. The more powerful the weapon, the more likely it will be used, and that includes their own children.

People who tend to get into enmeshed relationships with a spouse, and then lose that relationship, will often turn to their children in an enmeshed way. The person who is enmeshed with his or her children doesn't have a good sense of who's who—the child and the parent become one. A threat to one is perceived as a threat to another. People in an enmeshed, rageful feud with a spouse will describe their own children as being hurt by the alienated spouse the same way they describe themselves as being hurt by the spouse. They will then struggle in an endless campaign, not only at the expense of their children's emotional well-being, but at the cost of many thousands of dollars in legal fees as well, to keep their children from the offending parent, even when the other parent has never done anything to harm the children directly.

Carrying on a bitter feud with another person is a way to remain in an enmeshed relationship. The hallmark of enmeshment is a feeling of intensity. The intensity can be passionate love or passionate hatred, but it remains passionate. Neither Nicole nor Frank had much time for anyone else in their lives. They were kept too busy by plotting against each other, and dealing with the legal intricacies of their battle.

Even in situations in which parents who are feuding remarry, it is not uncommon for a feud with an ex-spouse to continue. I have seen many families in which the current husbands or wives actually feel jealous of the ex-spouses, because their current spouses spend so much time, energy, and passion feuding with their exes. When I bring them all together in the same room, the most recent husbands and wives almost seem peripheral. They usually remain fairly quiet, throwing in a word here and there in support of their current spouse, while the exes have at each other.

While feuds serve many functions, one of the most obvious functions in a feud caused by enmeshment is that the feud serves to maintain the relationship. The feud becomes the reversal of the popular adage "If you can't beat 'em, join 'em." In the case of an enmeshed, rageful feud, the adage becomes "If you can't join 'em, beat 'em over and over and over again." In a very real sense, this constant sparring between enmeshed partners is a way to stay attached, to remain "joined" with the other person even if they can't be physically present.

One of the easiest ways of understanding how rage is a form of enmeshment is to understand what enmeshment is not. Enmeshment is not an understanding, rational, compassionate relationship with another person. That would be what most people would want in a relationship, with moments of passion added from time to time to spice it up. Nor is enmeshment a detached, meaningless, nonrelationship between two people who have no feelings for each other. That would be a detached, disengaged relationship—not really a relationship at all.

People who are enraged with each other are anything but detached. Rage, while extremely unpleasant, is still a form of engagement. When two countries are engaged in war, they are in fact very tied to one another. To disengage, to ultimately separate and go your own way, you must also stop the hostilities.

ENMESHMENT AND CODEPENDENCY

The word "codependency" has been problematic for me as a psychologist and family therapist over the years. Many of my clients, having read popular books about being in codependent relationships, tend to misinterpret the point of these books. In particular, they often have trouble separating "codependency" from "healthy dependency." All relationships, by definition, require some dependency. If there were no dependency in a relationship at all, there simply would be no relationship—just two independent people who never need each other. If we never needed anyone, then whenever we felt weak, vulnerable, or imperfect, we'd only have ourselves to rely on. While that approach might work for some, it only permits a deep relationship with oneself; relationships with others become either nonexistent or superficial at best. Relationships become deep and meaningful to a large extent because we find that we *can* depend on another person to be there when we need him or her. That's the basis of trust, and trust is the foundation for any meaningful, long-term relationship.

Clients who have come to see me over the years often believe their chief problem is "codependency," and they seem to think that the solution to this problem is to become independent. To a certain degree they are right, but the difficulty lies in the fact that many of these people believe that becoming independent is the final, desired solution to their problems. What they don't realize is that by becoming independent they have only gone halfway in their attempt to be in a healthy relationship. What they have learned is how to go from being overly dependent to being overly independent. They have not learned how to balance healthy dependency with healthy independence, to be dependent on one's partner for certain emotional needs, while at the same time being an independent, separate person. This balance requires the ability to tolerate the pain of occasional loneliness and longing for another person, while at the same time honoring your need for privacy and separateness. It also requires the ability to give in to feelings of being needy and dependent, holding another person close and taking in feelings of warmth, comfort, and security. The key to this healthy balance is to be able to move back and forth smoothly between the two poles of mutuality—dependency and neediness on the one end, and individuality, independence, and self-sufficiency on the other.

DISTANT, SILENT WARS

When most of us think of family feuds, two types of families come to mind. One is the family that fights so voraciously and habitually that there seems to be no end in sight. The other is the family whose split has become a war of silence. In silent wars, the feud is marked by a lack of contact rather than endless battles. In some instances the contact has stopped completely, while in others the feuding family members may be forced into seeing each other, but eventually go out of their way to avoid each other.

When people respond to feelings of enmeshment by cutting themselves off from another person, they usually do so because they feel that there is simply no way of getting the other person to change. Many times they practice what I half-jokingly call "relocation therapy," and move as far away as they can from their family or from the party they feel has hurt them.

Checking yourself out and cutting yourself off usually engenders a feeling of immediate relief. "A change of scenery" can feel temporarily comforting for people embroiled in a situation from which they fear they can't escape. Whenever someone who is in an enmeshed relationship moves away, there's an initial feeling of freedom, but it doesn't last. Many people who run away from the source of the problem never do the necessary emotional work in order to gain the tools needed to handle the original wounds. Consequently, the wounds never heal and are left buried deep within, often to fester and then surface in a feud with someone else. Meanwhile, the problem of enmeshment, which was the source of the original feud, and the multigenerational patterns that helped create the original feud, also remain beneath the surface, only to rear their heads in some future relationship.

There are three ways in which "cutoffs" tend to influence the future. Each of these represents a common pattern. One way is that, because the original enmeshed feelings are never fully resolved, people who cut themselves off will remain emotionally attached to the people they have cut themselves off from. Future relationships will remain superficial at best, because the enmeshed person's primary attachment remains with the other enmeshed person, regardless of how intolerable and rageful that relationship may have been.

The second way "cutoffs" influence the future is that the original feelings of enmeshment are actually transferred to another person. In this scenario, people who cut themselves off move from one enmeshed relationship to another. The jilted person goes "looking for Mr. Goodbar," each time falling into a relationship that is equally as unhealthy.

The third way enmeshed people try to cut themselves off from each other is by means of what I call the "illusion of independence." In this scenario, people believe that because they have left the source of the conflict, they are no longer being dominated or influenced by the enmeshed relationship. In cutting themselves off, they righteously declare that they will *never let that kind of relationship happen to them again.* As a result, they go about their lives living the opposite way they lived before. If a previous enmeshed relationship was marked by hostility, then at the first sign of hostility in their new relationship, the person leaves, vowing never to do again what he or she did before.

Where this becomes most obvious is in a cross-generational enmeshed relationship. A child (let's call her Mary) grows up feeling enmeshed with her parents, who were overly intrusive and kept an extremely close eye on her every move. Mary decides that she's "had enough," and moves three thousand miles across the country in order to make a new life, outside her parents' sphere of influence. As time goes by, she falls in love and marries. When she has children, she decides that whatever was done to her as a child she will not do to her own children. Mary resolves with her husband to "do it differently," so as not to repeat the mistakes of the past.

By doing the opposite of what was done to her, Mary believes she is doing the right thing as a parent. Where her parents were constantly asking her what she did at school each day, Mary never asks, in order to give her child the "space" she needs. Where her parents checked her homework every day to make sure it was done correctly, Mary decides that such behavior is merely for the parents' benefit, so she lets her daughter become "responsible" enough to do it herself. Where her parents hovered over her friendships and dating, needing to meet and approve everyone beforehand, Mary lets her daughter hang out with anyone her daughter chooses.

What Mary doesn't realize is that by doing the opposite of what was done to her, she merely creates a mirror image of herself. A mirror image is, of course, the same image, except that it is reversed. Mary's daughter will have the same conflicts over dependency, feeling safe and nurtured as Mary did. Only instead of feeling enraged at being overly attended to and not being allowed to breathe, as Mary did, Mary's daughter will feel enraged at being unattended to and not being able to get the support, nurturance, and guidance she needed.

Emotional cutoffs as a way of dealing with enmeshment create the illusion of independence, but the truth remains that a person who does the opposite of what was done to him or her continues to be controlled and dominated by the original enmeshed relationship. If every time some internal voice tells you to do something, and you then do the opposite, you never learn to create your own voice. You only learn to resist someone else; and in the process, you continue to be controlled by that voice. What is most difficult for people in enmeshed relationships is to create a rational, compassionate voice of their own. This voice must learn to evaluate both the harmful and the positive aspects of past enmeshed relationships, and then caution against what is harmful in present ones, without "throwing out the baby with the bath-water."

A MULTIGENERATIONAL HAND-ME-DOWN

The feuds mentioned in this chapter have had at least one thing in common: They all sprouted from enmeshed roots. Yet enmeshment alone doesn't account for why a particular feud will occur when it does. In many families, for example, enmeshment occurs without erupting into a feud. The simple fact of having an enmeshed relationship, while it raises the chances for a feud at some time, cannot account for why some enmeshed relationships culminate in a feud and others do not. In order to fully understand why a feud occurs when it does, it's necessary to understand the multigenerational nature of the enmeshment pattern. Frank and Nicole present a prime example.

Nicole was the only child of two European-born parents. All her life, Nicole had a strenuous if not impossible relationship with her mother. She remembers fighting with her mother constantly, and Nicole blamed her mother many times for "ruining her life." When I asked Nicole just what it was that her mother did that upset her so, she told me that her mother was "overprotective," and that she had to know everything that Nicole did and everywhere she went.

While there were other clues to their enmeshment with each other, such as the constant feuding between the two of them that went on until shortly before her mother's death, these clues were all I needed to assume that Nicole and her mother were locked in an enmeshed battle. Understanding that most violent, resilient feuds, such as Nicole's feud with Frank, take at least three generations to develop, I asked Nicole to conduct a little experiment for me. She was about to visit her father, a quite aged but still mentally sharp retired farmer. Because Nicole did not know enough about her mother's childhood, I asked her to ask her father to tell her about her mother's childhood. In particular, I wanted to know about her mother's relationship with her own mother and father.

I wasn't surprised to learn on Nicole's return home from her visit that her mother was described as "extremely close" to her own mother. Nicole's father recounted how difficult it was to court his future wife, because she insisted that her mother accompany her everywhere. Nicole's father related how he had to pass the test of Nicole's mother's parents, and how difficult that was, because no one was going to take their daughter away from them. In fact, he even had to promise that he would not move to a far-off city after marrying his new bride!

Nicole's enmeshed relationship with Frank represented at least the second generation of enmeshment in Nicole's family. But what about Frank's family?

This information proved more difficult to obtain. That's because Frank had been completely cut off from his own parents, both of whom had died quite some time ago. Frank had one brother, but the two of them did not get along, and Frank had virtually no contact with him either. His family had a long, proud history, but one that Frank was completely disinterested in. He remembered his parents as strict disciplinarians, and he recalled that he couldn't wait to get out of the family, leaving the house to do odd jobs and work when he was sixteen.

Even with a minimal amount of information, I was able to determine that the extent to which Frank had nothing to do with his family was profound and unusual. The fact that he left home so early indicated that life must have been fairly horrible for Frank as a child. Frank acknowledged that while he remembered little from his childhood, he knew it was "pretty awful." He had no fond memories of his family life, only that his parents were strict and proud. He could not recall ever feeling warmth or safety. Although I wished I had some more information to confirm my suspicions, I assumed that Frank's isolation from his family represented a cutoff, an angry rebellion or reaction against the lack of warmth in his family. This, along with Frank's inability to detach himself from his rage at Nicole, led to my assumption that Frank, too, had an enmeshed rage stemming from the family he grew up in. His rage took the familiar form of a cutoff. I had no way of knowing how many generations this pattern traversed, but, again, I assumed the family history created a ripeness for Frank's feud.

Taken together, the histories of intense, enmeshed relationships converged to set off a time bomb in Nicole and Frank's marriage. Sadly, neither of them was aware at the time they were married that these influences were residing dormantly inside them both, awaiting the right moment to spring into a feud.

Seem far-fetched? Not if you take a closer look at how multigenerational patterns work.

The pattern is fairly simple. At some point, two people enter into an enmeshed relationship. Let's say for a moment that they are a father and a son. Let's call the son Harry. Perhaps the father in the family felt terribly isolated as a child, and had difficulty obtaining the love and affection he wanted from his wife. He therefore turned to his son Harry, and developed an overly close relationship. Because enmeshed relationships are always powerful and intense, and as a result of the father's need not to let his son grow up and leave him, Harry had trouble becoming self-reliant and coping with social pressures, such as dating. As he grew into an adult, Harry felt the need to leave home, but had great difficulty doing so. The world was too dangerous a place, he felt, but he still had urges to grow up, and he knew he had to leave home.

Because he felt so socially incompetent, Harry knew that he couldn't attract the "best catches" at his high school. The cheerleaders dated the jocks, and the smart and pretty girls dated the smart and handsome boys. So Harry searched for someone he thought no one else would be interested in. At first he met Susie, and asked her to the movies. She accepted, but when she tried to have a discussion with Harry, she discovered that he didn't have much confidence in himself, and wasn't too socially adept. Susie came from a family that provided her a nice mixture of warmth and support, along with encouragement to function independently and responsibly. As a result, despite not being the brightest or the prettiest girl in town, Susie felt good about herself, and couldn't see herself with someone like Harry. So she politely declined his future invitations.

Harry went headfirst into a deep depression, but to his credit he worked his way out of it just long enough to find a girl at school who didn't think too much of herself. Ironically, Elizabeth was quite bright and good-looking, but seemed to lack self-confidence. In fact, she seemed as frightened of the world and as frightened of independence as Harry did.

So it was no surprise that she turned down Harry's first invitation to go out with him to the movies. In fact, in an awkward telephone call, she told Harry that her mother wouldn't allow her to go out on a date anyway. But they started having wonderful phone calls, and eventually were able to go roller-skating together during the daytime. They found in each other a certain familiar ease. They could understand each other. They could talk about how they hated people, and how their parents were too intrusive in their lives. They became soul mates, and eventually married.

A preposterous story? Hardly. In this simple example you can find elements familiar to many couples who end up sharing a chunk of their lives together. But the story is important because it highlights a key principle in understanding how enmeshment echoes from one generation to the next. The principle can be stated simply: *People who have difficulty leaving home, growing up, and forging independent, self-confident identities tend to find and marry people with similar levels of difficulty.* When it comes to enmeshment, the formula states that the more enmeshed you are with someone in your family, the more likely you are to find someone to marry who is just as enmeshed as you. Harry and Elizabeth can both tell you that getting into a relationship with someone who is much more independent and self-confident than you can be difficult, but not nearly as difficult as staying in one. So even when someone is successful at attracting a "healthier," more emotionally mature mate, it is difficult to make that relationship last long enough to culminate in marriage.

This formula explains how enmeshment can traverse one generation, be passed from parent to child, and dictate that the child will find someone to be in a relationship with who is equally as enmeshed. What happens, though, when Harry and Elizabeth have their first child?

Neither Harry nor Elizabeth knows what it's like to be in a relationship that isn't overly intense. The only kind of relationship either of them had had was one in which one person was thoroughly dependent on the other. (The other relationships, you'll remember, didn't stick.) You can see immediately what kind of parents Harry and Elizabeth are likely to be. At the very least, they are not likely to be self-confident parents. Instead, they are likely to be anxious about "doing it right," much more so than most new parents. Having learned that the solution to one's struggles is to look toward others for answers, they might consult their own parents. If Harry's parents agree with Elizabeth's parents about how to raise a child, things might go well for a while. But if the in-laws disagree, Harry and Elizabeth will have to turn elsewhere. They may buy a book about parenting, but the particular book they buy might advocate something different from what the in-laws suggest. They might buy another book, but they might find that these two books contradict each other. The confusion is likely to set off a panic about parenting, and the anxiety they feel associated with being a parent will be felt and experienced by the child.

Sometimes when he's cold he will get a blanket, and at other times he won't. Sometimes when he cries he'll get taken into Mommy and Daddy's bed, and sometimes he won't. The result of not knowing what's going to happen from one time to the next is that Harry and Elizabeth's child won't be able to predict what's going to happen to him. When a child cannot predict what's going to happen, he feels unsafe in the world. These feelings of unsafeness lead to the child turning to an even greater extent to his parents for comfort. And a vicious cycle continues.

Harry and Elizabeth will know full well that their child is needy and not feeling safe, so they'll ultimately turn to the one thing they know best. They'll do to their child what was done to them, and they'll become vigilantly involved in every aspect of the child's life. They'll soothe the child's fears with nonstop affection and attention. This may prove to be a good thing, because children need to feel safe before they can grow up and explore the world for themselves, or it can become too much of a good thing.

A problem arises when Harry and Elizabeth's child decides to become independent, because this is something Harry and Elizabeth know nothing about. They've read the books, and they know this is natural—they may even boast about his precocious development, but their child's becoming independent threatens them to their very core. It brings out their own deep conflicts about trying to become independent from their own parents. Those efforts met with failure, and rather than master a sense of independence, they simply transferred their overdependence to their spouse. Never having learned to be independent themselves, Harry and Elizabeth feel terribly frightened by their child's emerging sense of himself as different from them. For Harry and Elizabeth, the unresolved fear of becoming independent, and the unresolved feelings of anger toward their parents and themselves for not ever mastering this milestone, are powerfully intense, unconscious conflicts. Unaware of the influence of these unconscious, intense feelings of anger, Harry and Elizabeth find themselves sabotaging their child's efforts to move toward independence.

This is the next principle: *The unconscious conflicts over dependency in an enmeshed couple result in a sometimes subtle but always powerful sabotaging of their children's moves toward a healthy balance of dependency and self-sufficiency.* The child experiences life as a dangerous undertaking; his only options are to become involved in an overly dependent relationship with someone else, or to avoid relationships altogether.

When Harry and Elizabeth's child grows up and tries to leave home, he will find someone equally as enmeshed, and then the whole pattern repeats itself. By the time the third, fourth, or fifth generation rolls around, unresolved conflicts over dependency become highly charged and intense. As each child grows up and marries into a family in which enmeshment is also passed on from one generation to the next, the intensity builds to a fever pitch, eventually erupting into a rageful feud.

Having said all this, it becomes clear why I insist that when family members are embroiled in a feud, it is rarely about the specific issue one or both people feel enraged about. Instead, it's about the accumulated rage that is passed from one generation to the next. Rather than merely trying to deal with the particular recent events that sparked the feud, both family members must be committed to understanding the multigenerational rage and deep family wounds they have inherited. Only then can resolution and healing take place.

Three's a Crowd

There were three of us in this marriage, so it was getting a bit crowded.

—DIANA, PRINCESS OF WALES

A HUSBAND AND WIFE WRAP THEMSELVES AROUND EACH OTHER, TIE THEMSELVES TOGETHER IN A TRUE LOVER'S KNOT, AND BECOME "THE red rose and the briar." Eventually, if they fail to hold onto the very things that make them two distinct people, there becomes no way to distinguish one from the other. A parent and a child become braided together like bread, so that tearing away one portion necessarily tears away at the other. These intense enmeshment scenarios set the stage for troubling family feuds. When two people strive to feel whole by merging into one, they dance to the melodies that have wafted through their family trees for generations.

There is another desperate dance that two people do, a dance that also finds its way from one generation to the next in an unmistakable pattern. In this dance, one of the two protagonists, rather than merging with the other, turns to a different partner, someone or something else. This entrance onto the scene of a third party forms the classic "eternal triangle." Perhaps the husband becomes overly weary from trying to make a marriage work, and comforts himself in a renewed relationship with an ex-girlfriend; or a wife turns to her child because she feels abandoned or smothered by her husband. Or a teenage girl, feeling the pressure of a parent crushing down on her, turns to a young boy, falls passionately "in love," and thus attempts to buy a ticket out of parental demands.

This *triangulation* is an involvement with a third party or activity in order either to fulfill needs that aren't met within the original twosome, or to escape from the feeling of losing autonomy and falling into an endless well of enmeshment. Triangulation is felt as the subtle, painful tug of an unwelcome third party. It can arrive on the scene in the form of a desperate husband, longing for the company of his wife, who feels useless and left out because she now has an intimate bond with their newborn child. Or a lonely wife, who longs for her husband's attention but can't seem to find him amid the haze of his relentless work schedule. Or a spouse who has an affair in a misdirected attempt to repair a marriage twisted out of shape by a parent, a child, a quest for money, or long hours on the road.

Triangulation always involves a form of running away to soothe one's troubles; whether that running away is in the form of a lover, work, an overly intense relationship with a child, an in-law, or a drug doesn't matter. Learning how to prevent and deal with triangulation is essentially the same process no matter what the source.

The damage that is done by this pattern of running away to some other person or activity in order to avoid the difficult work of creating a successful relationship can devastate a family. When children get pulled in between parents to create a triangle, they become confused and angry, not knowing what to do with all the mixed messages they are given. When alcohol or drugs are brought into a family to smooth over the inevitable wrinkles of family life, the results can shatter any semblance of peace or safety. When work or an affair is used as a way of avoiding marital difficulties, the very backbone of a coherent family is threatened. Eventually, any of these triangles—if combined with a history of triangulation in a family—will lead to a feud.

Nancy and Joe's feud with their mother was terribly painful for all involved. Nancy, a forty-five-year-old housewife, and her brother Joe, a thirty-nine-year-old salesman, were the only two children of Connie and Ron, who had been divorced since Nancy and Joe were teenagers. Both Nancy and Joe stopped talking to their mother about a year and a half ago, when they learned from their father that their aunt, Connie's sister Anne, had died from pneumonia. After receiving a phone call from one of Anne's sons, informing Connie that her sister Anne had died and inviting her to the funeral, Connie agreed to call her own children, Nancy and Joe, with the news and pass along the funeral invitation.

Anne's death came up in a telephone conversation between Nancy and her father Ron six months after Anne died. It was the first Nancy had heard of it—six months after the fact. In disbelief, Nancy's father asked, "Didn't your mother tell you about it?" When Nancy realized that her mother had neglected to tell her, she telephoned her immediately. When Nancy pointedly asked her mother why neither she nor her brother Joe had heard anything about their aunt's death, Connie demurely responded, "I'm sorry. I must have forgotten to tell you."

Nancy and her brother Joe were beside themselves with anger. Joe, who had already had many run-ins with his mother, said to Nancy, "To hell with it. She may be our mother, but can't you see she doesn't give a damn about our feelings? All she's ever cared about was herself. I have no need for her in my life." Nancy also experienced their mother's "forgetting" as a knife turning in her side, and she joined her brother in a rebellion of silence.

Sadly, it wasn't until several years later, as Connie herself was critically ill, that there was any hint of reconciliation—an ingenuine apology from her daughter Nancy while Connie was on her deathbed. Connie died with her son barely speaking to her, and both her children holding onto resentment and anger.

As far as either Joe or Nancy knew, there was one simple reason for their feud: Their mother neglected to tell them about the death of their aunt. What neither Joe nor Nancy realized was that the feud with their mother was the culmination of a long history of triangulation in their family.

In the years that Joe and Nancy's parents were married, their father Ron complained that there was no romance between him and his wife Connie. Bored with the marriage, he sought the comfort of long hours away from home at work. As a result, the children felt they had no father. They suffered from being on the outside of a father-mother-work triangle.

But there was another triangle going on as well. This triangle started as a deep competition between the two sisters, Connie and Anne. Dating back to a triangle between Connie, Anne and *their* mother, Connie and Anne always competed for their mother's attention. When Connie's children were born, they even competed over who could care for them better. It was Anne who won the competition, and Connie's children ended up feeling better taken care of by their aunt than by their mother. In this triangle, Nancy and Joe together were wedged between their mother and their aunt.

After many years of feeling abandoned by their parents, and being caught in between two warring factions, withholding the news of Anne's death was the straw that broke the camel's back. Because third parties were recruited in a misguided or unconscious attempt to smooth over the trouble spots in the marriage between Connie and Ron, and in the relationship between Connie and her sister Anne, neither of these relationships could be healed. Triangulation diverts the emotional energy away from the places that need that energy the most, so the work of getting through tough times in a family never gets done. Eventually, triangulation takes its toll and erupts into a full-fledged feud.

Early on in my marriage, I experienced firsthand the way triangulation weaves its web. Soon after the birth of our first child, my wife and I learned that our baby was not one to be soothed easily. Rocking, swinging, swaddling, holding, cooing, dancing until dawn—none of them worked. Only two things did the trick: nursing at his mother's breast, and long, bumpy car rides at night during which my wife and I sang poorly harmonized, jumbled strains of "Chapel of Love."

Hoping, like most fathers, to be an intimate partner in the raising of our children, I did what I could do to soothe a baby who could not be soothed easily. It didn't take long before I experienced deep feelings of frustration at not having the "equipment" necessary to soothe him. Both our son and his mother became entwined in a relationship in which she alone could soothe him, emotionally locking me out.

While my wife was awash in mother's milk, trying to find her own strength and individuality, I found myself increasingly preoccupied with work. I started to look longingly at other women, and lost patience easily with my wife. Used to having the bulk of my wife's attention, I became jealous of the attention our son received, although I tried to keep the jealousy hidden; after all, we were all stressed enough with the demands of a colicky newborn. Fortunately, as time passed and our son grew less dependent, we were able to weather this marital storm, and move on to other, so far less intense challenges.

Had we not weathered the storm of a new child entering into our lives, the results might have been the dissolving of a marriage, or the beginnings of a deep chasm that would have been difficult to bridge. To some extent, the triangulation of getting more deeply involved in my work can be viewed as a healthy adaptation to my uselessness at home. When a person can't get emotional needs met from one source, it often becomes necessary to look toward another source. Like most of life's paths, however, this one can be risky. When the new path becomes so engrossing that it prevents the traveler from doing what is necessary to "come back home" and resolve the problem that led him or her from home in the first place, the triangulation becomes treacherous fodder for a feud.

Often, moving closer to someone in a family who has a special need is necessary and inadvertently leads to triangulation. When a parent has a child who is born with congenital disabilities, suffers from a severe developmental disability, or who later develops a serious chronic illness, it is natural for one parent to focus most of his or her attention on that child. In the process, other family members often suffer. Other children, and sometimes an uninvolved spouse, feel neglected. In these situations, siblings of the needy child often make heroic sacrifices, knowing that it is the "right thing to do." They will often deny their own suffering, only to have it surface years later. Families who have a child with special needs are not only burdened by the child, but by the extra effort needed to attend to the needs of the other children in the family.

When no one in a family feels left out, triangulation doesn't occur. There is no triangulation when getting closer to one person in the family who is particularly needy is matched by an increase in attention to the others as well. But when getting closer to one person means neglecting another's needs, a destructive triangle sets in.

Triangulation also becomes destructive when it ends up distorting the roles of the people involved. Essentially, a child's role in a family is to act like a child while slowly learning to take on responsibilities of adulthood. One role of a parent is to create a feeling of safety so that a child can learn to take on these responsibilities. In the case of a family in which a child is particularly needy or ill, triangulation occurs when the ill child also becomes the source of nurturance for the parent. For example, rather than turn to her husband for support and nurturance, a mother turns to her ill child to comfort and support her. A father who spends all his time taking care of his son not only neglects his wife but begins to distort his relationship with his son so that time with his son becomes the only thing that truly feels comforting to him. This sort of role distortion ends up placing a heavy burden on the child, one that children are ill-equipped to handle.

While triangulation can occur among any combination of three parties, there are certain triangular relationships within families that occur repeatedly and often culminate in a feud. When triangles extend beyond or outside the family, they nearly always in some way reflect something going on amiss within the family. Typical "external" family triangles include the extramarital affair, and triangles with work, play, or friends.

PARENT-CHILD TRIANGLES

Harry, a seventy-year-old retired real estate broker, came to my office in a panic. He had the face of a man who was once boyishly handsome, but constant worry had etched itself into his forehead. He was a soft-spoken man, with a deep, gravelly voice that would squeak to reveal moments of distress.

At first, Harry's panic seemed to be about his health. He had been proud of his good health all his life, and viewed himself as young and vibrant until a fainting spell caused by high blood pressure landed him in the emergency room. Although Harry hated physicians, one sympathetic cardiologist to whom he took a liking recommended that Harry see a psychologist to "talk his troubles out."

Initially reluctant to talk, Harry didn't take long to settle in and tell me about his life. The coffee he requested sat untouched on the end table by his chair, as he did his best to describe his childhood. His parents were from the "old school," never interested in him or his feelings. Harry spoke haltingly and fidgeted as he brought up his only sibling, a younger brother named Sam who contracted polio at an early age, and who he "always resented" for stealing away their parents' attention. Although he was also angry at his parents, Harry seemed to try to hold back tears as he talked about his mother's death fifteen years ago, and his father's death two years later—which was when Harry's anger at his brother Sam came to a head. Spurred on by Harry's wife Sylvia, whose disdain for Sam was never kept a mystery to anyone, Harry meekly attempted to confront his brother for not doing his share of taking care of their infirmed parents during the last few years of their lives. Harry felt as though Sam had never pulled his weight, that the burdens on the family had always fallen squarely on Harry. Harry was convinced, as was Sylvia, that the only reason Sam ever contacted his brother was to ask him for money. Sam was not exactly a slouch, having earned a doctorate in chemistry and a second doctorate many years later in sociology. Yet, Harry told me with a sheepish grin, Sam's doctorates never taught him either business or common sense.

Harry, growing increasingly agitated, told me that ten years ago, after brewing with anger for three years, that he finally gave Sam the piece of his mind he deserved. I sensed that it wasn't easy for Harry to express his anger directly at anyone, so when I asked him to describe just what piece of his mind he gave Sam, I wasn't surprised at his response.

"Well . . ." Harry said as he fidgeted again, "I told him on the phone that he was irresponsible . . . you know, he blamed the whole thing on my wife. And I didn't give him any more money. You might find that hard to believe, but I held the line with him."

Harry's confrontation, however meager, and his statement that he would no longer provide his brother with financial aid, signaled *the last time the two brothers spoke, roughly ten years ago.* Their feud of silence followed on the heels of a long history of hurtful squabbles. Sam was all that Harry had left of a family, and their feud left him feeling empty and alone. Harry wove his recent health concerns into the tapestry of his family chasm, as he related his sadness to me:

I don't know if you can understand this . . . I don't want to make a big deal out of this, but I've always been concerned about my health, and I could have twenty years to go . . . But let's say I only live for a few more years. I don't know how I could leave without making some kind of amends. Not that my brother's a real terrific person. He's a selfish son of a bitch, and I know that if he weren't my brother I wouldn't want to have anything to do with him. But we were close when we were young, very young I guess. And he's really my only family left. He's really the only family I ever had. You know, you could never really talk to my parents, they wouldn't have that! I was much closer to my wife's family, and they're about all gone too.

And I really don't know if it's all my brother's fault. My parents weren't really the nicest people, although they were always good to my brother. But I think if I were to be real honest about it all, I'm sure he suffered too. My wife thinks I'm being too sympathetic, but that's Sylvia. She's suspicious that everyone tries to take advantage of me; you know, I've made a lot of money. I realize that this whole thing might be stupid of me, but I know that before I die I need to somehow get back in touch with my brother. Like I said, he's really all I have of a family, and for better or worse, right or wrong, I was brought up that family is the most important thing.

Harry's soft, slightly confused, and tentative tone revealed a deeply held desire to be part of a family. I told him that his venomous feelings toward his brother, however unpleasant, were nevertheless a powerful link to him. He took my suggestion well that perhaps it would make sense to take a closer look at how his family "did business"; the roots of his feud with his brother might extend beyond his brother's ability to take care of his aged parents or the jealousy Harry might have felt as a result of all the attention Sam received for his polio.

For Harry, the answers were revealed by looking up and down the generational ladder: up at the generation that preceded him, and down at the generation he helped to create. Harry knew very little about his grandparents, other than who they were and where they were from. Because he knew little about them, and there were few family survivors he could ask, we decided to look closely at the three generations that consisted of his parents, his own generation, and his children's generation.

As we talked, it became apparent that in each generation a "special child" was selected for special attention. In the case of Harry's primary family, it was clear that his brother, perhaps partly due to his having polio, received an overwhelming amount of attention and affection from their mother. As a result, Harry felt left out. Harry never before considered that this arrangement also left even his father feeling like a pariah in his own family, excluded from a relationship with his wife or either of his children. Harry's father, a gruff sanitation engineer in New York City, chose to work as a watchman at a garbage dump for long hours not only for money, but also because it most likely helped him deal with his inability to break the strong bond between his wife and his son Sam. He became wedded to his job and his social life with his friends, extricating himself from a marriage that offered him little.

When Harry looked down the generational ladder to his own children, it was easy for him to see triangulation at work there as well. His oldest son, first a beatnik and then a hippie, became involved with drugs at an early age. Harry and his wife became overly involved with this son, which in retrospect Harry believed only worsened the problem. Their other children told Harry that they felt completely neglected by him and his wife as they were growing up. Harry saw that by neglecting his own "good" children, he had done the same thing to them as his parents had done to him.

But the pattern of triangulation did not stop there. Harry even noticed his own children triangulating their children, to the detriment of their marriages and families. Harry saw his grandchildren as depressed and apathetic, and understood their feelings for the first time as emanating from a historical family legacy of triangulation.

Harry's feud is a good example of how many people in a family are affected by triangulation. When Harry's mother paid such close attention to Harry's brother, Harry's father felt left out of the picture, Harry felt left out, and in a strange way Harry's brother Sam also had a price to pay. Most children who are the "object" of the dance of triangulation suffer as well, because they feel overburdened. While they like the attention, they know that others are being left out, and they feel guilty. In future relationships, they often feel deserving of extra attention, but ashamed and guilty when they get it.

Harry first felt his distress in his body; his heart raced, he became dizzy and light-headed, and his blood pressure soared. For others, the mystifying effects of triangulation appear not in their own bodies, but in the behavior of their parents toward them, or, in Paula's case, in the behavior of her children toward each other.

Paula is an effervescent forty-five-year-old commercial artist who has spent the last twelve years of her life working out of her suburban home so she could be closer to her children. Her two children, an eleven-year-old boy and a nine-year-old girl, fought fiercely with one another over just about anything. The tantrums often escalated into full-fledged warfare. Even though Paula sought help in order to better manage her children's behavior, the severity of the children's difficulties led me to suspect that they were somehow carrying more than their share of the family's burden.

Paula described her relationship with her husband as "remarkable in this day and age." She remembered her parents, who died many years ago, as loving people. Suspecting that a feud might be lurking somewhere in Paula's background, I asked her about her own sibling relationships. After a wince and a long breath, Paula told me that she was the youngest of three children, and although she remained in friendly contact with her brother, she had not spoken to her sister for fifteen years. When I learned that she had been locked in a feud with her sister, I waited to see if Paula would realize on her own that her children were doing with each other what she and her sister had done for years. After she changed the subject, I pointed this "coincidence" out to Paula. At first she seemed taken aback, but as she sat and thought about it, she began to see the similarities.

Even this important realization didn't get to the heart of the matter. I was after the more deeply rooted pattern, so I asked Paula if she would consent to find out more about the particular habits her family acquired as it moved from one generation to the next. She agreed, and although she already knew a good deal about her family history, there were also large gaps because both of her parents had died almost twenty years earlier. She relied mostly on conversations with her older brother to help fill in the blanks. And because she was still reluctant to speak with her sister, she enlisted her brother to speak with her sister on the partial ruse that he was putting together a family history.

At first it seemed a far stretch for Paula to believe that the best thing she could do to help her children get along better with each other was to struggle to heal the intense sibling conflict in her own generation. Though she was loath to hear it, this meant dealing with the feud she had been having with her sister for the past fifteen years. Paula insisted that she would prefer a root canal, but when she understood that reconciling with her sister would break the patterns that she had learned so well from her early experiences as a child in her family, and therefore permit her to deal with her own children more effectively, she decided it was worth the effort.

Paula's family history revealed a very powerful pattern of intense sibling conflicts. In each generation the oldest child was triangulated, forming an intense bond with the mother while the younger children were neglected. This triangular pattern ignited sibling antagonisms and resentments, taking otherwise healthy sibling rivalry and intensifying it into sibling rage. In the family Paula grew up in, a triangle was discovered in which Paula's mother avoided dealing with her husband by getting closer to her son. As a result, Paula felt left out in the cold. What Paula hadn't considered before, though, was that her sister also must have felt left out. Their intense sibling rivalry was really a competition between the two of them for their mother's scarce attention. Paula came to realize that while they were both rowing against each other, they were both in the same boat—being "triangled out" of the mother-father-son relationship.

Paula was also able to see how she had repeated the same pattern with her own children. While she worked hard to give both of her own children equal time, she admitted to feeling a special bond with her oldest son. Paula's daughter was fighting with her brother in part to vie for Mom's affection.

As we discussed her family history in greater depth, Paula revealed that her anger toward her sister was something she carried with her all the time. I suggested that it was this anger, stemming from the triangular patterns of her own childhood, that was at the root of her unwittingly siding with her son against her daughter, which only served to fuel their intense rivalry with one another. Paula and I carefully orchestrated visits between her and her sister using some of the strategies discussed in the second half of this book, which eventually disintegrated their feud. Once she overcame her animosity toward her sister, Paula found that she was better able to help her children get along with each other. She was able to more clearly see her son's provocations, so her daughter felt less "ganged up on." And she found that she was better able to set limits with her children, feeling more confident in her role as a parent.

In Paula's feud, like so many others, triangulation operated in the background, weaving its insidious web in such a way that even the people embroiled in the feud had no idea of its existence or harmful effects. For both Harry and Paula, triangulation was a subtle influence, the tension between two people resulting in a third feeling either pushed out too far or pulled in too close. The multigenerational pattern of triangulation can also be set in motion in less subtle ways.

IN-LAW TRIANGLES

In one form of in-law triangle, a man may be in a highly conflict-laden relationship with his mother. Immediately upon getting married, he turns his "problem mother" over to his new wife to handle. As with a football being handed off to another player, all responsibilities for the care of the mother are now the wife's. The new wife is given the responsibility, either directly or underhandedly, of telephoning the problem parent regularly, remembering to celebrate and buy cards for birthdays and anniversaries, and making sure the parent has a relationship with any grandchildren that might come along.

In this sort of triangle, the husband usually plays a passive role, preferring to stay aloof from both his mother and his wife. He leaves it "up to the women" to have the relationship that he could never achieve with his own mother. The women can do one of two things: They could team up with each other and "triangle out" the husband, or they could join forces and team up to "fix" the cold and aloof son and husband. When the mother and daughter-in-law decide to leave the husband to his passive ways, this decision usually stems from a situation in which the new wife feels somehow disconnected or alienated from her own family, and joins her husband's family as a refuge. She then teams up with the "mother she never had," and because this meets a deep need for a mothering relationship, she settles with this and leaves the husband to his own devices.

In the situation where wife and mother-in-law join forces against the husband/son, the husband often feels betrayed and ganged up on by two women. While the husband may have felt good early on, when he is relieved that he no longer has to deal with his mother, his good feelings turn to bitterness and resentment as his best-laid plans unravel and eventually backfire. Now, instead of one woman to contend with, the husband/son has two. Where he might have felt particularly incompetent in dealing with the demands of his mother, now he feels doubly incompetent because he can't come to grips with either woman. He may even blame his wife for betraying him by siding with his mother against him, and the whole nasty situation might eventually form the groundwork for a feud.

Many men deal with their inability to cope with women by creating even more triangles, turning to work, superficial affairs, or very often to drinking or using other drugs. At times they seek out the company of other men to commiserate with, or they do the opposite and turn inward. This turning inward might eventually result in a severe isolative depression.

Occasionally, this pattern does a flip-flop, and it is the husband who unites with his wife's mother against his wife. This may happen at times when the wife begins to do some of the things with her husband that both he and his mother-in-law find intolerable. Perhaps it's a childhood or teenage habit, such as drug abuse, or a vicious, potentially life-threatening eating disorder, such as anorexia or bulimia. It may be a tendency to run away from life's problems by not holding a job, or philandering. The husband, desperate to find someone to turn to who understands his wife, calls on his mother-in-law, who shares his concern for her daughter. Unfortunately, the closer he gets to his mother-in-law, the more alienated and angry the wife becomes. Just as with the reverse situation, the wife feels betrayed and isolated.

This pattern can also occur when a woman attempts to break free from a traditional role, deciding to work outside the home, or advance in a career that might take her away from her family. Threatened by the change in the status quo, and perhaps fearing the loss of his wife, a husband might enlist the support of his mother-in-law in arguing that his wife is neglecting the children or her wifely duties.

POWER AND LOYALTY

The most pervasive in-law triangle occurs when a husband or wife fails to adequately "grow up" before leaving home and marrying, resulting in an overly intense, dependent relationship on a particular parent. While this seems to occur just as frequently with men and women, for simplicity this example will center on a man. Overly attached to and dependent on his mother, he marries, hoping that doing this will help him become emotionally independent. Still terribly close to his mother, he finds the woman he marries difficult to get along with, and perhaps inadequate in certain areas. After all, no one can live up to his mother. So instead of struggling to work out his difficulties with his wife, he turns to his mother for support and guidance.

In this scenario, the mother may also be dependent on her son (perhaps because he was part of a triangle involving his mother and father), and she encourages him to come to her with his problems. Even though she may know that this is potentially destructive to his marriage, that might be all right with her because, after all, no one can be good enough for her son (except her, of course).

The husband's loyalty remains with his mother, and his failure to shift that loyalty to his new family and wife ends up undermining their marital bond. She is powerless against the combined forces of her husband and her mother-in-law, and must yield authority to them. This problem becomes particularly acute and devastating when children enter the new family, because any hope of the wife growing into feeling competent as a mother is undermined by the mother-in-law, who—at least in her husband's eyes—maintains ultimate authority.

In many families, it is the father-in-law whose domineering presence crosses the generational line. Not uncommonly, a woman who "leaves home" with an adoring view of her father as someone who can do no wrong finds it difficult to tolerate her husband's imperfections. An adoring father of the bride might find it difficult to see any man as living up to his standards for a son-in-law. Whenever something goes wrong, the wife runs immediately to the telephone to contact her father, informing him of her husband's latest escapades. The father, especially if he maintains a strong, patriarchal role, makes the decisions and undermines his daughter's marriage.

This situation is not uncommon in families where the son-in-law is brought into his father-in-law's business. The father-in-law, not only the patriarch of the family but also the boss of his own successful business, becomes such a powerful figure that the son feels as though the only way he can grow up, earn self-respect, and have a sense of power and authority within his own family is to disconnect completely from his wife's family. This is difficult to do, because the dependency on them is often not only emotional, but financial as well. It becomes truly impossible, however, when the daughter's dependency on her father is so great that she sabotages any moves toward independence her husband makes. She too wonders whether her husband could ever fill her father's shoes, and consciously or unconsciously she makes sure he never gets the chance.

As a result of these in-law triangles, mothers-in-law and fathers-in-law find themselves wedged between their children and their children's spouses. Without a healthy resolution to these triangular relationships, the seeds are sown for a feud. There is no shortage of divorces blamed on intrusive in-laws. It takes a courageous attempt to break free of an overly dependent relationship with one's parents in order to navigate successfully the rocky waters of marriage.

Often, in-law triangles create an ongoing feud not only within the marriage, but also between the two corners of the triangle that consist of the parent in-law and the child in-law. As an attempt to break free of a domineering and intrusive in-law, either the parent in-law or the child in-law declares a war of hatred and competition with the other. The parent insists that the child in-law is not good for his or her child, and will do everything and anything to get the child away from the influence of his or her spouse. Likewise, the child in-law will insist (correctly) that the parent in-law is doing everything and anything to break up the marriage, and insists that she or he must fight to preserve the marriage and family. The child of the parent in-law, feeling caught hopelessly between two allegiances, often acts ambivalently. The war continues unabated unless the child whose parent is involved in the triangle takes some definitive stance.

CHILD-FOCUSED TRIANGLES

When two parents are unsuccessful working out their troubles, either by fighting overtly or by burying their feelings in a code of silence, they often turn to their children for consolation. Children become the likely targets of triangulation primarily because they are there, but also because it is easy to see oneself as a "good parent" by having an intense relationship with a child. The line between an overly intense, triangular relationship with a child, and merely giving a child what the child needs by way of attention and nurturance is often blurry, so it's easy to justify a triangular relationship. But many parents need no justification for triangulation; it is done automatically, without planning. In essence, all family members play an unconscious conspiratorial role, with children taking up the slack of intimacy where their parents left off.

Triangular relationships with children nearly always serve the purpose of turning attention away from parental disharmony. At times, marital disagreements about money issues, sex, and emotional availability transmogrify into disagreements over parenting. When a child is brought into my family therapy office, designated in one fashion or another as a "problem child," and I discover that the parents disagree about how to handle the child, it tells me immediately that I'm dealing with a problem of triangulation. It is remarkable how, when the *true source* of the parental disharmony is located and dealt with, disagreements over parenting vanish into thin air.

The absence of one parent in a family due to a divorce, death, or remarriage does not necessarily mean that a child will become triangulated with the remaining parent. Triangulation is always a distortion of the normal parent-child relationship, leading to an emotional overburdening of the child. When a parent dies or moves away, whether the children become triangulated will be determined by how the remaining parent deals with the loss. As long as the remaining parent deals with his or her grief within himself or herself, or turns to people other than the children for support and help, it is not likely that the children will feel the pressures and burdens of triangulation. It is only when a parent turns to the children for emotional comfort that the children feel overburdened, and a child-focused triangle rears its pointy head.

Variations of the child-centered triangle abound; the more clever the parents, the more creative the exact manifestation of this triangle. Generally, though, there are four basic formats that this triangle follows.

THE CHILD AS MARITAL PARTNER

In this form, one parent feels emotionally neglected by his or her spouse, and turns to a particular child to meet the parent's needs for nurturance. Usually, a particular child in the family is more susceptible than others. It is often the more sensitive child, or the child who already shows a preference for one parent or another. It may also be the child least likely to rebel against being in this position. In this scenario, the triangulated child eventually cooperates with the comfort-seeking parent, and the two become extremely close. This serves to alienate the remaining parent, who grows more distant over time. The parent who gets closer to the child eventually feels calmed down and soothed, and this parent no longer needs to attend to the marital difficulties that spurred the triangulation. The marital partner who is "triangled out" grows increasingly resentful, and eventually becomes even more distant and hostile.

THE CHILD AS DARTBOARD

In this variation of the classic parent-child triangle, the one parent who is left out in the cold due to the other parent's closeness with one of the children turns on that child. If it's the father who is triangled out, the father may blame the child for taking his wife away from him, or more likely, will find something egregiously wrong with that child and shove it down the child's throat. The child who is selected as the target will often share physical or behavioral characteristics of the mother, and these characteristics will often be the focus of the father's rage. In so doing, the father is able to express his anger toward his wife by criticizing his child. The child need not share these characteristics to be placed in this position; just the fact that the mother selected this child is often enough to do the trick. So long as the child is the dartboard for the parent's angry darts, the original marital discord remains masked and unavailable for discussion.

"Dartboard children," as I call them, suffer deeply as a result of their position in this triangle. As is the case with all children caught in a triangle, they end up feeling as though they are in a "no-win" situation; none of their choices appears to solve the problem. They could align with one parent, most likely the one parent who has gotten closer to them, and condemn the parent who is throwing darts. If the dart-throwing started very early on in the child's life, this will often guarantee that the child will side with the safer parent. But if the child at one time had a positive, warm relationship with the dart thrower, the child is hesitant to reject him or her outright. If the dart-thrower is the father, and the child is a boy, the son might feel as though he needs a father as a role model and be hesitant to reject him outright. If the dart thrower is the mother, and the triangled child is a girl, she too might not want to reject her angry mother.

Also, most triangulated children have some awareness, however dim, that the vituperation placed on them is displaced. When asked, they will often state directly that the dart thrower is "really angry at my mother." There is some solace in this knowledge, and it allows the child not to have to completely turn away from the hostile parent.

Feeling as though they can't completely reject either parent, dartboard children often internalize the conflict between their parents. While such a child may occasionally express his or her anger toward both parents, the protests go unheeded because the parents need the child to remain in that role in order to not face their own marital problems. Because children tend to incorporate aspects of each parent into their own personality as a normal developmental process, dartboard children hold onto an image of themselves as though they have two people residing inside themselves. The two parts of their personalities wage a war against each other, mirroring the war between their parents. As a result, dartboard children are often confused, ambivalent, and continually upset. They often fail to develop a sense of themselves as competent in handling life's conflicts. They become depressed as a result, feeling ineffectual and failing to develop a strong, integrated personality.

Occasionally these children take desperate measures, designed cleverly to upset the system. If they become depressed enough, or somehow manage to become enough of a problem, they notice that their parents might temporarily put down their guns and work together to deal with them. A triangled teenager might attempt to kill herself, hoping that if her parents see her as desperately in need of help they will work together to support her and thus put down their weapons. A triangled boy may resort to stealing, making sure he gets caught in order to mobilize his parents to work together. A girl may starve herself, becoming anorexic. While these children might still be the focus of their parents' attention, and their self-destructive behavior will only continue the attention being placed on them instead of on the parents' marital relationship, the child feels the sacrifice is worthwhile because at least the parents are now working together.

THE CHILD AS FOOTBALL

In this variation of the parent-child triangle, the child selected for triangulation is thrown back and forth between the parents like a football, as each parent vies for the child's favor and allegiance. In order to avoid facing each other, each parent focuses intently on one child.

Sometimes this takes the form of each parent declaring "I'm the better parent!" to the child, and then undermining the other parent's authority with the child. "You know your father doesn't like it when I buy you junk food, but we know he's too rigid about these things." "Your mother thinks these shoes look terrible on you, but *we* like them."

The child-as-football triangle is not about parents simply disagreeing. It's about parents who go out of their way to undermine each other, seeking the child's favor. As with all triangles, it's merely a subterfuge for the rage that exists between parents, and as with all triangles, it sets the stage for a subsequent feud.

The football child suffers most of the same consequences as the dartboard child. The child internalizes confusing messages, with one part of herself continually undermining another part of herself. She may become paralyzed with indecision or, more likely, harbor deep feelings of resentment and become extra sensitive to being betrayed in life. After all, she grows up in an environment where betrayal is the business of the day. As a result, she also might find herself having difficulty trusting others.

But the most characteristic state of mind of the football child is one of confusion, or a feeling of mystification. On the one hand, the football child—as opposed to the child who is used as a dartboard—is being told by both parents that she is being loved. On the other hand, she is constantly being told that the other parent is wrong. She is required to hold these feelings of anger toward the other parent inside her, to become a container for them. As such, even though she is told she is being loved, she ends up feeling a tremendous amount of anger, usually toward both parents.

As she becomes more sophisticated and thoughtful, the football child ends up realizing that what she thought was love and even favoritism was actually just a cloaked weapon in a war between her parents. She then feels angry about being used as an object, about not being seen as the unique individual she is, and angrily turns away from both of her parents.

THE CHILD AS PARENT

Parents who are particularly needy and insecure may turn to their children to take care of them. I am not talking about the normal process of aging, in which the "child becomes father to the man" as the older generation becomes physically dependent on the younger generation. What happens instead when young, healthy parents turn to their children to become their own parent? This generational flip-flop often occurs when young parents marry early, before they can become emotionally independent from their own families. Or it occurs when a young adult wishes to escape his or her family, and attempts to do so either by running off with the first person who comes along or by having a child.

During one of my internships as a psychologist, I was privileged to work with a group of teen mothers, teenagers as young as eleven years old who became pregnant and decided not to abort their children. Many of those children having children were doing so with the terribly misguided hope and expectation that their newborn child would somehow take care of them. "I got pregnant," I would hear them say, "so that someone would love me." The someone to whom they were referring was their newborn baby.

In many other cases, it's the husband or wife who becomes the "ticket out" of the family. The two children get married, expecting each other to become the parent. This formula seems to work well for the first few years, until one of the two starts to grow up and begins to resent the role of the parent. If the "younger one" can't grow up as quickly, the marriage is usually stressed beyond repair, and the couple breaks up. Someone, however, is left with the child or children, and if it is the emotionally younger of the two, that parent will turn to the child to take on the parenting role.

When this generational flip-flop happens, the parent begins to expect more of the child than the child can handle. The child does the housekeeping. The parent turns to the child for advice. The parent looks to the child to tell the parent what to do and how to run his or her life. Parents come crying to their children, dumping their own fears and troubles on their children's laps. Bedtimes become extended or violated, because parents need their children to stay awake for late-night talks designed to soothe the parents.

As a result, children lose their ability to be children; they can't depend on their parents for support and comfort, because the parents are too needy themselves. The child, burdened already by the social demands of childhood, feels overly weighted down by having to care for his or her parents as well. The child's deep anger, which can't be expressed for fear of losing his or her parents, simmers as resentment builds, and results in an overly intense relationship between parent and child.

This form of triangulation, in which one parent becomes emotionally dependent on a child, and the other parent fades from view, is remarkably common in families who feud. It is a particularly difficult form of triangulation to fix, because doing so requires "growing the parent up" in order to free the child from the burden of being stuck in the parent role.

The kind of feud that arises from these generational reversals, as is the case in nearly all feuds, is usually seen in more than one generation at a time. In fact, it is usually the child who is placed in the parent role, or "parentified," who responds by cutting himself or herself off from the overly dependent parent. The parent, in turn, is forced to get his or her needs met elsewhere, so then turns back again to his or her parent, and the pattern seems to reverberate through the decades.

STEPFAMILY TRIANGLES

An increasingly common triangle involves members of a stepfamily. The postdivorce situation often represents the continuation of a feud begun earlier on in the original marriage. Unfortunately, while many divorces appear to be attempts at ending vicious feuds, the legal divorce itself rarely ends a feud. Ex-husbands and ex-wives continue their deeply linked, enmeshed relationship by triangling in a child, and through the child the parental feud continues.

While divorce is complex, I have found over the years that as a general rule most divorces occur because one marital partner begins to get healthier and the other partner isn't willing to go along for the ride. Emotional well-being, for someone who has functioned neurotically for many years, can be a terrifying ride. Having to give up the comfort and ease of unhealthy behavioral patterns is no small task, and can lead someone down a road filled with unpredictable, painful potholes.

One of the saddest things about the decision to divorce for many feuding families is that some individuals harbor an illusion that the divorce will end the feud. I have found instead that very few bad marriages end up in good divorces. While there may be other good reasons to divorce, a legal divorce rarely ends a feud between two partners, especially when children remain a permanent link between the two parents. It has been said that you can divorce a spouse, but you can never divorce a child. If a child is involved in a triangle with his or her parents, a divorce between the parents does not ensure that the triangulation will end. Instead of fighting over which parent takes the child to the mall, the post-divorce fight becomes about which parent takes the child for Christmas. In addition, fighting about whose parenting methods are better continues long after a legal divorce is obtained.

For many parents, a significant part of picking up the pieces of their lives after a traumatic marriage and an equally traumatic divorce is an attempt to get romantically involved in a relationship with someone else. Most people make a conscious effort not to repeat the same mistake they made before, and search for someone who is at least superficially different from their ex-spouse. Most parents search for a partner who will have a good relationship with their children, and in fact, winning over the potential stepchildren is often a critical part of the courtship process for someone seeking marriage to a previously married man or woman (as, I believe, it should be).

In families where children have been triangulated, however, the new stepparent is often in for a surprise. Unresolved issues and battles from the prior marriage crop up, often in relationship to the child or children who are triangulated. The new stepparent feels increasingly like an outsider, as he or she feels the tension between the ex-spouses mount, usually over issues pertaining to the children.

Biological parents question a child's loyalty, as the child is pushed to take sides against the other parent. New stepparents, if they are not clear about what they are getting into, may be surprised to encounter the depth of their new stepchildren's ties to their other biological parent, even when the other parent may have been abusive and terribly harmful to the child.

Feuds involving stepfamilies often begin even before the remarriage takes place. The announcement of the remarriage itself is often enough to set off a feud between ex-marriage partners that may have been lying dormant. The entrance onto the scene of another man or another woman creates another triangle (original husband, original wife, and new marriage partner), and the feelings of animosity that may have been carefully compartmentalized by one member of the triangle now erupt when the new partner threatens to destabilize the peace.

Under these circumstances, the originally triangulated child may now be called upon to fill his or her original role as the funnel for one parent's rage against the other, and the original triangle erupts into yet another manifestation of the original feud.

But the stepfamily situation becomes potentially much more complex, as the number of possible triangles multiplies. As each parent remarries, a new set of in-laws enters the scene as well. Now, not only do the in-law feuds among the original marriage partners play a potential role, but the possibility of feuds among the two new in-laws on each side is also added to the equation. The possible number of triangular feuds among all four sets of in-laws becomes arithmetically staggering. Fortunately, however, despite the staggering numbers and the potential for a great number of triangles, most feuds that occur in stepfamilies fall into one or more of four types: the *wicked stepparent,* the *perfect stepparent,* the *ghost of the former spouse,* and the *grandparent triangle.*

THE WICKED STEPPARENT

This most common feud occurs when a child and stepparent declare open season on each other. Perhaps jealous of the new parent taking away Dad's or Mom's attention and affection, the stepchild blames the stepparent for intruding and casts her or him as evil. Hoping to regain the bliss that may have existed prior to the new spouse entering the scene, the triangled child does his or her best to destroy the new marriage. Similarly, from the new stepparent's perspective, the new child may represent a threat and competition for the love of the biological parent, and so the stepchild becomes castigated and even blamed for any marital discord in the new marriage.

In the meantime, the biological parent is caught between the proverbial rock and hard place. Owing primary allegiance to his or her biological child, perhaps even feeling some guilt for having put the child through a difficult marriage and divorce, and knowing that the child is not yet ready to fend for himself or herself in the world, the biological parent is loath to go against his or her own child. But also desperately wanting to make a new marriage work, and believing that it will serve the child best in the long run, the biological parent is also loath to go against his or her new spouse. In this triangle, the biological parent is the one who feels like a ping-pong ball, bouncing back and forth between allegiances. Yet, as is the case with all triangles, all parties to the conflict feel frightened and threatened as long as the feud continues.

THE PERFECT STEPPARENT

This feud arises out of the attempt that a stepparent makes, however noble, to become the ideal parent. Entering into a new family, the new stepparent seeks acceptance by all involved, and strives to become the best, most involved parent possible. Some stepparents enter families with the naive belief that it is the stepparent's role to fulfill all the functions of the missing biological parent. New stepparents often have to learn through trial and error that stepparenting is a different role from biological parenting.

At times, an unconscious competition exists between the stepparent and the ex-spouse. In the case of a new stepfather, for example, the new stepfather wants to prove to his new wife that he is a better father than her ex-husband, so he will go all out to be the best possible dad he can be.

The expectation that the new stepparent can somehow replace the "missing" parent may not just come from the new stepparent. Often, the biological parent believes as well that it is the role of the stepparent to fulfill all the responsibilities of the prior spouse. Explicitly or implicitly, this expectation is placed upon the new person entering the scene. The new stepfather's attempts at becoming the golden father to his stepson, or the stepmother's striving to become the supermom to the stepchild, is often doomed to failure.

The feud that unfolds from this triangle begins when the stepparent inevitably fails in some fashion. The supermom who is ultimately supportive begins to feel rejected as the stepchild takes advantage of the stepmother's openness and largesse, or the stepchild acts up rebelliously despite the kind gestures of the stepmother. Or, attempting to correct an overly lax attitude by a previous parent, a new stepfather comes in to discipline a stepchild as it should have been done before. When the stepchild ultimately rejects the stepparent's attempt to correct past mistakes, the stepparent fails. A feud erupts when the biological parent becomes deeply critical and rejecting of the "perfect parent," not because the stepparent attempted to be perfect, but because the stepparent failed in his or her attempts. The biological parent's unreasonable expectation that the stepparent succeed at doing the impossible and become the perfect replacement parent turns into disappointment, anger, and blame toward the stepparent.

Likewise, the stepchild becomes upset as the perfect parent attempts to get emotionally close to the stepchild. Some children feel as though this threatens their relationship with the noncustodial parent, that if the child allows himself or herself to get too close to the stepparent, the child will be betraying the parent who does not live in the household.

I have seen this triangle present itself most often when a father retains primary custody of his children and a new stepmother enters the scene. The father, who may be the primary wage-earner, is gone from home most of the time, and the primary parenting responsibility falls on the stepmother. The father expects the children to attach to her deeply, and despite the stepmother's best efforts to make that happen, the father blames the stepmother if she cannot get his children to love or mind her the way they do his ex-wife. As a result, every member of the triangle feels cheated; the stepmother feels as though she cannot have the love she wants from her stepchildren or the support she needs from her husband, the husband feels as though he can't have the effective mother he wants for his children, and the children feel abandoned by their father, who has left them with a stranger as a mother, albeit a very nice one.

THE GHOST OF THE FORMER SPOUSE

In this stepfamily triangle, a feud develops directly between the stepparent and the former spouse, triangulating the current husband or wife. It seems as if the ghost of the former spouse still resides hauntingly in the new family. In the case where the new stepmother feuds openly with the former wife, the current husband may covertly fan the flames of this fire, because to do so keeps the ex-wife's presence alive in the family. It also effectively transfers the feud that he may have had with his ex-wife to a feud between his new wife and his ex-wife. It is as though he has managed to keep the feud alive by hiring out someone to do his dirty work for him.

This feud is usually created by an enmeshed relationship between an original husband and wife that ends up in a divorce. Having mastered the pattern of enmeshed relationships, the husband goes out and finds another woman with whom to have an enmeshed relationship. The new wife, sensing her new husband's rage at his ex-wife, attempts to win her husband's favor by solidly taking his part in the battle with his ex-wife. As long as she can blame the ex-wife for all the troubles in the world, there can be nothing wrong with her own marriage to her new husband. Creating a common enemy has always been known as an effective strategy for avoiding conflict; in this case it serves to avoid conflict in one's own marriage.

A variation on this feud occurs when the husband is unable to let go not only of his rage toward his ex-wife, but of his affection for her as well. In fact, ironically, at times the new wife's declaration of war on the ex-wife may make it more likely that the husband, not having to bear the burden of animosity toward his ex-wife, will now feel more free to show the remnants of his affection toward his ex-wife. The closer he gets to his ex-wife emotionally, the more the current wife feels abandoned, frustrated, jealous, betrayed, and potentially vengeful. The husband's relationship with his ex-wife may be experienced by the current wife with feelings of betrayal, as if it were a kind of an emotional affair.

THE GRANDPARENT TRIANGLE

This less common but potentially highly destructive triangle occurs when a grandparent who has played a significant role in raising a child suddenly becomes left out in the cold due to the remarriage of a son- or daughter-in-law. While grandparents often play a central role in raising children in families in which parents are unable or too busy to do it themselves, their role is often magnified in a divorce situation. Following a divorce, both parents are often required to work and may have even less time to spend with their children. Grandparents step in to fill the gap, and the children involved become very close to their grandparents. When one parent remarries, it often becomes easier for the stepparent or biological parent to fill the primary parenting role, leaving the grandparent feeling "unemployed." If the grandparent is the parent of the former spouse, the remarriage leaves the grandparent feeling left out of the picture even further, and the grandparent may become highly protective of his or her grandchildren. Feeling threatened about being pushed out of the picture altogether, the grandparent wages a war against the former son- or daughter-in-law.

THE MARITAL AFFAIR TRIANGLE

Because they draw an unwelcome third party into the life of a twosome, extramarital affairs are always a form of triangulation. Whether it is an affair of the heart or the genitals, or an overly passionate attachment to work or a hobby, as a form of triangulation it always has a detrimental effect on the primary relationship.

While affairs are as varied as those who enter into them, those families in which affairs are common can often find their family history laced with them as well.

Jackie's affairs began *before* she was married. In high school, she was involved with two boys at once—the quarterback of the football team, a well-liked and respected student, and an irresponsible "druggie" from the wrong side of the tracks. Pregnant and uncertain which boy was the father, she married the quarterback to appease her parents. Needless to say, her first child turned out to look like the boy from across the tracks. Jackie and her ex-quarterback eventually became Jackie and her ex-husband, and the two of them became locked into a bitter feud that has lasted for twenty-five years.

Jackie's ex-quarterback became a firefighter who had no difficulty creating conflagrations at home. He was physically abusive toward Jackie and especially toward the oldest child, despite his earlier assurances that he would be otherwise. He tormented her verbally as well as physically, relentlessly accusing her of seducing other men. Finally, in anger and disgust, Jackie did have a series of affairs. Ultimately, the tumultuous marriage led to a tumultuous divorce. Their feud continued long after the divorce was finalized, moving the hostilities from the bedroom to the courtroom. Their fight over property ownership ultimately bankrupted Jackie; she declared to me once that her ex-husband would not stop fighting until he completely ruined every aspect of her life.

When Jackie and I discussed her parents' history, at first glance it seemed odd that her parents had been "successfully" married for nearly forty years. On closer examination, it turned out that while Jackie never thought of her father as particularly unfaithful, she had been clearly aware of his constant flirtations with waitresses, salesclerks, and virtually anyone of the opposite sex. Her father frequently debased his wife both publicly and privately. Although as a child she didn't feel particularly close to her father, Jackie felt a deep, almost inexplicable animosity toward her mother. The rage that Jackie felt toward her mother left her little time or energy for a relationship with her father. Her father continually put his wife down to others, and, as Jackie learned as an adult, went outside the marriage to meet his needs for affection and attention. While Jackie apparently wasn't aware of her father's exploits when she was a child, she discovered that her life was in many ways a replica of her parents' marriage, marked by abusive disregard for each other's dignity, and especially of the tendency to look outside the marriage for comfort when there was none to be found within the marriage.

Affairs are a form of triangulation, because one spouse turns to a third party to meet some need that should be met within the marriage itself. The need may be for affection, sex, attention, love, admiration, or sympathy, but it is a need that for some reason is not met by the appropriate partner. Of course, there is often much more to an affair than this; often, a tremendous amount of anger is involved as well, and that is one of the primary reasons why the partner who is having an affair often wishes to get caught. After all, if the partner having the affair doesn't get caught, it isn't likely to be as hurtful to the spouse.

It would be wrong to view affairs simply as weapons against unsuspecting victims. That would disregard the triangular nature of affairs. The partner having the affair leaves hints in order to be discovered, hints that despite great effort often go unnoticed. The so-called "victim" has a stake—often an unwitting one—in the affair. The "victim" in the affair sees the clues, and often refuses to take the hint. At times this is because the result may be too painful, and at other times it is due to a tacit, resigned acceptance. The "victim" may believe he deserves the betrayal as punishment for his own shortcomings, or he may feel that he is martyring himself in order to satisfy his wife.

The dynamics of an affair are often subtle and complex, but in most affairs, each partner typically blames the other. This recent exchange between Dean and his wife JoEllen occurred in our fourth meeting, after JoEllen had spent three sessions venting her rage at Dean for having an affair:

JoEllen (indignantly): As far as I'm concerned, there's no point in my ever trusting him again.

Dean (sighing): No matter what I do, no matter what I say, she just won't leave this alone. I know it was stupid. I apologized a hundred times.

JoEllen: Apologies mean nothing when there's no trust. You've lost my trust in you. That's all there is to it.

Dean: So there's no hope, then. So why are you still here?

JoEllen: I don't know why I'm here. The whole thing is stupid. I've had it with you.

Dr. H. (to Dean): So you're an asshole. So you're all to blame for doing a stupid thing, but you can't talk about how it came about that you did it. I don't think it's just about trust. It's also about responsibility. If you don't know how or why you did it, then what's stopping you from doing it again? And if you're likely to do it again, what good is an apology?

JoEllen (to Dr. H.): Exactly. Thank you. But I'm sure he has no idea what you're talking about.

Dean: I know what he's talking about. He wants me to take the blame. Yes, I made a mistake, but if you weren't so impossible to deal with all the time . . .

JoEllen: I don't want to hear this . . .

Dean: But if you want to get to the bottom of this, you need to hear this.

Dr. H.: You know, I'd love to hear about how impossible your wife is, but the issue here for you is how you managed to tell her that she was impossible. If you could tell her directly, maybe you wouldn't have needed to risk your whole marriage by having your affair.

Dean: I told her a million times.

JoEllen: You told me nothing. Nothing. Ever.

Dean: I told you a million times.

Dr. H. (to JoEllen): And what's your stake in his affair? What did you get out of it?

JoEllen: What are you talking about?

Dr. H.: I assume that because it took you so long to figure it out, there was something in it for you.

JoEllen: Like what? What could be in it for me?

Dr. H.: I don't know. Everyone's different. Strangely enough, for some people it's a sense of security. As long as their husband's cheating on them, they won't have to be affectionate. For some it's a setup. You know, if he screws up this big, it'll give you a great excuse to get out of the marriage without having to blame yourself.

JoEllen: That's crazy. That's about the craziest thing I ever heard.

Dr. H.: I don't think he could have done this thing without you. I don't think you're to blame for what happened. It was his stupid, irresponsible, desperate way of getting you angry. But what on earth could make him so angry that he would do something this stupid?

JoEllen (reluctantly, and after a long hesitation): Nothing I did or could ever do can excuse him.

Dr. H.: I'm not excusing him. He was wrong. How did you dance with him?

JoEllen: Maybe I never got angry enough with him.

Dr. H.: So he got away with a lot of crap all along?

JoEllen: A lot of crap. And I never knew how to stand up for him—I mean for myself, stand up against him.

Dr. H.: So he figured if he had an affair, maybe that would wake you up.

JoEllen: But I'm not his damn mother.

Dr. H.: So his having an affair was your little wake-up call to get tough with him. That was what your investment in it was, that was your stake in it.

JoEllen's relentless blaming of Dean can be viewed as his well-deserved punishment. At some point, however, after Dean takes full responsibility for the damage his behavior caused, JoEllen must examine her behavior as well if there is going to be lasting beneficial changes in their relationship. While JoEllen's passivity, her inability to confront her husband, did not cause her husband to have an affair, it was one element among others in their relationship that contributed to the affair. Ultimately, there can be no repairing of anything that's broken while the people who are trying to fix it spend their time blaming each other for breaking it.

This "blame game" keeps marriages furious and intense, just as an affair or series of affairs keeps marriages smoldering with tension. This thicket of intensity is what characterizes triangular feuds, and it is this intensity that is passed on from one generation to the next.

Imagine, for example, what it is like to be a child in a family in which a parent or both parents are having affairs. The furious exchange of blame between the parents creates an atmosphere of danger and fear for children. While the children may not know exactly what goes on behind the scenes (although they often do), they do know that Dad's or Mom's affections and attentions are being spent elsewhere, and that both parents blame each other for wounding the marriage. As a result, children learn that marriage itself is a dangerous proposition, and despite their knowledge of the dangers of triangulation, they often end up feeling compelled to repeat their parents' mistakes.

WORK AS TRIANGULATION: WHEN OCCUPATIONS BECOME PREOCCUPATIONS

Rick was a fifty-year-old advertising executive; being fifty and still surviving in advertising was an "accomplishment unto itself," according to Rick. His wife insisted that he come to see me with her, putting him on notice that their marriage was hanging by a thin thread that would likely break if he didn't agree to come in. The two had waged a war of silence for nearly two years, in which Rick's wife Estrella decided that the only way to survive with Rick was to create a life of her own. In the last two years, Rick's work hours had expanded to the point where he was home basically to shower, sleep, and change clothes. Estrella worked as a part-time fashion designer, and built a coterie of friends and acquaintances with whom she could spend her time. Estrella was Rick's third wife, and Rick was Estrella's second husband.

As the amount of time Rick spent in his business grew, his relationship with his wife became increasingly distant. Estrella told me that she could barely get his attention even when he was home, and that her frustration mounted to the point that she had no choice but to create a life of her own. As the two of them spent so little time together, Estrella found herself become increasingly aware of Rick's limitations as a husband, realizing things about him that she claimed she never knew when she decided to marry him. She eventually became so enraged at him that even if he did make the slightest efforts toward getting close, she quickly turned away from him in order not to decimate him with her rage. Feeling rejected, Rick buried himself even more deeply in his work.

After learning about the history of both of their previous marriages, it became clear that whenever the going got rough in the past, each of them managed to find some third party that provided an escape. While the triangle provided immediate relief, the marital conflict was buried only to rear its ugly head down the road. The end result was usually divorce, and a repetition of the pattern with the next spouse.

"Workaholism" is one of the most common forms of triangulation that lead to family feuds. It runs rampant as a form of triangulation, because realistic economic pressures make it easily justifiable. Many jobs and businesses truly do fail as a result of not spending the requisite amount of time and energy on them. Yet spending a tremendous amount of time on the demands of running a business or succeeding in a career does not necessarily mean abandoning the demands of a marriage. Work becomes a form of triangulation when the needs that would ordinarily be met by a spouse are instead provided by work. People become "married to work" in no uncertain terms; they think about work constantly, they grow romantically attached to work, their lives become dictated and dominated by the demands of work; they feel soothed and comforted by work; they feel spurned like a jealous lover when a competitor threatens their work; they feel emotionally supported and are given a sense of purpose by their work—all feelings that are possible, if not necessarily desirable, to obtain from one's spouse.

It is not that one's marriage should take care of all of a person's needs; in fact, that would likely lead to a hopelessly enmeshed relationship that also might lead to a feud. Instead, the idea is that work should not *thoroughly replace* a marriage as a source of emotional sustenance. When it does, the result is to increase the emotional distance between marriage partners to the point of ultimately destroying the marriage.

OTHER ADDICTIVE TRIANGLES

The term "workaholic" is an apt description for someone who uses work as a way of avoiding other problems, because the word underlines the addictive aspect of work. Almost any person or any thing can be enlisted as a third party in order to shift attention from the original source of pain in a family, and almost anybody or anything can be the object of an addiction.

On occasion, someone in a family will triangulate a friend or a social group, and become addicted to that person or group. He or she becomes obsessed with that person or group, and appears to take direction and solace from that group, thus avoiding the conflict in the original twosome. More often, people become addicted to chemical substances, such as alcohol, marijuana, or other drugs, which serve an identical function. These drugs offer the added effect of numbing the senses, making them not only an effective way to avoid pain and conflict, but a very effective way of not feeling as well. Devoid of feeling, the chemically addicted person loses all motivation to face the issues that need to be addressed.

When someone is addicted to a substance, it becomes such a powerful force in that person's life that it takes on a life of its own. When working with families in which one member is an alcoholic, I often designate an empty chair in the circle of family members for the "other family member"—the alcohol. It serves to emphasize what the family already knows—that for better or worse, the alcohol seems to have a place and a function in the family, even more powerful than other family members.

There is no doubt that people who are addicted to substances find that drug addiction in one form or the other nearly always runs in the family. Exactly *how* addiction runs in the family has never been established. While researchers try to find the gene responsible for alcoholism, no one has established that such a gene actually causes someone to become an alcoholic. The powerful yet subtle influence of family behavior patterns no doubt combines with any genetic predisposition to make someone likely to become addicted.

It is probably no coincidence that family trees that are riddled with triangulation down through the generations also seem to be riddled with substance abuse. Substance abuse is merely one method of creating and then sustaining a triangular relationship. In understanding how feuds develop, it's more important to note the history of triangulation than to note exactly what form the triangulation takes.

four

Wounds That Time Won't Heal

Give sorrow words: the grief that does not speak
Whispers the o'er-frought heart and bids it break.

—SHAKESPEARE, *MACBETH*

A CHILD DIES. A MAN LOSES HIS WIFE AND CHILDREN IN A CAR ACCI-
DENT. A TEENAGE GIRL, DISTRAUGHT BECAUSE HER BOYFRIEND TELLS
her he's no longer interested, overdoses on her mother's pills and dies.
A man who worked for the same company for thirty years gets laid off,
suddenly becomes ill, and, feeling as though he has no purpose in his
life, leaps off a bridge.

If the statistics are to be believed, very few of us have not in some
way been touched by a tragedy in our lives. When the tragedy happens
to a family member, the emotional impact is life-altering. We are
changed deeply, in ways that are likely to affect us the rest of our lives.

These traumatic events usually involve loss, although the loss doesn't
always come in the form of death. For some, it's the loss of a sense of
well-being, a loss of a feeling of safety, a loss of innocence, or a loss of
trust in others. The loss in learning of a diagnosis of cancer is enough
to radically change the direction of our lives, even though the cancer
itself may eventually be treated and cured. For some, the trauma may
be rape, or incest. In the case of rape, the victim feels a loss of a sense
of safety and self-assuredness in the world. In the case of incest, the
victim feels a loss of trust in others, a deep betrayal, and a loss of in-

nocence. The exact nature of the trauma may be different in each instance, but in every case the people involved experience a sense of loss.

Throughout life, the effects of these traumatic events linger, and can often be the spark that ignites a family feud. Many family feuds, seemingly inexplicable at the time they occur, suddenly take on meaning when placed in the context of a forgotten trauma. These feuds are fueled not by the specific events of the moment, but by an often hidden set of memories. These hidden memories can color a certain time of year so that subtle or powerful feelings left over from a past traumatic event emerge when that particular time of year arrives. Certain family members or others outside the family who may have been directly or even remotely involved in the original trauma may also spark reminiscences of the trauma. These traumatic events may be remembered consciously, and when they are, people become flooded with the feelings associated with the trauma. On the other hand, memories are frequently pushed beneath the surface, and while the actual memory of the event may no longer be present, the person feels the emotions associated with the events.

Such powerful emotions are often associated with a particular time of the year, and when that time comes around, the feelings erupt. Tempers flare, emotional outbursts occur, and feuds erupt usually without either party having a clue that their feelings are connected to the anniversary event. The intense feelings aroused by these events conspire with enmeshment and triangulation to ignite a feud.

ANNIVERSARIES OF TRAUMATIC EVENTS

It has been said that "timing is everything." Whether or not an event or situation turns into a feud will often depend to a large degree on timing. If the trauma hidden away in a family's history is someone's death, the anniversary date will create an overly intense moment in time. Two other occasions may create the kind of buildup of emotional intensity that can erupt into a feud: the birth date of the lost person, and when another family member reaches the age the person was when he or she died.

In most families, birthdays are important rituals in which the entire focus of the day is on the birthday boy or girl. It is a celebration of that child's life. Because birthdays are a celebration of someone's life, the day becomes a terribly painful one after the person dies. In some families, the birthday becomes a day of commemoration. Recently, the friends of a client of mine who died from complications of AIDS decided to meet annually on his birthday to remember him, to tell stories of his life, to look at photographs, and to celebrate. In other families, it becomes a day to forget, to push memories away into some corner of the mind so as not to feel the relentless, annual pain.

In families where parents, children, and siblings strive to forget, the birthday becomes a veiled cauldron of unexpressed grief. If the hidden memories themselves don't surface, the feelings of grief and tension bubble up unpredictably from beneath the surface of everyday life. I remember the time a client of mine reported to me how she found herself unable to sleep one night. She bolted out of bed at about five o'clock in the morning, got dressed, and decided to take a walk to a local coffeehouse that she knew opened early. On the way she passed a bookstore that was displaying a book about "motherless daughters," and when she saw the cover she burst into tears. She realized that this would have been her mother's birthday, had her mother not died from cancer when my client was a teenager. Her agitation and insomnia seemed to have been brought on by the partially blocked memory that this was her mother's birthday.

Gregory Bateson, a well-known anthropologist and one of the pivotal figures in the family therapy field, had two older brothers. The eldest brother, John, died at age twenty during World War I, and the second eldest brother, Martin, died four years later. Martin's death was the result of a dramatic, self-inflicted gunshot wound after being shunned by a young woman. His suicide, in bustling Trafalgar Square, occurred on the birthday of his older brother John. While no one can know for certain the extent to which the hidden grieving for his brother may have affected him, many "coincidences" such as these occur on significant dates.

One of the most celebrated facts about birthdates and their open and hidden influence has to do with the birthday of the United States, and the death of its second and third presidents. Thomas Jefferson, nearing death, inquired whether or not it was finally the fourth of July. When he was told that it was, he apparently closed his eyes and died. John Adams, the second president of the United States, died the same day as Jefferson, on the fiftieth anniversary of the signing of the Declaration of Independence.

But the symbolism alone of these acts doesn't account for the kind of coincidences that seem to occur in families on a more frequent basis. You may recall the story told in the first chapter about the client who, in group therapy, revealed that two generations of men before him in his family all shot themselves on their fortieth birthdays. He lived in despair at the thought of reaching his own fortieth birthday, nearly a decade away at the time.

The other, even more crucial, anniversary date has to do with the chronological age of the person who suffered the trauma. Mentioned briefly in the first chapter, this important factor in the development of a family feud exerts a powerful underground influence on when and how a feud will eventually develop. You might recall the story of JoAnne, related in the first chapter, in which JoAnne's father had a sister who died when she was seventeen. When his own daughter reached the age of seventeen, JoAnne's father became highly overprotective of her, a drama that resulted in a feud between JoAnne and her sister. Without knowing it, JoAnne's father created the conditions for his own daughter to lose a younger sister to a family feud, just as he lost his own younger sister to death decades earlier.

MULTIGENERATIONAL ECHOES

While it's not uncommon to see family feuds arise as a direct result of traumatic experiences being handed down from one generation to the next, the most common way that traumatic experiences ignite into a feud is much more subtle. In many families, the trauma in their history is hidden. These hidden traumas, when uncovered, can often be like the single artifact an archeologist discovers that links together two disparate periods in history, the missing piece in the jigsaw puzzle of time that makes the puzzle clear.

The missing piece in the puzzle may be any traumatic event, although it's usually some sort of major, life-changing loss of a loved one. It can be other losses as well, though, such as an accident leading to a major incapacity or coma, or the witnessing of the death or murder of someone else. The idea that the loss of a loved one two or three generations ago, someone whom you've never known or may have never heard of, can play a key role in your life and even determine your behavior hardly seems credible. Yet, when this idea is looked at in the light of how trauma affects each of us throughout our own lifetimes, and how the feelings that accompany those events get handed down to our children, some sense of how the pieces fit together emerges.

Philip was forty-six years old. He worked in a downtown New York camera store as a salesman. He had a soft face, with eyes that twinkled when he smiled, and a warm, gentle laugh that endeared him to his friends and customers. Married for nearly twenty years, he had two children, a seventeen-year-old daughter and a fourteen-year-old son. His wife was a schoolteacher, and the four of them had a good life together. They were able to live comfortably on both their salaries in a nice house on a tree-lined street in Brooklyn.

It was fall in New York, and there was a distinct nip in the air. Philip woke up, went through his morning rituals, and kissed his wife and two children as he left for work. On his way out the door, he barely noticed the oranges and deep reds of the leaves around him. He thought about the first snow, and wondered if his tires would hold out or whether or not he needed to buy new ones for the winter. There was nothing unique about this day, nothing that could have forewarned him that it would be a day that would change his life forever.

His workday was chaotic as usual, with barely any time for breaks. A steady stream of customers appeared at his counter, and the telephone rang incessantly, punctuating his repartee with the customers and disrupting any downtime that might have given him a chance to rest. At four-thirty, it was normally his time to begin to think about going home. It gets dark early at this time of the year, and his urge to go home would swell during his last half hour at work. Today, though, Philip was called to the telephone by a fellow salesman who had a twisted look on his face that Philip hadn't seen before. The salesman shouted out to Philip from fifteen feet away to come to the phone, that it was for him and that it sounded serious.

When Philip got to the phone, he heard his son's voice on the other end of the line. "Dad. Please come home quick, as quick as you can. Leslie took pills, a lot of pills. I called the police, but they're not here yet."

The store, the disembodied voices, the late-afternoon rush of humanity all disappeared. For this moment, there was only Philip and his son on the telephone. Philip shouted, "Did you call an ambulance? How is she?"

"The police said they're sending an ambulance. That was five minutes ago. Nobody's here yet."

"Did you call Mom?"

"She should be home soon. I called the school and they said she left already."

"How's Leslie? What's she doing?"

"I don't know. She's breathing, but I can't wake her up. I can't wake her up, Dad. I'm holding her. She's not waking up."

There was a short pause as Philip felt his own breathing stop. "Call the police again. I'm coming home. Talk to her, try to wake her up, but don't shake her. I'm coming home." Philip hung up the phone and glanced over at the salesmen who had gathered to listen to Philip's end of the phone call. One of them asked if there was anything he could do. Barely noticing, Philip shook his head and darted out of the store.

From that moment on, every routine obstacle to getting home felt like an eternity. Philip knew it would take nearly an hour in rush-hour traffic. Even though he took every shortcut he knew, the time it took to get home was nerve-wrenching. Philip realized that the future of his daughter's life would be determined while he was driving home. There was nothing he could do. The image of his daughter lying limp and helpless in his son's arms was more than he could bear. He tried to push it out of his mind, but the other images that arose in its place were just as terrible. Philip saw quick pictures of his daughter laughing, the two of them playing together. He saw her being held in his arms as a baby, being rocked to sleep by his wife. No matter how hard he tried, he couldn't stop seeing pictures of his daughter in his mind.

When he arrived home, no one was there. He drove up to his house, and saw neighbors milling around outside. One of his neighbors, a burly Italian man to whom Philip had never said more than a few words, waved to Philip and came over to the car window. "There's no one home. They've gone to the hospital. Coney Island, must be Coney Island."

"Thanks. Is everyone okay. How's my daughter?" Philip found himself pleading.

"I don't know. Better go to the hospital."

Philip feared the worst. The neighbor was grim, but Philip couldn't let himself believe anything other than that things were going to be fine.

At the hospital, Philip learned otherwise. Arriving at the emergency room, he found his wife and his son sitting on a bench, huddled with their arms around each other. He came over to them and knelt down in front of them. When they looked up, his wife looked deeply and forlornly into her husband's eyes. "She's gone."

The events that followed the tragedy of Leslie's suicide were all shadowed by the grief of losing a daughter. It was an event no one who knew Leslie would have predicted. In almost every way, Leslie was a happy, normal child. She was bright, with her father's warmth. Being the first child, she was prized by her parents, and her father especially felt close to her. Leslie had a huge, teenage crush on a boy at school. Her parents knew about it, but didn't make much of it. The boy had been telling her for two weeks that he wasn't interested in her, and Leslie was frantic about it. She telephoned the boy, and in an act of desperation, took two bottles of some pills that she found in her parents' medicine chest. She then went to her brother and told him what she had done, and even asked him to call the ambulance. She did not want to die. What she couldn't know was that it would take nearly forty-five minutes for the ambulance to arrive, and that was just enough time for the pills to stop her young heart from beating.

Philip, his wife and son, and all who knew Leslie had to find ways of coping with this tragedy. Life, although rapidly rendered meaningless, had to go on somehow. Bills had to be paid. Another child had to be brought up. The immense grief that they all felt had to somehow be tempered. A perspective had to somehow be found.

In the years that followed, Philip and his family felt as though they were living in a haze. Nothing any of them did felt meaningful. Each of them, in his or her own fashion, found ways of surviving. Philip's wife turned inward, although when she went back to work, each child with whom she worked seemed like a tarnished jewel that she hoped to polish. Philip's son began experimenting with drugs, and studied Eastern religions, trying to find a spiritual path that would give his own life some purpose. Philip went back to work, and got closer to his son. They attended seminars together and began to participate more in each other's hobbies.

Although the feelings of having been devastated by this loss softened in time, there was no doubt in any of them that they continued to live with a huge piece of themselves missing. If there is ever any doubt about the importance of a family in determining one's own personality, that doubt is erased when a family member dies. For Philip, losing Leslie meant losing a part of his purpose in life. It meant losing a world of hopes and dreams that could never be fulfilled.

As Philip continued to work and go through the familiar routines of his life, over time he regained a semblance of predictability and comfort. He compartmentalized the memories of his daughter, boxing them away just enough for him to manage his own life. But still, some times were harder than others.

Every fall, when the leaves began to change color, the memory of the fateful day he lost his daughter would intrude. Even when the memories finally were stored away successfully, Philip found that he began to feel differently when certain things happened. He had once looked forward to the nip in the air of winter; it gave him energy, and the promise of Christmas—the most financially rewarding time of the year for him. Now the signs of winter were met with subtle feelings of depression.

The phone would ring at work, and instead of the excitement of a potential customer and eventual sale, Philip found himself shying away from the telephone altogether. Instead, he preferred to work the counter, and asked the other salespeople to cover the telephones.

People remember through association. Philip remembered his daughter's death every time he encountered some element that was present on the day his daughter died. He remembered through the smell and chill of the air, the sound of the telephone ringing, the colors of the leaves on the trees. And he remembered even though he didn't want to remember. When he was able to strike from his mind the actual memory of his daughter's death, he was left remembering the feelings that surrounded it. He felt panic when the phone rang, and a sense of loss and grief when the signs of winter approached.

Leslie died when she was seventeen. For at least the next generation or two, and possibly even more, whenever a child in Philip's family reaches the age of seventeen, the parents will likely find themselves unconsciously intensifying the relationship with their child. For Philip's family, seventeen is now a sensitized age. Feelings of unresolved grief about Leslie's death will create tension and pressure in the family, making family members ripe for a feud.

ANNIVERSARY DEPRESSION

When someone feels grief or other intense feelings during a particular time of year, and when these feelings stem from memories of a past trauma that occurred at the same time of year, that person suffers from *anniversary depression*. Although this condition is labeled as a form of depression, feelings other than depression also surface around the time of the year that the trauma originally occurred. People may feel inexplicably agitated or upset; they may feel explosively angry or fearful. They may cling closer to their loved ones, becoming overprotective, or even overly possessive and jealous. Because most trauma involves loss of some kind or another, and because depression is normally the response to unresolved grief over a loss, the label "anniversary depression" has stuck.

One of the more interesting elements of anniversary depression is that most people have no idea that their feelings are related to the anniversary of a loss. Because there is such a strong need to bury, or at least to relocate, the actual visual memory of the loss, the feelings associated with the loss become disconnected from the actual memory of the event. Nevertheless, people end up having the same feelings they would have if they actually remembered and reflected on the memory.

Anniversary feelings surrounding past trauma don't necessarily occur on an annual basis. Because the feelings about the trauma are connected with the events that surrounded it, years could go by when those events don't occur. For example, if Philip were to move to Southern California, where there are very few deciduous trees and the colors of fall in New York are hard to find, he would not be reminded of his daughter's death and therefore might not have the anniversary feelings associated with it.

For many families, holidays take on a similar significance to birthdays. Holidays such as Thanksgiving, Christmas, New Year's, Easter, Passover, and other religious and cultural holidays are often times when the strength of the family is celebrated. Holidays can therefore become significant reminders of painful past experiences. The loss of a loved one always feels particularly devastating during a holiday when the family normally is all together.

For this reason, holiday celebrations can become a time when unresolved emotions escalate into a family feud. Several years back, a film entitled *Avalon* did a wonderful job dramatizing one family's feud. It occurred one Thanksgiving, when the father in the family finally gave up waiting for his chronically late brother to arrive for the family meal. All the guests had gathered, the turkey was sitting out on the table, and the father decided to go ahead and cut the turkey before his brother arrived. As a result, when the brother finally arrived to find the family already eating, he stormed out of the house vowing never to speak with his brother again. The act of beginning the family meal signified the final crucible of family loyalty and devotion, and years of accumulated anger between the brothers rose to the surface.

Whether or not a feud will emerge out of the groundwork laid by the anniversary of a traumatic loss, or a holiday season, often depends on three factors: gender, one's position in the family, and physical characteristics.

GENDER

In many families, gender stereotypes and expectations are very emotionally charged. Extra pressure may be placed on boys to become high achievers, to "follow in your father's footsteps." Girls may be expected to achieve less than their brothers, or aimed toward less influential careers. While the rise of feminism and greater parity of the sexes has diminished these influences, there are many families in which gender-related burdens continue to flourish. In some families, gender-related expectations are flagrant and open, while in others they have been made more subtle, but their influence remains.

Gender alone, aside from the questions of stereotypes or role expectations, can be a powerful determinant on future generations. In Philip's family, the experience of losing a daughter leaves a huge gap and a residue of intense feelings toward daughters and girls. As Philip's son grows up and marries, the first girl who is born will have intense feelings associated with her. She will inevitably be compared to Leslie. Philip himself and Philip's son will see in that child's eyes the eyes of Leslie peering out. The child may even be named after Leslie. Whether they are seen as a blessing or a curse, much stronger feelings and expectations will be placed upon this girl than if a daughter had not been lost one generation ago. The new girl, without necessarily even knowing about the legacy that came with her birth, will feel the intense, extra pressure placed on her. As a result, she will sense that she is being burdened by her parents' expectations even more than her siblings are. Should she fall in love as a teenager, her father (whose sister died in his arms), terrified of a similar outcome, will likely become exquisitely overprotective of his daughter. He may forbid her to see boys until she's much older, or go out of his way to warn her of the dangers of dating, or find some creative way of spurning or sabotaging any involvement with the opposite sex. No matter how he does it, she will feel especially "chosen" for this treatment, no doubt believing that it is unfair and wrong to be treated this way. She will have no choice but to rebel, or to somehow suffer in this overly intense thicket of emotion brought on by the death of someone she never knew.

BIRTH ORDER

Much has been written about the profound significance of the order in which people are born into a family. Like our gender, and the selection of our parents, it is something that is out of our control, yet a factor that deeply influences the course of our lives and our personalities. When it comes to creating the multigenerational conditions for a feud, birth order can play a crucial role. Birth order often combines with gender to create the intensity that can accumulate over several generations and result in a feud.

Leslie's death made those around her exquisitely sensitive and emotionally vulnerable at those times of year that reminded them of their loss. It even helped to create extra pressure on the girl born into the next generation, simply because she was a girl. It also created a special burden on the first child born to the next generation, because Leslie was the eldest in her generation. All the dreams, aspirations, and expectations placed on the eldest child in Philip's family vanished with Leslie's loss, or may have been transferred to her younger brother. But even if Leslie had held a different position, if she were the youngest, or somewhere in the middle, the position she held would have become a position that consciously or (most likely) unconsciously would have become overly sensitized and infused with tension.

Family psychologists, who over the years have examined countless charts that graphically portray multigenerational family histories, have seen an unmistakable and remarkable pattern occurring. *The child who is born in the same position as the person who was lost through death appears to have a greater burden placed on him or her.* This burden can often become the underlying cause of a family feud.

Returning once again to Leslie, it's not difficult to see how the anniversary of her death might instigate feuds in future generations based on sibling position or birth order. If Leslie's brother married and had a boy, instead of a girl, additional pressure would still be placed on this child, not just because the eldest typically has more pressure placed on him, but also because he had the same position that Leslie held. If a second child were born, the older sibling–younger sibling conflicts that normally arise between children would remind Leslie's brother of his relationship with Leslie. These interactions would bring to the surface his carefully boxed-away feelings and memories of him and his sister, and those feelings would likely translate into increased pressure on the oldest child.

If Leslie had been the youngest child, or the second-born child in a larger family, Leslie's brother's children who shared the same position would feel the extra pressure placed on them by virtue of the memories and deep feelings of their father for his sister.

PHYSICAL CHARACTERISTICS

If a particular child happens to have similar physical characteristics to a person from a prior generation who was tragically lost, it's very likely that this child will elicit the intense feelings associated with the unknown figure from his or her past. While these may be conscious associations, I'm often amazed at how unconscious such associations can be.

I see a family of four women, one mother and three daughters, who live together in the same house. Two of the three daughters are children from the mother's first marriage, while the third is the daughter of the second marriage. During one recent meeting, the mother turned to me and looked at me with pleading eyes. She sincerely wanted to know why, no matter what she seemed to do or think, she was unable to stop hating her second daughter. Knowing that the second daughter, Cheryl, was physically quite different from her sisters, I ventured a simple guess and asked the mother whom Cheryl looked like in the family. It didn't take but a moment for the mother to state that Cheryl looked very much like her biological father Ned, the man with whom the mother had had a rocky and completely unresolved love-hate relationship. I asked her to do an experiment, in order to confirm or disprove my "wacky theory." I told the mother that each time she was aware of her rageful feelings coming to the surface, she was to turn to her daughter Cheryl and say three times, "You are not Ned." She was then to monitor her feelings and tell me later if she felt them dissipate. The wacky theory and the wacky experiment were successful.

SEXUAL MOLESTATION

Many of the people I see in my practice who are involved in family feuds have a history of being sexually abused as children. The experience of being taken advantage of at an early age by an adult no doubt has a profound influence on our relationships as adults, and is also likely to create a deep schism in the family. The family feuds that occur as a result of sexual molestation are ultimately best understood by understanding the multigenerational nature of sexual abuse. The trauma of sexual abuse demonstrates the power of traumatic events to traverse the generational line, creating deeply divided and feuding families in its wake.

The fact that sexual molestation occurs in generation after generation in the same families defies common sense. One would think that having experienced the devastation of sexual molestation oneself or having witnessed it in one's own family, the victim or witness would take extra care to make certain it never happened again. Yet those who have witnessed sexual abuse or been molested often find themselves unconsciously creating the conditions for sexual molestation in their own family.

Freud and his followers call it the "repetition compulsion." Feeling compelled to repeat the same behavior patterns is considered to be an unconscious attempt to "work through" or master the emotional agony of the past trauma. Painful childhood experiences are pushed away from consciousness, "repressed," and left to reside in lost chambers of memory until someone feels safe enough to bring them to the light of consciousness.

When someone doesn't feel strong enough to overcome the pain of a traumatic childhood experience, that experience begs to be reckoned with. In an attempt to come to grips with these painful incidents, people unconsciously enlist a multitude of creative strategies. One of these is to orchestrate one's adult life to resemble the life one had as a child. A parent might unwittingly attempt to resolve the pain and conflicts of his or her own childhood by placing his or her own child in circumstances similar to those of the parent's childhood. The children of these parents become the vessels into which they pour their own conflicts, and the parents vicariously struggle to repair their own history as they watch their children play out the painful drama from their own past.

Monica is a thirty-year-old television company executive. It was difficult to discern when her feud with her father began. She had felt angry with him for years, ever since she was a child, although she remembered a time when she was much younger and they were both very close. Her anger with her father increased after Monica's mother died, after she made an attempt to get closer to him by trying to be in closer contact with him. He "neglected" to return Monica's phone calls, and Monica felt completely abandoned. The loss of her mother was terrible enough, but her father's refusal to keep in touch with Monica added insult to injury.

Monica found herself getting more and more agitated, and her relationship with her lover was becoming strained to the limit. Monica wantonly exploded with rage toward her partner, for no apparent reason. During this time, Monica began to have disturbing dreams, in which she "remembered" her father coming into her bedroom at night and getting into bed with her. These nocturnal recollections became more vivid over time, until Monica came to believe that they were actual memories from her childhood in which her father fondled her. Eventually, she remembered telling her father to stop, which apparently he reluctantly did, insisting in the process that Monica not tell her mother.

In order to verify that these recollections were not inventions stemming from her anger toward her father, Monica telephoned one of her sisters who shared her bedroom as a child. Her sister confirmed Monica's suspicions and reported that she had been in psychotherapy trying to come to terms with her own anger at their father.

Monica joined a therapy group dealing specifically with healing the injuries related to being a victim of sexual abuse. In this group, Monica learned that perpetrators of sexual abuse were often victims themselves. Monica did not want to talk to her father directly about this. At that time, she had no relationship with him and had no desire to attempt to start one again. She had been spurned too many times in the past. Her mother was no longer alive, and so there was no way of asking her mother about it. Fortunately, however, her mother had a sister who was still alive, an aunt whom Monica felt comfortable confiding in.

Monica's discussions with her aunt were eye-opening. She learned that there had been a well-kept secret in Monica's mother's family. Monica's aunt disclosed to Monica that she too had been a victim of sexual molestation by her father, and that although she was never certain if Monica's mother was also victimized, Monica's aunt told Monica that "knowing our father," Monica's mother most likely had been.

Monica realized that her own mother had kept this a secret throughout her life, even up to her death. Monica too had a secret—the same secret—and had kept it from her mother when Monica was a child, as well as from herself throughout most of her adult life. The mystery that Monica wondered about was why she remembered her secret when she did, and whether or not the recollection was connected with her rageful behavior toward her lover. There might well have been an anniversary date tucked away that Monica couldn't identify, or perhaps the challenge of greater commitment and intimacy in Monica's relationship with her lover might have uncovered fears of abandonment linked to her prior abuse.

Monica also wondered about the feud with her father. It was clear to Monica that her anger toward him stemmed from his abuse of her. Those frightening nights in Monica's bedroom had never been discussed between them. Monica boxed them away in a remote corner of her memory, while continuing to have a relationship with both of her parents during her earlier years. No longer having a mother she could turn to, Monica struggled with the question of whether or not she should once again make herself vulnerable by trying to make a relationship work with her father. Even after remembering the horrible events of her childhood, Monica felt alone in the world without parents, and a part of her wanted to have some sort of relationship with her father. Whether or not she was able to accomplish some sort of reconciliation, Monica felt at this point that at least she understood the roots of her family feud.

For Monica, as is often the case in situations of abuse, there was a direct link between the events of her childhood and the events of her mother's childhood. Somehow her mother wasn't able to prevent the events that haunted her own memories from occurring to Monica. While no one knows for certain which factors are responsible for transmitting sexual abuse from one generation to the next, there are usually at least three things going on: mate selection, denial, and family myths and secrets.

MATE SELECTION

While most anyone may be capable of doing certain things to others under certain extreme circumstances, there are clearly people who by virtue of their personalities may be more apt to do harmful things than others. There has been considerable research into the personality characteristics of those who molest children, for example. They tend to be emotionally immature, as well as physically unaffectionate and emotionally distant toward their spouses, and are often victims of abuse themselves. They often have deep emotional problems, and are cut off from social relationships. Alcohol and drug problems frequently play a part. But why do people choose to be married to people with these characteristics?

To some extent, it is because people tend to marry those with whom they believe their marriage will succeed—people who share similar levels of emotional maturity. As mentioned in the second chapter, people tend to shy away from those whom they don't feel match their own emotional level. There is also the old cliche that men marry women who remind them of their mothers and women marry men who remind them of their fathers. There is some psychological truth to the cliche. When their spouses don't act the way their parents did, men often spend the rest of their married lives trying to get their wives to be like their mothers and women spend the rest of their married lives trying get their husbands to be like their fathers. This adage may be cute when you apply it to the positive aspects of one's parents, but the adage becomes painfully acute when it is applied to mothers or fathers who damage their children.

DENIAL

Humans have an extraordinary capacity to repress things they don't want to see. It's a built-in survival mechanism that allows us to deal with the most devastating catastrophes. Most important, denial serves to protect us from having to deal with things we aren't yet ready to deal with. If a mother, for example, allows herself to see what is going on between her husband and her daughter, she will have to deal with her own guilt over failing to protect her daughter, as well as her bad judgment regarding who she selected as a mate. She would have to face the fact that her husband may not be the person she needs him to be, and would have to face the terror of possibly living without him (or, deciding to remain with a man who molests children!). Even more painful, she would have to deal with the feelings of possibly having been molested herself. If she has built up solid walls of denial in order not to have to deal with these feelings from her own childhood, then she will have to build up the same walls of denial in order to make certain she doesn't see what's going on in front of her eyes, or just behind the bedroom door.

When a husband or child experiences a wife or mother in denial of that which is going on around her, it delivers some powerful messages. One message is that, if the mother is to be believed, what the child believes is going on must not really be going on. This leads to the victimized person feeling crazy, as though there is something wrong with how he or she perceives reality. Another message is that, if the child acknowledges what is happening, then the mother is either crazy or, if not crazy, she is engaged in an act of supreme betrayal. The third message is closely related to the last one: If the mother is allowing this to go on, then she is a conspirator, and as such bears much of the blame. But father also sees that mother is in denial, and to him his wife's silence is a passive endorsement of his own activity. He reasons that, since on some level she knows what's going on, she must approve of it. Her silence, born from the womb of her denial, allows the molestation to recur. Through the insidious process of denial, the conditions for trauma are set into motion and passed from one generation to the next.

FAMILY MYTHOLOGY AND SECRETS

The third way in which the effects of traumatic experiences are made to linger from one generation to the next is through the family's cunning use of secrets and family myths. Sometimes the myths are simple, such as "There's no abuse in this family," but sometimes they're even more complex and dastardly, such as "There is nothing in this family that we can't talk about." Nearly all families have myths and secrets which exert tremendous pressure on members of the family who don't buy into them.

Traumas that are "gone but not forgotten" are powerful forces that, like an underground stream that opens to form the mouth of a waterfall, can be the hidden roots of family feuds. They appear, often out of nowhere, as outbursts of raw emotion or increased sensitivity. Ordinary disappointments, like someone showing up late for an appointment, getting a no to a request, forgetting to make dinner, or neglecting to invite someone to a party, become imbued with the added sensitivity caused by the early, unresolved trauma. Little things become big, and fights that normally are ignored or resolved turn into passionate feuds that divide and shatter the family.

Whether the trauma was a hidden history of abuse, the loss of a loved one, or even a painful, unresolved prior relationship, the feelings remain inside us and linger until we feel safe enough or pressured enough to let them out. Unless the feelings associated with these traumas are acknowledged, discussed openly, or turned into productive attempts at reconciliation or forgiveness, they may continue to haunt the family and erode feelings of cohesiveness and safety, ultimately erupting into a family feud.

five

Family Myths
and Secrets

We spend our years as a tale that is told.

—PSALMS

THERE IS NO TRUE BLOOD THAT HOLDS A FAMILY TOGETHER, NO REAL FLOW OF RED AND WHITE CELLS THAT FORGES A LINK BETWEEN FATHERS and mothers, parents and children, sisters and brothers. The glue that holds a family together is not a tangible bond; it is a bond that is constructed with the mortar of ideas, beliefs that link one member to another, and each member to the generation before it. These beliefs arise from the stories we hear and tell about each other. It is our stories that also make each of us individuals, different from the next, stories that tell the tales of our lives, our adventures, our loves and failures, our enemies and successes.

When we erase our stories in an attempt to forget our past, we become lost in an alien world. Without our memories, we don't know who we are. It is the family stories we hear and tell that give us our identity and our unique place in the world.

Stories about our family come from two places—our own memories, and other family members. We can hold those stories close to our hearts, choosing to share little with the world, or we can actively share them with others, helping to create strong legends about who the family is and what its place and purpose is in the world. These stories, when taken together, form more than a simple record of who is related to whom; they form the trunk of the family tree. The family's stories are the core of its legacy, the defining center from which its branches—its smaller stories—emanate.

Although I see my own family's legacy as a gift I would like to give my children that I hope they will someday come to appreciate, I have taken an interest in my own family's story primarily because it enriches my understanding of myself. The better I know their stories, the more I understand who I am. As I took pride in my own academic achievements, I humbled myself with the story of having come from "a long line of cabdrivers and garbagemen." It was a way to be proud of my past while at the same time showing off my accomplishments with humility.

We tell our children stories of their relatives' lives in order to teach them who they are and who we would like them to be. We teach them moral lessons, such as "stay away from drugs," lest they end up wasting their precious talents "like their Uncle Jack." I tell my children the story of my own Uncle Sol, who was the family "Santa Claus," how every Chanuka he would open the trunk of his car and let the children choose whatever toy they wanted. It was not a story about material wealth, because Uncle Sol had very little. It was a story about his generosity and his kindness. My sister, an actress, teaches my children about how to handle their own stage fright by telling them stories about how she would get so nauseous before a performance that she would feel like vomiting, but that once she was onstage she would forget all about her anxiety by focusing on her role. The advice to focus on your role is simple, but placed in the context of a story it feels less like advice and becomes compelling.

While we attempt to teach our children by telling them our stories, it is ultimately our actions by which we are judged. When the stories we tell about our family match our actions, we leave our children with a sense of integrity. They can then take pride in being part of a family that lives according to its values and beliefs. But when we fail to practice what we preach, our stories become mere propaganda, sources of our children's skepticism. As a result, our children fail to trust us, and we fail in our major function, which is, I believe, to provide them with a sense of safety.

Family feuds often result from actions that don't match our family stories. These stories are often reinforced by grandparents and great-grandparents, and as such become powerful forces in children's lives. As children grow up discovering that the stories that they are told about their family fail to match their experience of the family, they lose their trust and end up feeling betrayed. Somehow, the family's "dominant story" doesn't match the family members' behavior, and as a result, one's place in the world becomes precarious.

There are at least two ways that a family's stories can create a feud. One way is to repeatedly tell a story about a family that doesn't match the truth of the family, and the other is not to tell an important story when it is needed to explain a family's actions. In the first case, a family myth is created, and in the second case, a family secret is perpetrated. Both myths and secrets place an undue burden on family members, under the weight of which I have seen families crumble.

Nearly every family with which I've worked over the years has some myths about themselves and the families from which they descended, and there are few families that don't have some secrets. Yet when working with families torn apart by deep chasms, an inescapable fact begs to be noticed: *Nearly all of them have an abundance of secrets and myths.* When feuding family members can finally feel safe enough to reveal their myths and secrets, it can clear a path of understanding, which then can lead to reconciliation.

FAMILY MYTHS

A myth is an unconscious conspiratorial story, shared by family members and usually passed down from one generation to the next. Given that family members are often so different from one another, and that each family member typically has his or her own view of "the truth" about the family, myths are remarkable things. A myth is such a strong, pervasive story that for the most part it actually transcends individual family members' points of view.

But the relationship between a myth and the truth is rarely simple. It's not really accurate to say that a myth is merely a lie, because for some members of the family the myth may well be the truth. The myth that "everyone in this family is successful" may be true for one person, but not another. One person may feel successful in her endeavors, while another may feel like a failure inside, but because of the family mythology, the person who feels like a failure doubts herself even more and tries to make her feelings conform to the myth. While she struggles to conform to the myth that "everyone is successful," she often ends up resenting her family because she feels as though she simply can't fit in.

A myth is an illusion, more like a movie than a lie. A myth is like a film portrayal of a family, scripted well in advance and projected on a screen for the family to see and hopefully believe. Some family members buy into the myth, while others may reject it. If all family members were to reject the myth, there would be no projectionist, and the myth would fail to take hold. But if enough family members are willing to play along, and the myth serves to meet enough family members' needs, the family members believe in the myth to the extent that they believe the "movie" is real.

While certain family members may aspire to live up to the family's myths, the myth itself seems to have a life of its own, and it doesn't necessarily relate to the feelings, needs, or personality of any particular individual in the family. Besides being a broad generalization, a myth is also a distortion of some real aspect of the family, and family members are expected to assume specific roles within the drama that the myth's script requires them to play. Whether or not a particular family member wishes to play the role, or whether or not the role fits the family member's personality, is irrelevant to the family myth.

THE PURPOSES OF MYTHS

Myths exist in families usually as a protective device, as a way of keeping family members safe from a perceived threat. In the very common family myth that "no one in this family has a problem with alcohol," the belief that no one drinks excessively not only protects the alcoholic from being discovered and therefore having to face the reality of the destructive behavior, but it also protects other family members who may feel dependent on the alcoholic for emotional or financial support. In this sense, myths are mechanisms of denial, serving to protect the believers of the myth from the pain and heartache that would arise from facing the truth of their family.

Myths protect by covering over or hiding serious problems. "This is a close, happy family" is a prevalent myth in families that are eventually broken up by a feud. While this myth may help to avoid the pain of dealing with one's own sadness or hurt, it also covers over the family's inadequacy in recognizing and dealing with the unique feelings of each family member, one or more of whom might be troubled.

On the other hand, myths can also serve the purpose of motivating family members. The common myth that "everyone in this family is successful" not only serves to help particular family members avoid the pain of failure, but is also meant to encourage family members who might lack sufficient motivation to succeed.

THE EFFECTS OF MYTHS

In families in which myths are pervasive, certain family members may end up feeling disillusioned. The late psychiatrist R.D. Laing called the experience of living in such families one of "mystification." Being mystified is more than just a feeling of confusion; it's a feeling of even being confused about being confused. This feeling of being mystified occurs because the family member knows and experiences one thing while he or she is being told another. The family members conspire to perpetuate the myth, and the result is that the particular child or children who experience the opposite are being told essentially that they are crazy. A child, for example, who experiences the family as a dangerous place goes to Dad or Mom for support and is told in no uncertain terms that the family is safe. The child who is frightened of her alcoholic father's unpredictable rages is told by her mother that "Dad's fine, he just had a hard day and needs some time to sleep it off." This is done to support the myth that "there is no alcoholic in the family" and that nothing unusual or frightening is going on. As a result, the child is essentially told that her fears are unwarranted, that they are not based on reality, and that therefore something is wrong with her perceptions.

The writer Bonnie Friedman described a family "secret," which in actuality was more of a myth than a secret. It describes an aspect of the mystifying effects of myths.

When I was growing up my family had a secret. My sister was fat. It was the one thing you were not allowed to say. In an argument you might say many nasty things, but never this. It would be too painful. It would kill her. She could never forgive you. It was too mean. And yet it was the most obvious thing about her, maybe the most important . . . Of course in a way there was no need to discuss it. It was what one could not for a moment forget. By not discussing it, though, it was as if one must see Anita but not see her. We saw her and didn't see her, we spoke to her and didn't speak to her, we loved her for who she was and we refused to acknowledge who she was. Are all secrets this obvious?

The child in such a family faces a dilemma. Which reality is real? The one I perceive with my own eyes and ears, or the one that I am being told is true? Wanting and needing to believe his parents, the child doubts his ability to perceive reality, and is left not trusting his own perceptions. The child moves forward in the world with a feeling of self-doubt. He also lives in a state of unreality and confusion, as though the world is a mystery that cannot be solved. The child often stays in a strange sort of limbo, caught in a mysterious puzzle that cannot be solved. This "mystified" state often leads to deep insecurity.

An alternate response to living in a family in which there is a pervasive myth is to go along with the myth, and build up a strong wall of denial of one's own. This method can work well for a while; as long as you adhere to your family myths, you won't challenge the other family members' beliefs and you won't feel the discomfort of having to battle their view of themselves. But in order to do this for long, the person caught up in a family myth must learn how to cut off his own feelings and perceptions so well that they won't end up intruding on his own peace of mind. While this might work well within the family itself, it may become a problem when adjusting to a new relationship, or joining a new family through marriage. The new family might not play by the same rules, and walls of denial and cut-off feelings can be problematic when a new partner attempts to get close to you. When creating a family of your own, cut-off feelings can often lead to marital problems.

MYTHS AND FEUDS

Family feuds arise when the mystified child attempts to grow up, come to terms with his or her own insecurity, and find a place in the world. This child, who may now be well into adulthood, has only a few choices if he is to increase his feelings of security. He might withdraw from his family altogether, preferring not to deal with his relatives at all, in order to shelter himself from further feelings of mystification. He might try a head-on approach—confronting his family members with their myths. In this situation, most family members steadfastly deny the truth of their family, preferring instead to hold onto the family myths in order to protect the feelings of safety that their myths afford them. The person who tries to confront his family members with their myths is likely to risk even greater feelings of mystification and insecurity by their continued adherence to their myths. A third option is to raise the ante altogether, not only exposing the myth for what it is, but also insisting that the family finally face the truth. This radical approach often feels necessary in order to preserve one's own sanity, regardless of the effect on the family. Depending on the family's response to these approaches, any one of them may result in a feud.

COMMON MYTHS

To paraphrase Walt Disney, "as long as there is imagination" there is no end to the myths that families can devise. Yet certain myths appear more often than others in the therapy office. It may seem ironic that one of the most common myths in families that feud is the belief that "this is a happy family." This all-purpose myth is designed specifically to ward off discontent at any level for any reason. Negative emotions or critical beliefs are forbidden, merely defined out of existence. The "happy family" myth shields the family members from any pain whatsoever, and the family acts as though everything is just fine, all the time. The prohibition against pain is pervasive, and the family members conspire to act as though everything is all right, regardless of the reality of the situation.

As long as all goes well, families can function with this myth for a long time, although the myth can be stultifying for children's emotional development. But when things go amiss either within the family, or in an aspect of one family member's life, the strain on this myth can destroy a family. An extraordinary example of the unraveling of this myth can be found in the film *Ordinary People,* in which a family cracks under the weight of the loss of one of their sons in a boating accident. Although such a trauma would rock any family to its core, rather than struggle through the devastating feelings together, the family in this film uses the "happy family" myth to enable them to avoid talking about the loss at all. Eventually, the weight of their tightly suppressed feelings shatters the family altogether.

Similar to the "happy family" myth is the "close family" myth, in which open expression of some feelings is permitted, as long as no one in the family threatens to leave or become distant in any way. The mythically close family subverts any moves toward independence, even when certain family members may feel like it's time to grow up and leave home.

In such a family, any efforts children make toward independence are met with either overt or hidden sabotage. The world is painted as too dangerous a place to survive in on one's own. Moves toward independence are met with predictions of failure, and children are encouraged to stay at home, often to take care of parents. Relationships that might lead to marriage are routinely disapproved of, unless boyfriends or girlfriends are interviewed and pass the "dependency test." This test requires that the outsider not be too dependent or close to his own family, and that he appear unlikely to succeed on his own. This would assure that he would then join the family, and not take the child away through marriage.

Often, this myth is bolstered by financial incentives not to leave home. Such tangible bribes may include offers to take over the family business, or follow in the footsteps of one or both parents. Potential sons- or daughters-in-law are accepted only if they can be seduced into the family business.

In families where the "close family" myth is in place, children are disowned if they don't toe the line, which is often only a strategy to attempt to keep them home. If the disowned child does return home, stating she or he is willing to accept the terms the family has to offer, the wayward child is again accepted. A family feud can break out when one child decides that it is better to grow up than be dependent on his or her family forever. In breaking away, this child is taking a courageous first step toward disavowing the "close family" myth, but often still has some way to go before achieving true independence.

ALCOHOL OR DRUG ABUSE MYTHS

Many feuding families are plagued with substance abuse, the drinking or drug habits of one or more members. The drinking or drug abuse is not kept a secret, and often it is evident to everyone in the family that there is a real problem. Despite overt evidence to the contrary, however, the family members are forbidden from discussing the drinking or drug abuse openly, because to acknowledge this would force the family members to deal with the painful feelings involved with its exposure. The alcoholic or drug addict is usually the last to accept what he or she already knows, openly denying that there is a problem while simultaneously pouring another glass of bourbon. Often family members dance to the tune of the alcoholic's denial, fearing perhaps that the cost of exploding this myth would be greater than holding on to the myth that there is no problem.

In families in which one or both parents are alcoholics or drug addicts, children grow up fearing that to expose the myth would risk their own safety. Sensing that it is forbidden to talk about the problem, they carefully sidestep the issue, learning how to carefully avoid the subject at all costs. Exposing the myth might not only lead to violence, causing direct harm, but children also fear that to expose the myth might lead to the breakup of the family. The alcohol or drug abuse becomes such a predominant force in the family that it seems to occupy a space all its own, like another family member who from time to time shows his or her ugly face around the house. Because Dad or Mom clings to this other family member, it is tolerated for the sake of keeping the family together.

I remember several years ago receiving a phone call from a past student of mine named Beth. She was a thirty-year-old teacher who was studying to become a marriage counselor. She called me because she felt that she and her sister Rose had feuded long enough; they barely spoke to one another, and when they did they fought miserably. Although she and her sister were both married, at my suggestion she brought her sister and mother in for a meeting. As Beth described her family, the myth that there was no alcoholism in the family took its toll. I remember her telling her mother:

"You know what it was like for us? Neither of us could talk about it. Even now, after all that's happened in our lives, even with our own families, it's hard to say out loud that Dad was an alcoholic. Me and Rose used to pray together that someone would let us talk about it, but even when we prayed we never mentioned the "A" word. We prayed that you'd pay attention to his drinking and do something about it. But it was forbidden. You didn't even have to say anything to us. We thought that if we mentioned it, even a little bit, we'd break some sort of a rule in the family. You always told us that everything was okay, but nothing was ever okay. I thought I was nuts. I thought maybe I was the crazy one. All I knew is that I had to get out of the house. But I'm still not safe. That house is inside me. I think it's inside Rose and me both, and now that we're on our own I think we're avoiding each other because it reminds us of that house and Dad's drinking."

Again, family feuds arise as a result of the damage done not by the drug abuse alone, but by the myth that it is not a problem. Family members conspire to pretend that this "ugly force" is not really in the house, even when its influence is ruling the roost. In order to take part in this conspiracy, a family member must put aside her own perceptions. She must place into doubt her reasoning and feelings, and fail to trust her personal knowledge of the drug's influence on herself and the family. To go along with this, or any other myth, requires a magical belief that everything is okay when it isn't. To doubt the myth, on the other hand, is to face the reality of the family. It requires confronting those who are telling you that you are crazy for believing that there is a problem. Breaking the myth open jeopardizes your position in the family, because you become the spoiler, the one who brings pain and discomfort down on the family's feigned well-being. Ultimately, by attempting to shatter the family's myth, you risk excommunication from the family.

EVERYONE IN THIS FAMILY MUST BECOME WEALTHY, POWERFUL, AND SUCCESSFUL

While there are many methods of becoming financially successful, the most common method is inheritance. Families whose wealth goes back many generations pass on compelling stories about the great and influential characters in the family's past. A tremendous pressure is often exerted on each successive generation to continue the family tradition of acquiring great wealth and power. This pressure exists not only among financially wealthy families, but also in families in which there is a strong legacy of professional identity. I remember being surprised once during a retreat I facilitated for medical school residents when I asked the neophyte physicians to tell me what their reasons were for going to medical school. Rather than hearing stories of altruism, prestige, or financial motives, the most common response was that "my father (or mother) was a doctor, and I was just expected to become one as well." Usually, an expression of thinly veiled sadness accompanied this response, a recognition that this was not a path they had chosen for themselves, but one that was chosen for them.

One physician whom I saw as a patient did not cover his sadness. He told me in no uncertain terms that he felt miserable, and hated his life. He felt as though he had no place in his family, because in his heart he hated being a doctor. The only reason he became a doctor, he told me, was that he had no choice.

"It was never about what you wanted to be when you grew up. No one ever asked us what we were suited for or interested in. The only choice was what *kind* of doctor we'd be, and really, we were all expected to become surgeons like my father and his father. So he got his way. There are now three more doctors in the family, and I'm the runt of the family because I decided to become a pediatrician. To me at least there was honor and dignity in taking care of kids, even if there's no money in it. But the truth is, I never wanted to be a doctor. But you just didn't bring something like that up in my family."

In such families, acquisition of status, power, wealth, or other success is not based on the individual wishes or needs of any particular family member, but instead on a strong multigenerational myth that in order to be a member of this family, you must perform at this predetermined level. Failure to do so would certainly risk rejection from the family. If the rejection isn't an outright one, it might be in the form of a powerful disappointment that a particular child did not live up to the unwritten but clearly defined family standards.

Bucking the myth of the successful family can be a powerful lead-in to a family feud. Some children who grow up in these families merely "resign" under the weight of the pressure, choosing to leave the family and break off relations before they are broken off angrily by others. More common, some children grow up attempting to meet the family standards outwardly while inwardly rejecting them. They achieve the requisite status but find themselves sabotaging their own success through risky investments, gambling, or other means. Their anger about living up to someone else's standards boils to a point at which they break off from the family altogether, constructing a feud just to cope with the fallout of this myth.

YOU CAN NEVER SUCCEED IN THIS FAMILY

Just as sad, and perhaps just as prevalent, is the way some families encourage failure. "No one in this family ever amounts to anything" is just as powerful a myth as the one proclaiming that everyone must be successful. Neither myth is based on the individual needs or wishes of any particular family member, and both myths are pathways to potential feuds. For those growing up in a family where failure is mythologized, moves toward success are downplayed and sabotaged. When a child becomes successful, she often feels as though she must hide her own success, out of fear that she will be rejected by her family.

Some children, wishing to break free of this myth, create a family feud in order not to disrupt the prevailing family story. In these families, children are afraid they will shame their families if they succeed. Those who succeed often believe that family members who previously failed will be shamed by their success. Similar to the days when teenage girls who became pregnant had to leave their hometown "to visit a relative" on a prolonged journey in order to avoid the shame of pregnancy, successful children often have to leave town to avoid the "shame" of success.

When a child from a family with a dominant "failure myth" grows up to become successful, she might also feel ashamed of her own roots and have difficulty associating with her family. A feud can be a way of covering up or avoiding this shame, because it is easier to justify one's distance with a feud than to deal with the feeling of shame toward one's family.

This is exactly what happened when Barbara, a forty-three-year-old executive in a retail chain, found herself in a conundrum about whether or not to go home to a twenty-fifth anniversary high school reunion. She wanted to go to the reunion, but she had had no contact with her family for many years, and no desire to have any contact. When asked why, she told me a long story about a feud she was having with her sister and her parents. Despite her feud, she didn't want to slap them in the face by traveling fifteen hundred miles and not at least seeing them. As I tried to get to the patterns in her family that supported her long list of complaints about the family, Barbara turned tearful.

"I think the hardest thing, and you're probably going to put me away for saying this, is that I'm ashamed. I'm not so much ashamed of them, but I'm ashamed of myself. I know that's crazy, but if you lived in my family you'd understand. It's that I've become so successful. I drive a nice car, I can afford nice clothes, I probably earn more money in a year than they have in a decade. You weren't allowed to be successful. Well, it wasn't that you weren't allowed, it's just that, it's not us. You know? It's not that money is evil or anything, it's just that it would be like showing them up or something. You're just not supposed to amount to anything in my family."

As we discussed her feud, it turned out that the more successful she became, the more difficult it was for her to talk to or relate to her family members. As a way of avoiding them, she manufactured a list of minor complaints that she enlarged into major conflicts. After several fights, she decided that she wanted to have nothing to do with them. The decision about whether or not to attend the high school reunion forced her family back into the spotlight, and after articulating the myth and putting it in the context of something that had existed for generations in her family, Barbara was able to return to her family.

NO ONE IN THIS FAMILY IS "SICK"

In families where the draw of the gene pool is unkind, certain children enter the world with a propensity toward a severe physical or psychiatric condition. One of the most blatant of these is the condition known as schizophrenia, in which disturbances in thinking are often combined with bizarre behavior. There is a tendency for schizophrenia to appear as children make the transition to adulthood, usually in the late teens or early twenties. Other "schizophrenia-like" conditions, such as childhood autism or certain developmental disorders, often appear as children develop the ability to communicate with others.

In many families in which a child or young adult has a severe psychiatric illness, the child's illness is confronted head-on and there is an aggressive attempt to learn about the illness, treat it as well as one can, and obtain support from groups designed to assist families with such members. The needs of others in the family are attended to as well, in the realization that it is often the siblings and "healthier" members of the family who suffer nearly as much from a lack of attention.

But some families—usually those that exhibit a multigenerational pattern of psychiatric illness and denial of that illness—subscribe to a myth handed down from one generation to the next. This myth prescribes that no members of the family are "sick" at all. The belief in that myth takes on religious proportions, so that whatever illness may be visible to the rest of the world simply does not exist in the minds of family members.

While this may seem like an uncommon myth to those who have never witnessed it, it is widespread. It is a myth that yields the kind of strenuous denial that permits parents to be told by relatives, school officials, neighbors, and doctors of every stripe that something is wrong with their child, and yet go right on believing and acting as though their child is no different from any other healthy boy or girl.

I have seen this myth exert such a strong influence that family members actually believe their seriously disturbed child, who may hallucinate or completely withdraw from the world, is emotionally healthier than their husband, wife, or a child who is doing well in work or performing well in school. The extremely withdrawn child may be described by a parent as simply shy, or the child who actively hallucinates or throws violent temper tantrums may be called merely obstinate. As a result of this myth, "healthier" family members find their own view of the reality of their family severely challenged, leading to a feeling of being "mystified," as mentioned earlier. Family members who challenge this myth are ostracized, and family feuds ensue.

These are just a few of the myths families create out of their need to deny emotional distress and protect each other from having to face the pain of having an imperfect family. Other common myths include: "This is a safe family. You can talk openly to anyone in this family without worrying about the consequences." Many families suffer from the myth that "Everyone in this family is equal; this is a democracy." Regardless of the specific content of the family myth, the consequences of the clash between reality and myth can do sufficient harm to family members to eventually precipitate a feud.

SECRETS

Having seen what happens when family members create false stories, we now turn to the equally powerful effects on families when they hide their true stories. Secrets in families are not uncommon; in fact, it's hard to find a family that doesn't have some secrets lurking in its closets. Yet, as I mentioned earlier, one chief purpose of a family is to create an environment of safety for children to grow up in. It is this feeling of safety that leads to a trusting attitude toward the world, an attitude that allows children to grow up learning how to appropriately lean on others while overcoming obstacles and taming the world's monsters. And trust itself depends on openness, on the knowledge that what you see is what you get. Hidden stories, secrets that are kept in order to protect a child from troubling information, ironically can result in damaging that child's sense of trust and safety.

In families that feud, secrets run rampant. I often get the feeling that the family is like a field, and the stories they tell are the vegetation. Their secrets are like weeds, unwanted growth that seems to spring up everywhere. So, while most families have an occasional weed in a lovely garden, feuding families tend to have vast areas of weeds growing out of control, prohibiting the growth of healthy vegetation. Typically, in families that value openness (while respecting each person's needs for privacy), secrets tend to be few and far between. The openness policy, when practiced judiciously, is one of the best insurance policies against family feuds.

THE DIFFERENCE BETWEEN MYTHS AND SECRETS

The myth-making process in families is often subtle. Family mythology is handed down from one generation to the next, and family members often effortlessly believe their family's myths. Those family members who actively create their own myths do so without planning or foreknowledge; they come to believe their myths in a thoughtless, almost accidental way, taking on beliefs that seem to protect them from the threatening feelings that the truth would engender.

On the other hand, families in which *secrets* prevail often have to go to great lengths to perpetuate their masquerade. For the most part, keeping secrets is not easy; it goes against our human nature to reveal the truth. As politicians of late can attest, withholding information can be more complex and dangerous than simply revealing the incriminating information.

Myth-making is a form of self-betrayal, because the propagators of family myths actually believe the stories they pass along. Keeping a family secret involves knowingly betraying another. In essence, myths are fictions while secrets are lies. Lying requires an intent to deceive another. Holders of secrets intentionally deceive, although they may proclaim altruistic motives. Myths are essentially not lies, because when one successfully deceives oneself there is no intent to deceive others.

THE PURPOSES OF SECRETS

People keep secrets from other people in their family for a variety of reasons. The most common reason is to protect others from hurt. Keeping things quiet is thought of as a way to shelter those who, for one reason or another, can't handle the truth. Shielding them from a troubling secret is believed to be a way of protecting vulnerable people from unnecessary pain.

In my own family, the death of my grandmother when I was twelve years old was kept from me for some time. My parents thought it would be unnecessary and hurtful for me to attend the funeral or any of the services associated with her loss. Yet what they didn't know was that, by keeping the truth from me, they were depriving me of the opportunity to express my grief and to participate in a communal healing process. Consequently, I had to hold my grief inside myself with no means of coping with my loss. It wasn't until I was a mid-life adult that I discovered that I had had two siblings, one who died in utero and another who died shortly after birth. The knowledge of these losses was also thought to be too difficult for a young child to handle, so my parents waited until much later in my life to tell me about them.

In many families, traumas such as these are hidden from the children, even if the children are full-grown, in the belief that having to face them would cause great pain. The suicide of Henry Fonda's first wife Frances was not disclosed to either of his children, Jane or Peter. Jane was said to have heard about the death of her mother six months later by reading about it in a movie magazine. Suicides, criminal behavior, incestuous relationships, extramarital affairs, abortions, pregnancies resulting from affairs, serious illnesses, and drug addiction are often kept from family members because it is believed that knowledge of these situations or behaviors would hurt others unnecessarily.

It's not uncommon for a woman to keep her close ties to other women from her husband, out of fear that if her husband knew how close she was to her friends, it would threaten her husband's sense of security and competence. Similarly, husbands and wives often keep the intimate details of their marital struggles secret from their closest friends, out of respect for their spouse's dignity, or to protect their spouse's vulnerabilities. I can't count how many times in family therapy sessions I've heard family members beg other family members to keep their family lives secret from the rest of the world, in fear of being shamed, embarrassed, scrutinized, or judged.

Mothers (and occasionally fathers) sometimes keep secrets from their spouses, such as when a child does something wrong, in order to shelter and protect their children from the wrath of the other spouse. While these secrets may appear to be a betrayal of the parental alliance, it is an arrangement that is often well accepted and tolerated in families.

Husbands whose self-esteem depends on their being the breadwinner will often keep their business failures secret from the rest of the family, sheltering them from the pain of what's hoped will be a temporary setback.

The secrets we keep from our families, the information we withhold in order to protect others, are often thinly veiled attempts to protect ourselves. Concern for others' often serves to disguise self-interest; if we can delude ourselves into believing that we are merely attempting to protect others, then our own self-interest becomes lit in the glow of nobility. Keeping one's own financial malaise from the rest of the family, for example, may appear to be a charitable act; but it also protects one from the shame and embarrassment of facing one's own failures.

Sometimes the self-protection of a secret is simple and obvious, such as when we refuse to tell someone our age because of our own vanity.

More often we keep secrets from others because it offers a shield against feeling the pain of our own failings, and facing the responsibility for our own self-destructive, greedy, or shameful actions.

Many family members keep secrets from other family members in order to protect the family from societal disapproval. Homosexuality is often undisclosed due to the belief that revealing it would embarrass and harm the family in some way. Families who pride themselves on their material wealth may not disclose their own financial troubles for fear that the family name will be tarnished. Similarly, the criminal activity of a particular family member will be hidden in order to protect the honor and dignity of the family.

Secrets are often kept to maintain a hierarchy of power and influence. Two people who share a secret have a special bond between them, and their knowledge gives them a certain power over those from whom the secret is being kept. The old saying that "knowledge is power" translates to the fact that those who are "in the know" have more power than those who are left "in the dark." One way to elevate yourself above others is to set yourself apart by keeping secrets. Certain children are often elected by one or both parents to know something the others aren't told. Automatically, the child feels honored by this level of increased trust, although sometimes the child also feels awkward about betraying her siblings.

A special bond is created when two people share knowledge unavailable to the older generation. Siblings at times soothe themselves by keeping secrets from their parents. Siblings can feel comforted when they know that their brother or sister shares some intimate detail that is too risky for their parents to find out. The secret club and the secret password are designed to create a sense of specialness that separates one group from another, an "in" group from an "out" group.

In some families, secrets are used as a weapon against family members who are overly intrusive. Enmeshed families are breeding grounds for secrets, because keeping secrets is one way a family member can keep other family members out of his or her "business." If there are no locks on the bedroom doors, people may create emotional lockouts of those whom they feel intrude on their privacy. Secrets provide the emotional deadbolts that can be turned when the danger of intrusion becomes too great.

THE EFFECTS OF SECRETS

While secrets are not always harmful, when they appear in great numbers in families it is usually a sign that something troubling is going on. This isn't always the case, such as when a teenager keeps a few "small secrets" from her parents, such as sneaking into a movie, or talking on the phone to someone she was told not to talk to. Occasionally, when one family member keeps a lot of secrets, it may be more a sign that this particular family member is going through a rough spot in his or her development, having some conflicts at work, school, or with peers. But when several family members have a plethora of secrets, this usually implies that there is a feeling of danger in the family, that the family isn't a safe place in which to discuss personal matters openly. When sitting with families that seem to collect secrets like flies on a horse, I often feel haunted by their awkward silences. Their silences are like Wite-Out on a page, covering up and censoring the most provocative and telling details of their lives.

Even one secret can have a profound impact on a family. Let's say, for example, that a child is born out of wedlock, or that a child in the family was the result of a pregnancy that occurred from a prior lover or husband who left shortly before or after the baby was born. In order to keep this fact a secret, a parent may alter her or his story, thereby falsifying the family's history. In order to avoid being caught in the lie, the whole subject of family history may be avoided, depriving the child of a sense of belonging.

When a family's history contains significant secrets, there is a tendency for the subject of the past to be avoided altogether. When the secret involves a particular relative, intense feelings may arise whenever that person is mentioned, and the secret-holders may go out of their way to avoid discussing that aspect of family history at all.

If the secret is important enough, the holders of the secret will do whatever they feel is necessary to avoid disclosing it. If they should feel their secret is in danger of being found out, their anxiety level will rise, causing them to further distort their past and become more entangled in a web of lies.

Secrets, like myths, have a mystifying power. Those outside the loop sense that something isn't being told to them, and as a result they feel confused. Recently, I worked with a family in which the father was feeling suicidal. Fearing that talking about his feelings would hurt his wife and daughters, he kept his suicidal feelings a secret. Still, one of his daughters, who was particularly close to him, sensed his depression. But whenever anyone asked the father how he felt, he would always give the socially appropriate response, denying that anything was wrong. As a result, the daughter felt crazy—mystified by the fact that she sensed her father was terribly sad and overwhelmed, even though he claimed not to be. She also started feeling very depressed herself and had no idea why. Finally her father revealed that he was considering suicide. Discovering this "secret" provided the daughter with an explanation for her own depression, and gave her a sense of relief at being able to validate her own feelings. Deeply concerned for her father, the daughter no longer felt crazy once he revealed the truth about his emotional condition.

When two people are very close, they become so sensitized to each other's feelings that each often shares or "holds" the other's feelings. In this family, the daughter not only felt mystified by her father's denial of his true emotional state, she also felt so close to him that she felt as though she had to hold her father's feelings. When he took on the responsibility of his own feelings, he reclaimed them, and his daughter no longer had to experience those feelings for him. Revealing his secret saved his family from having to deal with the mystification that can eventually lead to a major family trauma.

For some family members, the presence of injustice within their family is the source of great rage. While most mature adults agree with President Carter's astute observation that "life isn't fair," families are where we learn our first lessons about justice. When a family functions in such a way that some people have information and others do not, it is an insult to a child's budding sense of justice. This indignant stand waters whatever seeds of feuds may have already been planted.

Those who are on the outside of the secret are not the only ones to suffer. When secrets bind two or more people together, those who share the secret often share a sense of guilt as well. Knowing they are excluding and hurting others, knowing they are "breaking a rule," can leave them feeling ashamed and guilty.

Keeping secrets, fortunately, is not easy. In order to keep a secret, family members must often alter their own behavior. In order to cover up alcoholism, for example, family members must go to extremes, making up lie after lie to hide their alcoholic behavior. It's not uncommon, for example, to believe that a man is having an affair with a woman, because every Friday night he fails to come home until early the next morning. Eventually, the truth surfaces that this was the night that the "sober" alcoholic routinely fell off the wagon, and he went to stay with a friend in order to sleep it off, rather than go home and face his family. As the old saw goes, one lie often leads to another, building up to a crescendo of deception that can shatter trust beyond repair.

SECRETS AND FEUDS

Usually, feuds erupt in secretive families when the pressure caused by keeping secrets combines with the patterns discussed in earlier chapters. While a history of keeping secrets alone can push a family to a feud, especially when the history is a multigenerational one, most feuds that I have seen come about as a result of a mixture of the patterns already discussed. Secrets combine with triangulation, enmeshment, anniversary reactions, and a multigenerational history to ignite a feud.

Similarly, a combination of the untoward effects of keeping secrets can also lead to a feud, even when secrets are not revealed. The mystifying effects of secrets, combined with feeling left out of the loop and a feeling of not belonging, can lead a family member to angrily break free, using a feud as a vehicle.

When family secrets involving important issues are finally disclosed, those who have been lied to often feel so betrayed they want nothing to do with the perpetrators of the lie, and a family feud is set in motion. Because secrets are willful acts, requiring effort to create and enforce, those on the outside of the secret feel misled and alienated. Their sense of betrayal sets the stage for divisions in the family that can last over a lifetime. "I never knew what my two brothers were up to," one family member might say. "They always colluded against me, and I've been terrified of them ever since." It's not uncommon to hear feuding family members recite a litany of events and situations in which they were left out of the communication loop. After years of explanations and arguments, those from whom secrets were kept still reel from these wounds.

If revealing a secret can often lead to the kind of disruption in a family that will result in a feud, one wonders if it's just not better to keep secrets. It's true that revealing secrets often leads to hurt feelings and deep wounds, but the revelation of a significant secret is often the first step in healing those wounds. When secrets are not revealed, the result is often a paralysis of the family. If secrets are being maintained, whatever created the need for the secret in the first place remains. The secret functions like a crack in the foundation of a building. As time goes by, more secrets may be added, the original secrets grow deeper and more profound, and the building eventually collapses.

COMMON SECRETS

SEXUAL ABUSE

Sexual abuse is more common than nearly any other secret within feuding families. Sexual abuse can involve any member of a family, and while it is not at all limited to abuse between father or stepfather and a female child, this certainly appears to be the most common form it takes. While I will refer to this form when discussing sexual abuse, the statements I make are relevant to either gender.

When sexual abuse occurs in a family, many people are wounded. For most, the physical violation of sexual abuse is not nearly as devastating as the emotional violation of the relationship. The sexually abused victim is robbed of dignity, robbed of a sense of safety, and robbed of the ability to trust those who are supposed to protect her. Secrecy is an integral ingredient in sexual abuse. Without secrecy, most sexual abuse would never occur, and if it did, it certainly wouldn't continue over time.

The most common secret in sexual abuse is that of the existence of the abuse, which the perpetrator forces the victim to keep. This secret is often enforced through verbal threats. The simplest threat is the statement "Let this be a secret between the two of us." The power difference between the perpetrator and the victim is often enough for this statement to carry the weight of a frightening threat. Stronger threats, such as "If you tell your mother, it will kill her" lets the victim know that not only is she responsible for not betraying the perpetrator, but somehow she must also be responsible for not hurting her mother or her parents' marriage, and for keeping the family intact. Then there are even more threatening statements, such as "If you tell your mother, I'll say you're crazy and put you in a mental hospital," or "If you tell your mother, I'll make sure you never live to see another day." The secret that is kept between the perpetrator and the victim is the very glue that holds the pieces of the nightmare together, allowing the abuse to continue.

Often, other additional secrets are involved in sexual abuse. Once the initial secret is revealed, there are different ways that family members choose to handle the disclosure. For some, the abuse is such a shameful disclosure that the mother threatens the victim to keep it a secret within the family, so that no one outside the family will discover it. This secret then serves as a further betrayal, making the victim feel even more responsible for doing something dirty, something that must be hidden. It also prevents the family members from getting the help they need in order to deal with this violation.

In some families, the disclosure of abuse results in the breakup of the family. I have seen many families in which the mother remarries, and her second husband (the new stepfather) then makes advances toward the girl who had already been victimized by her own father. The victim's mother may then confront her current husband, or she may choose to keep this a secret, not wishing to "fail" at a second marriage. She then enjoins the twice-victimized daughter to not reveal the secret to anyone, including her new stepsiblings. This secret then paralyzes the family completely, with the victimized daughter feeling that she cannot reveal her own victimization, and therefore cannot protect her stepsiblings from suffering the same fate. The stepsiblings become acutely aware that there is something that cannot be discussed, and they feel betrayed because they know something is going on in the family that they are not being told about.

For most victims of abuse, there is a simple formula: Either the mother chooses to act like a mother and protect her child, or she sides with her husband against her child. Those parents who choose to side with the perpetrator by denying that there is a problem, refusing to deal with it, or refusing to believe the child, force the child to feel betrayed by both the perpetrator and the parent who fails to protect her. Feeling as though she has no one in the world she can trust, the victim of sexual abuse then turns away from her family, either refusing to interact with them at all or interacting in only superficial or angry ways. The victim may choose to engage her family with the bitter, resentful, enraged feelings of a feud, or she may simply move away from the family altogether, harboring deep feelings of resentment in a silent, enraged stand against them.

For many victims of sexual abuse, there is simply no alternative to a family feud. Unless the perpetrator is willing to acknowledge and face up to this terrible act, and unless the entire family can break the reign of terror by confronting the abuse openly, a family feud may be inevitable.

THE EXTRAMARITAL AFFAIR

The extramarital affair exemplifies the power of secrets to wear away at the fabric of a family. If it were not for the secretive aspect of an affair, it would be hard to call it one. An affair made public becomes a part of a redefined relationship, what in prior decades was referred to as an "open," or nonexclusive, marriage.

While secrecy is a necessary ingredient for an affair, it is not the reason people have affairs. As I mentioned in the chapter on triangulation, people have affairs for as many reasons as there are people who have them. Therefore, an affair might end because the reason for the affair no longer exists. The secrecy of once having had the affair, however, may linger for quite some time. That secrecy might well cast a long shadow on the family, and be intimately involved with the maintenance of a feud. Larry, a forty-six-year-old insurance salesman, had an affair with his secretary seven years ago. Even though his wife never learned about the affair, he ended it after two months, seeing the damaging effect it had on his marriage. Ending the affair, however, was the beginning of a feud with his secretary, who remained enraged that Larry didn't split up with his wife. Although she found a way to become someone else's secretary, she remained in the office suite, and the tension at work was palpable.

"The thing that kills me the most," Larry revealed, "is that I can't find a way to get close to my wife. The affair is over, it's done. But I know if I told my wife about it, our marriage would be over. She'd never get over it. But keeping this secret is killing me. I feel like every day is a lie."

Even though Larry's feud is with his ex-secretary, the secret of the affair is now making it difficult for him to get close to his wife. When combined with other marital problems, this might eventually lead to a feud with his wife as well.

Even though the secret of an affair may ultimately be exposed, I have seen marital partners actively support the secretive nature of the affair even after it has been exposed. It's not uncommon for a woman who has had an affair to tell her husband about it, continue to have the affair, and prohibit the husband from contacting the man with whom she is having an affair. In other words, while the affair has been unveiled for the husband to see, he is now asked to keep her secret for her, not allowing him to discuss the affair with "the other man." I have known many women who have discovered the extramarital preoccupations of their husbands, and who then refuse to confront "the other woman," in a sense keeping a new secret and protecting the man who is cheating on her. While the most important part of the healing process needs to occur between the spouses, conspiring not to contact the third party often reflects the betrayed partner's unwitting complicity in the triangle, or a simple lack of courage that might reflect a level of passivity that is destructive to the marriage itself.

Revealing one secret doesn't necessarily stop someone from creating others. As families and couples continue to weave one secret after another, they create a "culture of secrecy," in which the courage to face the truth is never developed. Maintaining this culture creates a breeding ground for feuds, because not learning how to face the truth makes the likelihood great that eventually someone will get hurt deeply by feeling betrayed.

When the extramarital affairs of a husband or wife are ultimately exposed, it's common for the affairs to be kept a secret from the children. They are often believed to be too young for this sort of sordid information, and the secret is designed to protect them from seeing their parents in too fallible a light, or to keep from exposing them to information about sex and relationships when they are too young to know about this kind of information.

More likely than not, children do know more than their parents think they do. And when they don't know about the details, they experience the feelings associated with the affair—the tension in the family, the distance between Mom and Dad, the anger between the two parents. Once again, the secrets in the family have the effect of mystifying children, ultimately leading to feelings of alienation.

ADOPTION

It was once believed, not too long ago, that children who are adopted would be better off not knowing about it, because it would make them feel "different" and perhaps feel less loved if they knew they weren't the "real" children of their adoptive parents. Fortunately, this view has fallen out of favor, but there are still some holdouts who innocently believe that not talking about the facts of adoption is a better policy than talking about it.

Not talking about adoption when a child may be curious about it, or withholding information about the adoption, is tantamount to keeping a secret. Revealing a child's adoption status when the child becomes a teenager or later can only cause that child to feel lied to and betrayed. Someone who is caught in the mysterious place between knowing and not knowing his or her birth status is likely to feel confused and wonder about whether or not he or she belongs in the family. The secret of one's adoption status can lead to a feud the way any other secret can—through mystifying a child and through the child feeling ultimately betrayed and left out of the loop.

THE CHILD IS NOT YOUR CHILD

If a child is born out of wedlock, or is the result of an extramarital affair, the truth surrounding the fatherhood of that child is often kept a secret. One such situation was discussed in the first chapter of this book. In these situations, the biological father may or may not know that he has fathered a child. The marriage partner may or may not know. And the child himself or herself is the least likely of all to know.

Mothers who risk exposing the secret rightly or wrongly fear that to reveal the truth might end the marriage. It's difficult for anyone to find the courage to face this stark reality. Once a secret has been kept from someone for many years, the holder or holders of the secret must face the difficult choice of whether or not to reveal it. Not to reveal the secret runs the risk of the child eventually finding out the truth, at which point he or she will have to confront the parent's long-term deception. If a parent does reveal the truth, the child still feels betrayed, having been lied to for many years. This feeling of betrayal might be deep, but the revelation of the truth permits the healing process to begin. There can never be a healing process as long as secrets remain.

Family feuds can erupt at any of several points in the process. Simply as a result of feeling mystified for many years, and experiencing the accumulation of mistrust in the family, a child may angrily detach from the rest of the family. A feud can erupt when the secret is revealed, because at that point the child has to face many years of being lied to. What seems like a no-win situation at first must be viewed as the beginning step on a long journey toward reconciliation and healing. When the situation is viewed that way, it becomes possible to become much closer to those by whom someone feels betrayed.

ALCOHOLISM

Virginia Satir, a key figure in the history of family therapy, used to tell a story about the boy who asked his father, "Papa, why do you stagger when you come home at night?" Before his father could answer, the mother broke in, reprimanding her son with a "Shhh!" When Satir asked the mother why she silenced her son, and if her husband did indeed drink, the mother said, "Yes, but we don't want the neighbors to know."

Alcoholism is a prime example of how something so obvious to all members of the family can be kept a secret from those who are not supposed to know. It is often the "bull in the china shop," stomping through the family, wreaking havoc in its wake. Family members are often exposed to the alcoholic's unpredictable violent episodes, emotional tantrums, unchecked bursts of anguish and raw emotion. At the same time, certain family members conspire to keep the alcoholism a secret.

The secret of alcoholism in the family is similar to the myth that "there is no alcoholism in this family." The key difference, of course, is that the myth of no alcoholism is a fabricated story created so that all members of the family don't have to face the facts. Alcoholism that is kept a secret is usually a secret between the alcoholic adult and his or her spouse. (Both parents may also be alcoholics, of course, or there may be a lone teenage alcoholic who keeps the alcoholism a secret to himself or herself.) The remaining family members are lied to. While both the myth and the secret create a feeling of mystification and confusion, the secret of alcoholism is eventually experienced as a greater betrayal, because it is a willing, premeditated lie. It may be well intended, but the fact that it is a planned, conscious effort makes those family members who are left out of the loop feel deeply betrayed by the rest of the family.

In many families, the secret of alcoholism is never divulged. In others, the devastation caused by the alcoholism forces family members who are left out of the loop to pay attention to it. The secret is eventually divined by those left out, and at that point each family member will choose to deal with it in his or her own way, usually based on the role he or she plays in the family.

For many, being left out of the loop is enough to fan the angry, resentful flames of betrayal. This deep resentment can then cause a deep chasm in the family, especially when other key multigenerational factors enter into the picture.

HOMOSEXUALITY

Secrets in families often reflect the taboos of the culture in which they occur. Alcoholism, drug abuse, and extramarital affairs are just a few of the issues that people often feel ashamed of, despite their prevalence in our society. Homosexuality is another issue that often brings discomfort to families. Myths about homosexuality run rampant in society, and they often result in family members feeling ashamed and embarrassed as they struggle to accept the fact that one or more of the children (or parents) identifies himself or herself as homosexual.

I'm currently seeing a family unravel as they try to deal with their son's homosexuality. The nearly thirty-year-old son had lived at home until very recently, when he decided to get an apartment with a young man with whom he had been having an intimate relationship. Although he identified himself as homosexual, he was always reluctant to talk about it with his family members, who were deeply religious and essentially felt that homosexuality amounted to an evil choice. He felt close to his family, and didn't want to risk losing their nurturance and love.

So Martin did what many homosexual men and women do—he kept his homosexuality a secret from his family. This tactic "worked" for a while, in that it permitted him to feel accepted and loved by his family. But eventually, Martin felt as though he was living a double life, and the deception began to wear away at his peace of mind. He slowly began to break his code of silence and inform members of the family one by one. While, predictably, no one was surprised, their reactions were as Martin feared they would be. His father wrote him a letter telling him that he had to make a choice between his "immoral lifestyle" or his family; he could not have both.

In Martin's situation, as is so often the case, exposing the secret of his homosexuality forced his family members to face their own insecurities and to test their own values. It was a crucible, a test for the family members to see if they could hold together and weather the storm created by having a homosexual relative who leaves the closet. Martin's religious family members failed to accept him, and exposing this secret caused feelings of great embarrassment and shame for them, especially while attending church. In a letter we worked on together, Martin asked his family members if they could accept him for who he was, a person who happened to be a homosexual. They did not have to approve of his homosexuality, but he hoped that they could love him. Using the biblical terminology his family members took comfort in, he hoped they could separate "the sinner" from "the sin." His father wrote back a scathing and angry letter, essentially stating that he wanted no further contact. As a result, Martin felt betrayed by his family, who could not accept him for who he was. It also challenged Martin's belief in his family's love for him, and eventually led him to take the stand that the only way he could have integrity was to live his life his way, even if it cost him his ties to the family.

Martin felt as though he had no choice but to refuse to respond to his family members or initiate further contact with them in any way. They did likewise, and the seeds of this family's feud took hold, growing into a nasty weed that infested what could have continued to be a loving, if not entirely accepting, family.

MONEY

Secrets involving money are one of the most common types of secrets between family members. Husbands and wives often keep their financial affairs from their spouse, and even when money matters are openly discussed between partners, information about money is frequently kept secret from the children. As with other secrets, money problems are often kept from children in a misguided attempt to protect them. Parents see their children as burdened enough by the challenges of school and social pressures, so why burden them more with problems that they have no control over?

It is true that some children, particularly those prone to worrying, will take on the anxiety of their parents' money fears. But the reality remains that children have sensitive enough antennae that, despite their parents' attempts to keep money troubles a secret from them, they will sense their parents' anxieties and worry regardless. The difference between knowing the content of the secret and not knowing is that when children have some idea what their parents are worrying about, they are less likely to feel confused by their parents telling them that everything is okay, when in fact they sense that everything is not okay.

The secret of money troubles, like most other secrets, contributes to a feeling of alienation and distance from one's parents, because children often sense that their parents are being less than candid. When money problems are kept secret from spouses, mistrust and a lack of safety are fostered between them. Mistrust, lack of safety, alienation, and distance are powerful ingredients in the recipe for a feud.

TRAUMA

Life holds many surprises, some pleasurable and others potentially disastrous. The child who dies, the loss of a lifelong ambition, the suicide of a friend, the murder of a next-door neighbor, a senseless killing in a drive-by shooting, an accidental drowning, the appearance at your door of a child who claims to be yours, the unexpected lawsuit that destroys a lifelong business, a rape, and the intrusion into your house of a stranger are traumatic events that often change our lives and shape our personalities in unpredictable ways.

Parents will keep from children, and from each other, whatever they believe will be too much for the others to handle. For some, the secret becomes the drug that helps to anesthetize the pain of the trauma. Sharing the news of the trauma with the family would only spread the pain to others, so instead of using the family as a source of comfort and support, the family becomes a distant group of familiar faces who must be protected.

This ostensibly noble effort is often in reality a self-centered attempt to protect oneself from feeling the effects of the trauma. When a trauma occurs, people have a way of shutting down their feelings in order to protect themselves from an emotional overload. We go into an emotional shock that often looks to others as though we don't care or aren't affected by the trauma. The truth couldn't be more different; in fact, we are so deeply affected that our emotional world shuts down. It is an inborn "circuit breaker," designed to keep our bodies going while our minds attempt to grapple with the devastation of the trauma.

Once we share the news with others, we know they are likely to react. If they aren't as close to the trauma as we are, they are less likely to go into shock than to express their feelings directly. When those around us express their feelings openly, we are confronted with the need to not abandon them and to comfort them, or at least to commiserate with them. By connecting with them, we are forced to reexperience our own emotions about the event. Some people are so afraid of their own emotions that they prefer to "keep it to myself," instead of sharing the trauma with others and risking whatever feelings might come up.

Of course, as with so many other secrets, it takes tremendous effort to hide from plain view something as large as a traumatic event. Directly or indirectly, the news is likely to leak out. When it does, those whom the secret was designed to protect are likely to rebel, and to feel hurt because of being left out.

DISEASE

Another common family secret is a chronic or acute disease of one of the family members. Diseases that may seem invisible to the naked eye, such as certain stages of cancer or AIDS, may be so devastating to the family that those who know about the condition often keep it a secret from others. The person diagnosed with the disease may be the only one who knows about it, and may choose to keep it from the rest of his family. Frequently, the seriously ill person will select only a few trusted family members to tell, in fear that the reactions of other family members will make handling the disease even more stressful. Not only does the illness-bearer have to hold the knowledge, pain, and struggle of coping with his own disease, but he is also faced with the burden of dealing with the feelings of others in the family.

In some cases, other family members may be informed about the disease, but the one with the disease is kept in the dark. This can happen when the person with the illness is older or very young, and it is believed that having knowledge of the disease may cause greater distress.

Most often, though, the person with the disease is informed about her condition, and one or two key family members are told as well. The decision to keep the knowledge away from the others, such as children if it is a parent who may be ill and possibly dying, or the siblings of a child with a severe disease, is often made, once again, in an attempt to protect the others from the emotional pain that would ensue. As with other secrets, there is a tendency in these situations for those left out of the inner circle to feel betrayed rather than protected. They often feel insulted that they are not considered competent enough to handle the news, or denigrated, as though they are not important enough in the scheme of things to be included in the secret. Similarly, when some family members know and others do not, the stage is set for divisions in the family to emerge. One creative solution is for the seriously ill person to have the few trusted friends or family members hold the responsibility of initially communicating with the others, thus freeing the ill person to focus more directly on taking care of his or her own immediate needs in the most nurturant environment possible.

When combined with enmeshment, triangulation, or other patterns that are handed down from one generation to the next, myths and secrets in families provide a fertile breeding ground for feuds. The inescapable fact is that families who are feuding have significant myths, a multitude of secrets, or a few pivotal secrets that remain undisclosed. Even when secrets are disclosed, feuds can erupt because those who have been kept in the dark often feel betrayed.

Myths and secrets can often work together. They can both emanate from a powerful wish to avoid the more painful aspects of life. They can both be potent ways of coping with shame, embarrassment, and humiliation. Those of us who inherit mythologies from the generations before us must work hard to conquer them, and those of us who keep secrets must learn the courage to face the truth if we are ultimately to heal our families' deep divisions.

Great Expectations

Blessed is he who expects nothing, for he shall
never be disappointed.

—ALEXANDER POPE

IF, AS SHAKESPEARE SAID, "ALL THE WORLD'S A STAGE," THEN SURELY
OUR FAMILIES ARE THE ACTORS' WORKSHOPS, PROVIDING US OUR EAR-
liest education in how to master the scripts and roles we are given. The
dramas of family life are played out daily, some of them raucous melo-
dramas, filled with passion and crises, others seemingly perpetual
tragedies. As actors in our family's dramas, we can become stereotyped
and ineffectual, or we can become dynamic and flexible, learning to
move from role to role with grace, precision, and timing.

The family's "script" is the set of expectations, often handed down
from generation to generation, placed on each family member. A family feud is a family drama that frequently takes shape as a result of one
or more family members getting stuck in their roles, making it difficult to break free of the family script. The roles we play and how we
play them are intricately tied to the development of a feud, as the recent feud between Allison and her sister Jennifer demonstrated.

Allison, a thirty-year-old nurse, called me to discuss some of the
difficulties she was having with her family. Although Allison was hap-
pily married, she and her sister, who normally had a close relationship,
had not been talking to each other for about two years. Her sister Jennifer, a year younger, had in fact divorced herself almost completely
from her own family, speaking only occasionally to her mother. After

discussing the family briefly with her on the phone, I decided that the situation would best be handled by trying to gather the whole family together. While Allison agreed, she said that she thought Jennifer was not likely to attend. I suggested that Allison tell her mother to tell Jennifer that she was needed to help fix a family problem. Allison's mother was instructed to let Jennifer know that Jennifer's silence and refusal to talk to the family got the message across that something was terribly wrong in the family, and that we needed Jennifer's guidance in order to figure out what it was and how to fix it.

As I had hoped, the whole family agreed to come, with the exception of a younger brother who was away at college. Allison was an attractive, well-dressed woman with straight black hair that she occasionally tossed to the side as she spoke. Articulate and strong-voiced, Allison began by explaining that she was worried about the fact that Jennifer seemed to want to have nothing to do with the family. With tender tears welling in her eyes, Allison talked about how close she had felt to her sister as a child, and how she didn't want to lose that closeness. Allison didn't know what she had done so wrong, and why Jennifer insisted on giving her the silent treatment.

Jennifer, although just a year younger than Allison, appeared considerably younger than her sister. With a pained expression on her face, Jennifer softly and angrily accused both her sister and her father of being the cause of her lifelong misery. Their fifty-two-year-old father Larry uncomfortably began to give some of the family history, when he was interrupted by his wife Mary, who, like Allison, spoke confidently. Mary explained that her husband had always had a hard time with Jennifer, that from the moment Jennifer was born Larry would do anything for her, but that Jennifer always put him off. As Mary paused, Larry jumped in to say that he felt as though he was never good enough for Jennifer, that no matter what he did he could never get close to her.

As our meeting went on, I learned some critical facts. First of all, Jennifer was born and remained physically small, and was described by Allison as "appearing to be weak." Curiously, no one said that she was actually weak, only that she acted that way. At another time during the interview her father described her as "helpless." I later learned two crucial points: Jennifer was often at the center of her parents' arguments with each other, both of them disagreeing about how to treat her. Jennifer was triangulated in her family, the child whom her parents isolated to contain their own marital difficulties. Allison was astute enough to see that Jennifer garnered a tremendous amount of attention for acting like the weak and helpless child. I also learned that both Jennifer and her father were the middle children in their families, sharing the same birth order. As the middle child in his own family, Larry was often vying for the attention of his parents.

When I asked Larry to describe his childhood, he became agitated and revealed that both his parents were alcoholics, and that he felt ignored as a child. He said he had to become rebellious and angry to get their attention, and to this day he acts that way toward his parents. At this point, Jennifer turned to her father and, raising both her voice and an angry finger at him, shouted that he was also abusive to her as well, and scolded him by telling him that he shouldn't have taken out his anger toward his parents on her. Muttering under her breath, she turned away and said, "It's all too late now anyway."

When the family members fought with each other, it followed a typical pattern. Allison elucidated the pattern as follows: "When Mom and Dad argued, usually about Jennifer, Mom would get real serious. I knew she was real upset and worried. When Mom got worried and serious, Jennifer would do almost anything to get attention; usually she'd become sick, helpless, or real lazy. Mom would then coddle her, you know, try to make her feel better, and then Dad would get real upset. He'd tell Mom that she was 'babying' Jennifer, and Dad would go through the roof. I think Dad pushed Jennifer too much, and I know Mom was trying to protect her from Dad's anger."

Later, Allison admitted that both she and her brother "fell into the same trap," and ended up treating Jennifer like the baby of the family, catering to her every whim. Allison continues to see Jennifer as "the weak one" needing extra attention and support.

The feud between Jennifer and the rest of the family began, it turns out, at just about the time that Allison was getting married. Allison's marriage, the first marriage among the children, took all the attention away from Jennifer and placed it on Allison. Jennifer never admitted openly that it was hard for her to deal with the spotlight shifting from her to Jennifer; in fact, Jennifer didn't seem to be aware herself how hard that was for her. All she knew was that she was angry at everyone in the family, and that she felt fed up with them. Struggling to figure out why she found herself so angry, Jennifer decided that she had had enough of being the baby in the family and that it was time to make it on her own. Unfortunately, having been the baby in the family all her life, she didn't have much of a clue about how to handle life on her own. Angrily blaming her father for being abusive toward her, and angrily blaming her sister for abandoning her (by getting married), Jennifer had no idea how to leave her role of the family baby behind. Her only option was to strike out against her family angrily, and struggle to make it on her own. This angry quest for independence became a protest march, a feud in which she took her passive role to an extreme by breaking off almost completely with her family.

From our first meeting, the family's script became apparent. While Jennifer was certainly enmeshed with her parents and triangulated with them as well, she also took on a powerful role. Despite being the middle child of the family, she took on the role of the youngest child, insisting that she be treated as the baby.

Each member of Jennifer's family had a role to fill. Jennifer found that the only hope she had for her parents' attention was to act weak and helpless, becoming the family "baby." Allison, on the other hand, secure in her position as eldest, became the successful, strong, competent child who could do no wrong. Jennifer's father was trapped in the role he acquired from his childhood of being the tyrannical rebel, and Jennifer's mother, playing out a role she learned well as a child, was the competent, nurturing protector. Eventually, as Jennifer struggled with her own independence, and as she faced her sister's marriage and "abandonment," she played her passive role to the hilt by avoiding the family altogether, while simultaneously struggling to free herself of her assigned role. Allison, as the competent one who could do no wrong, called the family together to help fix the situation, although it was Jennifer's mother who eventually had to bring Jennifer in to the family therapy session in order to face the family's problems.

In this family, each person had to be shown the role that he or she was playing, and how playing that role hurt not only the family as a whole, but how it hurt each of them as individuals. They were encouraged to break out of their rigid family roles and treat each other differently. Eventually, Allison learned how to treat her sister as an adult, and not "assume" she would react as a baby. Jennifer also learned, though it took some time, how to move beyond the angry, rebellious stage in her noble quest for emotional maturity and independence.

The roles we play in our families, and how we play them, can determine whether our families will fall into the deep crevice of a feud or successfully struggle to weather most storms. Roles are powerful expectations we place on ourselves and that others give us to act and think in a certain, patterned way. These expectations, while necessary, can limit our options in a complex world. The more limited we are by our roles, the more difficult it is to respond flexibly to life's demands and to the demands of our family. We get stuck—immobilized—and we may need to create a feud just to break free of our roles. Or, by remaining rigidly entrenched in our roles, we fail to respond effectively to another family member's behavior, and a feud ensues.

Imagine, for a moment, what happens when, after years of living away from home, and even after years of having raised your own family, you come to a family reunion, perhaps at Christmas. If you're like most people, you immediately fall back into the role you had as a child, sometimes to the amazement of your spouse and children. The eldest brother in the family, resentful of the attention received by the youngest daughter, finds himself scolding her for not having good table manners, despite the fact that she is now thirty-five years old with two children. The youngest daughter, despite now being a successful executive, finds herself dismissing her accomplishments and putting herself down because in her family she was not thought of as someone who would amount to anything.

In times of severe crises, or major transitions in a family's life, the roles we played as children often come back to haunt us. When the death of a family member is near, and the family comes from distant points around the country or the globe to be near the dying family member, inevitably and almost shockingly the family members revert to their childhood roles. The adult who as a child was the rebellious and angry one will criticize the doctors and the medical care; the nurturer and caretaker will soothe the dying family member, as well as the other family members, and the isolated family pariah will disappear into the woodwork.

My wife once asked me, early on in our marriage, if I noticed that every time I visited my parents I would lie down and complain of having a headache. I garnered attention as a child by having severe headaches, and despite my relative good health as an adult, I managed to have a headache whenever I went home. The role of the sick child was a difficult one for me to break in my own life, and even more difficult to break when I was around my family.

Roles are not necessarily destructive unto themselves. The roles we play in our families are necessary in order for families to function. The mere job of moving a family through the maze of a complicated world often makes roles crucial to the survival and integrity of the family. In any complex organization, roles help to make the organization flow smoothly and function well. On a farm, in a factory, or in a family, some people need to manage and make decisions, while others must follow. Those born physically strong will be called upon to lift heavy machinery or plow fields, while those with greater intellectual skills might manage the budget.

The roles we play and learn so well within our families are those we take into the world as we venture outside our families. Eldest children of large families, used to managing large households, typically become successful executives, business owners, or leaders. The family clown often becomes a successful socializer, and the sickly child often becomes a dependent follower. Although many factors determine how we function as adults, family roles are often crucial in establishing how we interact with others throughout our lives.

Understanding just what our roles are and how they came about can go a long way toward uncovering the mystery of a feud. Carol, a bright, twenty-four-year-old waitress and student, told me that her feud with her family was a complete puzzle until she understood her role in the family:

"The whole thing was bizarre. All my life I was healthy. I never complained. I played by the rules. I was a track star in high school. My parents were great. They came to practically all the meets, and they always cheered me on. When I got sick, they just disappeared. I was furious—I always thought I had a loving family, but when I got this Epstein-Barr virus and couldn't walk, they were nowhere to be found. At first they actually thought I was faking it! But then they just disappeared—no phone calls, no showing up at my apartment, nothing. I said to hell with them and refused to call them. I told my friends that they were 'fair-weather parents,' that they only loved you if everything was going okay. But that wasn't it."

I asked Carol what she thought was going on.

"Lying in bed, I realized it was all about my sister. She was always sick, she was always the one who got their attention for being weak. I had to be strong. I guess I was the source of their strength, or something. But I finally understood what was going on. I violated a sacred family rule. I was the healthy one, the athlete, the strong one. My sister was the sick one. When I became sick, they couldn't understand it. So they just abandoned me."

In Carol's family, the role of the "sick child" belonged exclusively to her sister. Seeing how well her sister was cared for by her mother, Carol assumed that when she got sick her mother would do the same for her. What Carol didn't realize was that her role as the healthy child was the only role her parents could see her in, so when she became sick it challenged the rest of her family to change their views. Clinging tightly to their scripts, the family had no way of reallocating roles, and a feud broke loose.

HOW WE GET OUR ROLES

The roles we play in our families come about as a mixture of three elements: We are assigned them either by others or by circumstance; we choose them ourselves; and they emanate from our particular personality characteristics.

Some roles are handed out automatically, depending on our age and gender. For example, the role of mother is assigned to the woman in the family who gives birth to a child. Along with the role of the mother come all the expectations, beliefs, and values that this particular woman has incorporated into her views of motherhood. Her husband (a role the man took as soon as he entered into the marital contract) also has his beliefs about what it means for a woman to be a mother, along with what goes into being a "good" mother and a "bad" mother. Husband and wife might not agree on these role definitions, and as a result they will need to work out their differences together. When men become fathers, they go through a parallel role adaptation of their own.

Similarly, the first child automatically takes on the role of the only child, to be followed perhaps by the role of the eldest child. The child's gender will determine whether or not the role is to be that of son or daughter, and will ignite whatever expectations the parents and others have about sons and daughters.

Other roles in the family are defined less by one's position in the family than on the person's behavior, social status, or personality characteristics. These roles may have to do with one's power in the family, such as the role of leader, follower, or scapegoat. Power and control are also evident in the roles of manipulator and mediator. Roles might have to do with one's personality characteristics, such as the shy one, the sickly one, the depressed one, the joker, the nurturer, and so forth.

Roles are also created by how we decide to handle others in the family and how we deal with the crises and stresses of growing up. For example, someone might find that he gets paid attention to in a family when he acts like a victim. The victim role, when effective for a long time, becomes repeated and incorporated into one's personality. Another person might find that by blaming herself, she gains sympathy, so she learns to play the role of martyr, willing to damage herself instead of inflicting any discomfort on others. Someone else might find that when he shuts down his emotions completely, he gains respect and admiration in his family, so he becomes hyper-reasonable. He learns to play the role of judge, or mediator.

Sometimes, especially when all the other roles appear to be used up, people make their impact on their families by becoming the rebellious one. The role of "rebel without a cause" becomes ingrained, the rebel doggedly determined to protest against the status quo. The troublemaker, the angry one, and the pessimist are all similar to the rebel.

Many families have at least one child who becomes the "Goody Two-shoes." This "good child" can do no wrong, and the role is often played to the hilt. The prince or princess is a similar role, as is the parent's "pet."

In some families, the script that is written calls for someone who is not only good, but goes beyond goodness to be a rescuer, or savior. This person actively seeks out trouble spots in the family and becomes the comforting ear and soothing voice for those who need her or him. Those people who end up in the "helping professions"—psychologists, nurses, social workers, counselors—often had the family role of rescuer as a child.

Our life circumstances often determine the degree to which our roles become cast in stone. Children whose parents become unavailable either through death, abandonment, or divorce, or simply because of their emotional distance, often cluster together. They develop roles among themselves; one might be the strong leader, another the helpless, sickly one. One might be a stubborn, strong-minded isolationist, while another might be a social butterfly. Their roles comfort them in the face of loneliness, and add a sense of teamwork and togetherness in the face of despair.

MULTIGENERATIONAL ROLES

The expectations placed upon each of us by our parents often reflect the expectations that were placed on them as children. Roles, like triangulation, enmeshment, myths, and other family patterns, echo from one generation to the next. The pressure placed on the oldest male child to succeed is often a tradition handed down through the generations. The traditional female role of nurturer and caretaker often reflects not just a societal expectation, but the expectations of generations of women which were incorporated into the very fabric of the family.

The experiences we have while we grow up, however pleasant or distasteful, forge a strong impression about how we believe things should be done in families. When we set out to create our own families, these expectations leak out of our pores regardless of how we try to keep them at bay. Often blindly, we catch ourselves repeating the same epithets our parents threw at us, shaking our heads in bewilderment, muttering to ourselves, "I told myself I'd never say that to my children." These messages, for better or worse, help to create the roles we expect our children to play.

Sonia's role as the sickly child was well established by the time I began to see her family. A twenty-five-year-old graduate student in religious studies, Sonia had been to many doctors for symptoms relating to chronic fatigue. Even though the tests she received came back negative, the most recent set of doctors she saw agreed to treat her as though she was hypoglycemic, prescribing a rigorous diet.

As I got to know the family better, I learned that Sonia's father had been estranged from his parents' family for many years. Sonia's father, Rafael, was the youngest son in his family, and his biological mother died when he was only five years old. For the next five years, he was raised by his father and his grandmother. But after those five years, his father remarried, and all the children in Rafael's family rebelled, with Rafael being the most outspoken. Rafael believed his stepmother was leading his father down a destructive path, and he began to avoid them both. No doubt angry that his stepmother was trying to occupy the precious and revered position his mother had held, Rafael left home and cut himself off from his family as soon as he could.

Rafael's older sister Liliana became very close to Rafael, and began to serve as a substitute mother for him. Liliana was described as a quiet and shy child who, following their mother's death, started to have psychosomatic symptoms that continued to plague her throughout her life. Liliana, the oldest daughter and caretaker in the family, seemed to have the same symptoms as Rafael's daughter Sonia, who also happened to be the oldest daughter in her family.

In Sonia's family, as is the case with so many families, family roles seem to be handed down from one generation to the next. As the similarities between Sonia and her aunt Liliana were pointed out, Sonia revealed very clear memories of her aunt's repeated bouts of weakness, and saw her own symptoms as mirror images of those she saw in her aunt. In Sonia's family, the way an eldest child cares for the rest of the family, the way in which an eldest daughter functions, seems to be tied up with the role of being the sick child. While at first glance it might seem unusual for someone to carry both the caretaker and the sickly role, it isn't uncommon for someone to rebel against a prescribed role by alternately claiming its opposite. The perennial joker may become quite depressed, the baby of the family might insist on being a leader, and so on.

Rafael's feud with his father had yet to be repeated in the next generation, but the stage was being set. Should one of Rafael's sons take on the role of rebel, as Rafael had done in his original family, and should Sonia's role of the sickly child keep her incapacitated, as it did her aunt Liliana, the entrenched roles might limit their options in a crisis, and lead to a repetition of the same kind of division that shattered Rafael and his siblings' relationship to their father.

CULTURAL INFLUENCES

The roles we play and the roles we are assigned never occur in a vacuum. Society at large informs and feeds the roles we play, and modifies them to the extent that each of us allows it to. A key element of the society we grow up in is our cultural heritage. For some of us, our cultural heritage is strong, especially if we grow up in an ethnically homogeneous neighborhood, such as a barrio, a "Little Italy," or a ghetto of one brand or another. Growing up in these worlds, we feel not only the direct influence of our parents and immediate family, we also feel the indirect influence of the culture that lives through them. When, for example, one of Tevye's daughters in *Fiddler on the Roof* chooses to marry a Gentile man, Tevye exclaims that she is betraying not just her father's wishes, but the imperatives of her culture and her religion.

When looking at the roles we play in our families, it's important to consider these cultural influences as well. Doing this becomes even more important when we seek to understand the cultures our parents and their parents lived in, as we try to learn how our own roles come about. In traditional Spanish, Indian, and Italian cultures, girls tend to be given a strong caretaking role, often serving as substitute parents for all the children, including older brothers. The historical legacy of the Irish includes a strong agricultural dependence on men, combined with severe famine, which some historians and sociologists believe led to an overprotectiveness toward sons. Some sociologists have observed that American and British WASP cultures tend to emphasize more equality among siblings when it comes to doing household chores than in other cultures. Jewish and Asian cultural influences underline the critical importance of education, especially for boys.

It would be a mistake to consider the roles that have been handed down from prior generations without taking a close look at whatever cultural context these expectations developed in. These cultural influences can exert a powerful and often unconscious force on the expectations we place on ourselves and others in our families. Opening these cultural expectations to conscious examination gives us the freedom to choose the extent to which we may want to alter them, or retain what we find valuable in them.

I have seen family feuds develop as a result of attempts to cross powerful cultural boundaries. The daughter of a Jewish concentration camp survivor deciding to marry a Moslem Arab, the son of a recently emigrated Vietnamese family shunning his parents' emphasis on academics by abandoning his studies to become a gymnast; these violations of cultural expectations can become fertile soil for chasms in the family. The battleground of cultural assimilation can also be understood as a war between roles. The fifteen-year-old Armenian girl asks: "Do I take the role of a modern American teenager, free to date whomever I choose, stay out late at night, and engage in premarital sex, or do I adhere to the role of the Armenian girl from the old country, loyal to my parents' wishes, remaining a virgin until I'm married?" Similar questions arise when any set of powerful cultural expectations mixes with another. A few years ago, a twenty-five-year-old Armenian woman told me about her feud with her family.

> *I knew when I did it that it would all be over. Americans don't really understand that when you date one of them you give up your own family. They wouldn't speak to me. Even my younger sister, who I thought at least would understand, sided with my parents against me. But I should have figured that she would. She's like that, she's one of them. That's her choice. I just couldn't live that kind of life. Now I have no life. I'm a slut in the Armenian culture, but in the American culture I have no family. And that's really hard, because for an Armenian, family is everything. But there's no going back.*

HOW DO ROLES LEAD TO FEUDS?

How family members handle their particular roles often determines whether or not a family feud develops. There are basically three ways roles can become destructive: if the roles we are assigned in our families don't match our inborn personality characteristics, if the roles we are assigned become so entrenched that "role rigor mortis" sets in, and if we become so overburdened by a variety of roles that we lose track of who we are. When one or more of these three things happen in a family, especially in combination with a multigenerational pattern of enmeshment or triangulation, a feud is likely to loom on the horizon.

WHEN ROLES DON'T MATCH PERSONALITIES

Roles that are handed down from generation to generation may collide with the inborn temperament of those to whom the roles are given. Not uncommonly, for example, the eldest son is expected to take on the "star quality" of the highly successful father, who himself might have inherited these strong expectations from his father. If the first son is born without the temperament to carry this responsibility, perhaps because he lacks the necessary intelligence, drive, or vision, he may fail to fill the role that is given to him. Similarly, a shy, withdrawn child may lack the requirements for filling the role of the successful salesman, which may have been assigned to him even before he was born. The mismatch between a child's inherent personality and the roles the family assigns to him or her can be one cause of extreme family tension.

I met Ronnie over ten years ago, but I remember her spirited demeanor and her masculine features well. She was a certified public accountant, in her early thirties, who had played softball since she was a child. Her relationship with her father was nearly nonexistent, and she rarely spoke to her mother. She revealed easily that she had always been a tomboy, and that caused great concern for her parents. Her father always wanted a girl, and Ronnie's interests in traditionally masculine activities seemed hard for him to accept. Her mother, too, seemed to grow increasingly frustrated with Ronnie, especially because her pursuits of traditionally masculine interests didn't abate. In fact, Ronnie despised wearing dresses, wasn't really interested in dating, liked her hair short, loved sports, and was a math major in college. When Ronnie decided to get married, she hoped that her parents' attitudes would change. Although they attended the wedding and seemed to like her husband, there was no change in their cold, rejecting attitude; the damage had already been done.

Ronnie was clear that she was comfortable with herself. Her source of sadness was that she had no family to rely on, no one she could turn to the way her friends did. At times, the hurt was so great that it turned to anger, and ultimately Ronnie decided that she could no longer continue quietly "courting" her parents when they didn't seem to budge. She simply stopped having anything to do with them.

When the roles we are assigned are a poor match with our genetic lot, the result is usually a feeling of alienation, a feeling of not belonging in a family. The father who needs his effeminate son to be "a man" will push his son to do "manly" things that his son has no interest in. Consequently, the son feels unappreciated and unloved unless he is able to jump through his father's hoops. This conditional acceptance leads to feelings of low self-esteem, to feelings of having to "be somebody else" because who you are is "not good enough."

The mother who needs her daughter to follow in her own footsteps and be a powerful executive will be repeatedly disappointed when she sees her daughter engaging in passive, dependent roles. A parent who needs his or her child to become an accomplished musician, and discovers that the child has no musical talent, may harbor a deep disappointment that translates into the child feeling unaccepted and unworthy. As problems and stresses on the family inevitably occur, these expectations backfire and the child launches a campaign of resentment that can easily culminate in a full-fledged feud.

WHEN ROLES ARE TOO RIGID

The biggest danger arises when we become so fixed in particular roles that we are unable to bend them when life requires us to. A child who is a "good son," who routinely does what he's told, and waits patiently for his just rewards, may fail at being a provider or husband unless he is able to become more assertive and outgoing. Roles that are learned well serve us well when the situation we're in calls for the kind of behavior that the role permits. But it becomes just as important to learn how to shift from one role to the next. A large repertoire of roles tends to lead to greater success in achieving our goals, as long as we have a sense of how these roles form a coherent whole. (Just playing roles, without having a sense of our own core identity, leads to a feeling of being lost in the world.) As is so true in all aspects of life, moderation is the key. Too few roles leads to a failure in the ability to handle life's many challenges, while too many roles leads to chameleonlike behavior in which one's guiding personality and integrity can get lost.

The more rigidly one's role is cast, the more difficult it is to break out of it. Roles can become so ingrained that some people find breaking out of one is one of the most difficult tasks they encounter. What happens in a family when one of its members becomes seriously needy, but the role they feel they must play prevents them from making their needs known? As the youngest child in my family, I grew up clinging to the role of the "good child." I firmly believed that it was a necessary role for me to play, that the family situation would not survive if I didn't play that role. When severe troubles erupted with either my brother or sister, I was left to give my parents some source of solace. Unfortunately, the role I played did not allow me to have needs; I believed it would have taxed my parents beyond their limits, a belief they continually reinforced with direct statements such as "Thank God you're a good kid. I don't know if I can stand any more grief." Whatever pain or suffering I might have experienced as a child I was required to hide from my parents, effectively making it difficult to share my needs with anyone. Breaking free of the "good child" role, with its attendant requirements of keeping my needs buried from others, required a conscious effort to share my emotional needs with others, to learn how to talk about my needs, and to learn how to accept being taken care of by others.

The more rigidly people cling to their roles in a family, the more difficult it becomes to forge a unique personality as an adult. Like an actor who is afraid to disagree with the director's interpretation of how his role is to be portrayed, some children feel that if they challenge their prescribed roles, they will be challenging the integrity of the family. Children who feel this way are usually right. Families in which roles must remain rigid tend to shatter like glass when children attempt to alter their roles. Healthier families, those in which individual personalities and needs are seen and honored, tend to welcome changes in roles as a sign of a developing personality. In healthier families, the whole family climate changes as each child moves through different roles on the way to adulthood.

"Role rigor mortis" sets in when we are given messages that we must behave a certain way whenever certain situations arise. Attempts to find new solutions are met with disdain by those in power in the family, and are discouraged. When a child comes home from Little League practice and says that his coaches are mean, and that he doesn't want to play anymore, one parent might call his child a "quitter," and insist that the child tough it out. Toughing it out becomes the one and only solution to adversity. Even if the child begins to ponder other options, this parent clamps down and insists that the child is just trying to get away with not facing up to a tough situation. Another parent might encourage a child in the same situation to look at all the options: having the child talk to the coach, having the parent talk to the coach, reporting the coach to his superiors, having the parent hang out at practices to see if the coach behaves the same way, switching teams, or even quitting. The former parent encourages a linear, single solution to problems, while the latter parent encourages a more fluid, creative, problem-solving approach to the world.

When a family member feels stuck in a prescribed role, he or she might find it very difficult to develop an authentic personality. And when family members only know an individual relative by the role that person plays, they may react with distress when that individual attempts to break out of the role.

ROLE STRAIN

We all wear many hats and play different roles in life. In fact, our culture has brought us to the point where many of us play so many different roles that psychologists have begun to label the consequences of this lifestyle "role strain." A woman may wake up in the morning, and by the time bedtime has arrived she's played the role of mother, wife, corporate executive, secretary, maid, friend, and romantic lover. A man might spend his day with a parallel set of roles, and both might find themselves moving back and forth among all of them.

Families suffer when people in the family carry too many roles, leading to role strain and to confused loyalties. Changing roles too many times in a day leads to the sense of not knowing who you are. When Lewis Carroll's Caterpillar asks Alice how she is, Alice responds, "I . . . I hardly know, Sir, just at present—at least I know who I was when I got up this morning, but I think I must have changed several times since then."

Wearing too many hats can become so unwieldy that balancing them all on one person's head becomes overwhelming. The weary husband, tired after a long day at work, comes home and barks orders at his wife. She turns to him and coldly reminds him that he's not at work anymore, and not her boss. The overworked mother reports to work and finds it difficult to focus on her job while she tries to remember who's picking up the children after school.

Families can also suffer when family members carry too few roles. A woman may be an excellent mother, but unless she also can be a good lover or a good breadwinner her family might suffer. Similarly, a man may be an excellent breadwinner, but if he fails at being a good father, husband, and lover, his family will suffer as well. When people fail to take advantage of important roles that are available to them, their families may succumb to "interpersonal arthritis," an atrophy of unused life.

Not taking on important roles can be dangerous to families in other ways as well. Some parents, for example, fail to take the authoritative stance necessary for effective parenting. They underfunction as parents by being overly passive. Similarly, a parent can be overly authoritarian and fail to provide nurturance and comfort.

POWER AND ROLE REVERSAL

Being a parent is a role, as is being a child. Unfortunately, many parents too often act like children, and too many children are forced to play the role of parent. In many families, when parents *habitually* act like children and children are *consistently* forced to act like parents, an important and destructive role reversal takes place. Sometimes, parents who are too immature to be parents often look to their children to parent them.

When parents become overburdened with the demands of their own lives, they will often leave to their children decisions that their children aren't mature enough to make. In the vast majority of families I have seen in which children seem to run rampant and are out of control, the parents insist that somehow they don't need to or simply can't discipline their own children. Essentially, the children end up being in charge of the family, with the parents helplessly complaining about the situation.

This reversal of the parent and child roles wreaks havoc on families. Children, who may initially savor the freedom, end up feeling insecure, not taken care of, and overburdened. They simply don't have the life experience to be either their own or their parents' caretaker. In response to their anger at not having limits placed on their behavior, they become rageful and out of control. They "scream" in order for someone to hear their wish to be structured, and then scream louder when no one pays attention to them. The parents, who may make meager attempts at structuring their children, often feel that setting limits on their children's behavior is abusive. Most likely their reluctance to discipline their children is a result of their own family history. The children, sensing their parents' weakness, panic, and the cycle of out-of-control behavior continues.

Role reversal leads to family feuds when children who have been forced to act like parents decide that they want to grow up. Not knowing how to be a child, and feeling awkward wanting to be a child in an adult's body, such "parentified" children blame their parents for cheating them out of a childhood. They begin to refuse to take care of their parents, and their parents angrily reject them for not taking care of them. Parents and child come to loggerheads, and each side refuses to have anything to do with the other.

GENDER ROLES

Ever since my college experience of chivalrously opening a door for a woman resulted in her stopping dead in her tracks, refusing to go through the door as a protest of my sexist gesture, I've been acutely aware of gender stereotypes. Yet in the quarter century that has passed since that moment etched itself in my memory, I've seen very few changes in the extent to which gender exerts a powerful influence on family life.

"Liberated" fathers will insist that they place no extra burdens on their sons to achieve, yet can't resist scolding them from the sidelines when they don't "look sharp" on the baseball field. "Liberated" mothers likewise insist that they assure their daughters there is no job they cannot do, yet they privately wince when their daughters decide to become firefighters. While the struggle to raise children in a nonsexist way continues, it's often difficult to escape the subtle expectations that are carried over from previous generations, in spite of our best efforts to overcome them.

Many families exhibit role expectations based on gender that are not at all subtle. The more rural areas of the United States, which account for half of the nation's population, continue to subscribe to strong gender-specific expectations. Similarly, families in which gender-specific expectations are deeply ingrained in their culture will often openly declare very different expectations for men than for women in the family.

Strong gender stereotypes can create harm in a way similar to how inflexible roles in general create harm. Boys who are raised in families that shun "feminine" traits in males never learn how to nurture others, express their feelings, or share and cooperate with others. A "good cry," and tenderly cuddling with a baby, are virtually forbidden acts. Likewise, girls who are raised in families that insist on rigid gender roles lose the opportunity to think of themselves as competent, competitive, independent breadwinners. The thrill of a competitive athletic victory, or the sheer delight of a masterful demonstration of wit, is prevented by parental expectations to act "like a lady."

The child who rebels against strong gender-related expectations is often seen as going against family tradition, and some parents feel betrayed and disappointed by this rebellion. This child must either conform, regardless of how alien or awkward it may feel to do so, or risk alienation. When placed in the context of triangulation, enmeshment, and other factors, this scenario may well lead to a feud.

In a marriage, failure to shift between traditional gender roles can lead to devastating consequences. A man who insists on being waited on hand and foot becomes helpless when his wife becomes disabled, goes away for a while, or decides to move away from her own traditional role expectations. Likewise, a woman who is used to depending on her husband as the breadwinner will be ill-equipped for coping with his disability or death, or the dissolution of the marriage.

The feud between Jeff and Bonnie was a nightmare. Married for over forty years, this couple in their late sixties fought day and night. I often thought to myself that their fighting *was* the marriage; they seemed more wedded to chaos and animosity than to each other. While there were other important elements in their feud, one of the most powerful was how the multigenerational inheritance of role-related expectations became a source of conflict for them. It worked simply: Jeff expected Bonnie to act in every respect like a traditional woman. Bonnie expected Jeff to act in every respect like a traditional man. Neither of them did either. Jeff, who had been on state disability due to chronic back problems and diabetes for many years, refused to work. Bonnie, who had been a private music teacher for many years, refused to do anything for Jeff or anything around the house. While they fought about nearly everything, the common theme was that Bonnie should learn how to take care of Jeff and to do more housework, and Jeff should "grow up and get a job." Jeff wanted to be taken care of, the way "a woman is supposed to take care of a man," and Bonnie also wanted to be taken care of, the way "a man is supposed to take care of a woman."

Ironically, the arrangement they did have with each other worked out fairly well; Jeff stayed at home and did the housework, while Bonnie went out and brought in the revenue. Yet both resented deeply having reversed the traditional roles they experienced as children. They both believed that they were being betrayed, even though they had a system that otherwise worked well. Their rigid adherence to gender stereotypes fanned the flames of their already intense feud.

BIRTH ORDER

The roles we play, and whether or not those roles contribute to a family feud, are often affected by our birth order. None of us have a choice about the order in which we are born into a family, yet our birth order can have a profound influence on our personalities and on the roles we play. While our serial rank among our siblings doesn't necessarily determine every last thing about who and what we become in life, there are some factors that appear to be fairly universal. Very few people disagree these days about the crucial importance of our earliest years in developing our future personalities. If you are the first child to enter your family, your experience of those first few years will be very different from the experience of the next child to arrive on the scene. Firstborns enter a brand-new family, having their parents completely to themselves, with no one else to compete for their attention.

When it comes to birth order, there are only a few situations you can be in. You can enter the family first, in which case you are granted the mixed blessing of being the eldest child. Your parents can stop production there, making you also the prized possessor of the title "only child." Another possibility is that you'll be the last person to be born in the family, in which case you acquire the position of "youngest child." The last possibility is that you'll end up somewhere between the first and last, in which case you are a middle child. The term only applies literally when a family has an odd number of children, but the role of middle child is shared by all children placed somewhere between the first and the last.

One complication to this scenario has to do with your gender. Whether you are born a boy or a girl can have a big impact on whether or not you are considered the eldest, middle, or youngest, because at times the second child may be a boy, and the "eldest boy" might afford some of the benefits of the eldest category. Similarly, the youngest child status may differ to some extent if you are the youngest boy or the youngest girl.

The second complication has to do with the number of years between you and your next youngest or oldest sibling. If there are more than four or five years between siblings, it's almost as though a new generation begins. If your family has an oldest child, and the next child comes along one or two years later, then the third comes along five years after that, perhaps soon followed by a fourth, it's almost as though the third child becomes the eldest of the next group of children. Similarly, the larger a family gets, the more likely it is that the eldest children will take on characteristics of the parents to the younger children. It's not uncommon for the youngest children in a large family to say that they were closer to their eldest siblings than they were to their parents, because it was the eldest children who did most of the parenting.

OLDEST CHILDREN

Oldest children share many characteristics. Typically, they tend to make good leaders, having had that position in their families. They can be highly responsible and conscientious, and due to the high expectations placed on them by their parents, they often have lofty ideals and high ambitions. Because they are often used to having their parents' spotlight all to themselves, especially prior to the next children coming along, they often long for the spotlight as adults. According to psychological research, eldest children tend to be somewhat conservative in the manner in which they present themselves to the world, and at the same time they are often boldly willing to venture into new and uncharted territory.

Many new parents often feel tentative and confused about their own parenting abilities. As a result, they often give their eldest child confused and confusing messages. Eldest children, as the recipients of both high parental expectations and confusing messages, tend to either overcome this burden and excel, or succumb and feel like failures.

THE YOUNGEST CHILD

Youngest children are the only children who never had to deal with the spotlight taken away from them. They never have the experience of being replaced in their parent's eyes, so they often harbor a feeling of being especially prized. Youngest children, especially if they come from a large family, have others around to take care of them, often at their beck and call. Not having to take responsibility for caretaking others, youngest children often retain the feeling of being "babied" long into adulthood, sometimes expecting others to take care of them. Their siblings often resent them, because they see them as spoiled, given more latitude and not having to take care of other children.

Because they never had to take care of others, youngest children often possess a certain feeling of freedom, not being weighed down by the burdensome responsibilities of caretaking. This freedom from burdensome responsibility, along with a sense of specialness, often leads youngest children to remain prima donnas, but at the same time gives them the opportunity to be creative. Two of this country's great inventive minds belonged to two youngest children—Thomas Edison and Benjamin Franklin. Neither of them cared much for responsibility, but both were extremely prolific and creative.

Youngest children tend to be more comfortable following others than leading. At the same time, their prized position as the center of the family's attention often gives them a more carefree attitude toward life. This attitude, along with a lack of leadership and a sense of entitlement, can make it difficult for some youngest children to achieve success in a highly competitive or cutthroat environment.

MIDDLE CHILDREN

Middle children are sometimes referred to as the "lost children," not having the prized position as the eldest or the coddled position of the "baby." Yet very often it's the middle children who succeed in many of life's more challenging tasks. Being in the middle affords them the opportunity of having experienced at one time, however briefly, being the prized baby, while also dealing with the frustration of being re-placed by another. Typically more even-tempered than their counter-parts on the extreme ends of the family, they often develop excellent negotiating skills, learned as a tactic of survival in their families. They learn to understand the intricacies of power, how to have power over others and how to be subservient to others as well. Some middle chil-dren even learn how to master their obscurity, using it patiently in life as a tool for achieving their goals.

In families where conflict runs rampant, it's often the middle children who are able to negotiate compromises. Because there is less focus placed on them, they can use their relative obscurity to defuse some of the ten-sion in the family. As a family therapist, I often turn to middle children to help me break down some strong family patterns, because they are often the most skilled at reading the family's subtle power grabs.

ONLY CHILDREN

The most unique characteristic of only children is that, because they have no siblings, they tend to be more comfortable with adults, often seeking their approval. As only children grow up, they face the chal-lenge of learning to deal with peers, or with others who are close in age. They also share many of the qualities of eldest and youngest chil-dren. They may have the determined sense of responsibility of eldest children, while at the same time feeling a sense of being prized, spe-cial, and even entitled, as many youngest children feel.

BIRTH ORDER AND FEUDS

The feud between Christa, a forty-six-year-old court reporter, and the rest of her family is a good example of how someone's birth order can become a rigid role that can lead to a family feud. As the youngest child, Christa learned her role as "the baby" well. She played it to the hilt, and everyone in the family willingly played along. Even though her three siblings were jealous of the special attention she received, they recognized that the baby role was her birthright, and they catered to it.

The problem came when Christa tried to break free of her role as the baby. Because it left her ill-prepared for life, she found it difficult to cope with life's stresses as an independent woman. While the baby role worked well in her family, it didn't work in the world of work. When she was sick as a child at home, others came to her rescue and catered to her every need. When she became sick at work, she neglected to call in, came to work late, and expected that the service she worked for would understand. Instead, no one cared much, and she lost her job.

Christa's struggle to liberate herself of her assigned role was an internal one. She eventually understood that her family role would not serve her well in her life. Yet while she eventually understood and rejected her role, it was all she knew. If she went ahead and rejected her role completely, she would feel lost, not knowing who she was. Even though she desperately wanted to break free of the chains her role imprisoned her in, her role was a familiar enemy. Just as Jennifer did in the family mentioned earlier, Christa had to learn how to "grow up" by seeing herself in a more self-reliant light.

Family feuds related to sibling position occur from time to time as a result of a child entering into a competition for a prized position. One common form that a feud takes occurs when the youngest child refuses to give up that position after a new child enters the family. Some children are so closely tied to a parent that when a new child comes along, all hell breaks loose. At the beginning, a sincere effort is sometimes made by the parents to help the youngest child accommodate the new baby's arrival. The youngest child is coached to feel useful by the parents, who attempt to make it a positive experience in every possible way: "Now you'll finally get to have a younger brother or sister to play with," or "Won't it be wonderful to help Mom and Dad take care of a new baby?" Perhaps an older sibling will add sardonically, "Now *you'll* have someone to boss around."

Despite their parents' best efforts, newly replaced youngest children sometimes don't give up their prized roles easily. I have worked with many families in which these early "replacement wounds" are carried well into adulthood, and at times even to the grave. Some children will develop extreme symptoms in order to maintain a focus on themselves. Severely anorexic children "starve themselves" to get the attention they once received as youngest children. Aggressive, hyperactive children might develop all sorts of pseudoproblems, such as becoming accident prone, or having difficulty reading or learning in order to regain their position as center of attention. These symptoms might develop into a full-fledged feud when they fail to garner parental attention.

• • •

Clearly, growing up in a family is not an easy job. Wearing too many hats can overwhelm us and hurt the quality of family life. Wearing too few hats can create a stiff, unidimensional approach to life, an atrophy of potential in which our children grow up feeling like their options in life are limited. Being too flexible with one's roles can lead to a feeling of being lost and confused, and being too rigidly stuck in a particular role can lead to the need to rebel. It may seem like a losing battle no matter where you turn.

Yet it's important to remember that feuds tend to emanate from *extreme* positions, from family situations in which role expectations follow these patterns in exaggerated ways. These extreme positions aren't necessarily fixed in stone, and flexible parenting can mitigate their potential damage. When a young boy seems to have effeminate characteristics, a macho and homophobic father might attempt to "turn him into a man," but eventually realize his efforts are unsuccessful, give in, and buy his son the doll he always wanted. Or the mother who finds herself torn apart by conflicting loyalties because she is working two jobs and raising her children by herself might wake up one morning and decide to quit one job, sacrificing some of her income to devote more time to her children.

Expectations turn into feuds only when the expectations are so deeply embedded that they seem irreversible. In a feud, there is almost always a pattern of entrenched role expectations that exists over three generations or more of the family's history. And almost always it is the combination of destructive role expectations with the other elements discussed earlier in this book that eventually leads to a family falling apart. Feuds erupt when family members feel trapped in their roles, when the only way out is to either angrily break free of the family altogether, or to create a series of disruptions—ongoing protests designed to slowly soften the steel grip of the roles we were cast in as children.

Unlike the genetic coding that is woven into our chromosomes, the patterns handed down from one generation to the next in our families can be changed. We can work to prevent family feuds from developing in the families we came from and the families we create. We can also struggle to heal the wounds that might be festering while we are in the midst of a family feud.

From Feud to Reconciliation

ONE OF MY FIRST INTERNSHIPS WAS LOCATED IN A COLD, STERILE BRICK BUILDING ON THE OUT-skirts of Los Angeles called MacLaren Hall. It was (and still is) the place where police and social service workers take children who are removed from their homes due to severe abuse or neglect. After a brief orientation, I was assigned several children with whom I was supposed to work. Not knowing how and where to begin, I retired to a small office to study the children's charts. The charts were usually thick, and they contained reports written by the social workers who came to the children's homes before making the thankless decision to take these children away from their parents. (In writing this last sentence, I found myself hesitant to use the word "parents," so I briefly thought about using the common, more generic term "caretakers." That word was even more preposterous.) The social workers' reports were descriptions of what they found in the homes, and I remember the cascade of alternating emotions I felt as I pored over those extensive reports, which often ran thirty pages long. Page after page of horror greeted me; children who were routinely burned by cigarettes, strangled and tied up with extension cords, sexually molested by a series of strangers while absent parents were prostituting for drugs and drug money. These starkly written series of facts and observations were at first intriguing, but the intrigue quickly turned to revulsion, then outrage, until the disgust turned into sheer pain and I would start to sob, closing the chart without reading the rest because I simply couldn't take it. Yet I only had to read about these events—I didn't have to live them.

I often found myself wondering what would happen to these children. Would they grow up and turn into the same sort of pathetic characters as their parents? The answers often lay just a few feet down the hallway, in the rooms where the children slept. There I would find sweet, frightened children, desperate to trust but obviously unable to do so, children so deeply emotionally burned, yet amazingly so attached and filled with yearning to be back with the very same people who hurt them so badly. Some, I'm sure, did turn out repeating the cycle of abuse, while others were saved by adoptive parents, a social service system that occasionally worked, treatment centers, group homes, and therapists. Some, I'm sure, were saved by some incredibly resilient kernel with which they entered the world, some remarkable spark that simply couldn't be dimmed by a childhood filled with torture.

A few years later, I began working with adults, many of whom had histories similar to those that I read in the social workers' reports. Some were filled with rage toward those who scarred them so deeply, while others were more forgiving. How could those children manage not to be filled with rage? How could those children whose early lives were so filled with torment manage to find a path out of the forest of blame that they no doubt lived in for many years?

For many of those children turned adults, and for many of those whose childhoods were less damaged but still find themselves brimming with rage over childhood injustices and horrors, the path out of blame was one that was walked and discovered on their own. Most had help along the way, usually from concerned and caring therapists or from someone who took an extraordinary interest in them and their well-being. The work of a therapist, I quickly learned, was to help someone steer a shipful of hurt away from an island of blame to a more liberating place of responsibility and justice.

No therapist, however, can steer this ship for someone else. We are not captains, we don't make the decisions or even take the deep risk. We are more like navigators, using our charts and diagrams, compasses and knowledge to advise the captain on how to get from one place to another.

This is not to say that everyone who has been abused as a child will end up feuding with a family member. Or that every feud can be tied to some earlier form of child abuse. Nearly everyone who is in a feud with a family member does share something with those who have been abused, though, and that is the feeling that a terrible injustice has been done to them. Many people who feud do acknowledge intellectually, however, that the feud is a two-way street, or that no one meant to maliciously hurt them. In the case of child abuse, as is so often the case in situations in which there is an ongoing feud, the abuse of power, the lack of respect for each person's dignity or point of view, yields a strong sense of blame and self-righteousness. It's the need to move through the complex web of blame and self-righteousness that people who have been abused and people who are feuding have in common.

The second half of this book is meant to give you the tools you need to move beyond your feud and into more caring, mutually rewarding relationships with your family members. It begins with a description of the navigational tool most family therapists find essential in understanding families, a tool that places your family in the all-important multigenerational context. The next chapter is designed to help you move from a position of blame to one of responsibility. Following this, I discuss the steps to forgiveness, and the important role forgiveness can play in reconciliation. Once you understand these concepts, you then need the courage it takes to confront those with whom you are feuding. The chapter titled "Creating the Climate for Change" discusses important facts to remember about the situations you choose as you repair your family feud. In the last chapter, I discuss when reconciliation may not be appropriate, and what to do in those situations.

How to Create a Genogram

If you want the present to be different from the past, study the past.

—Baruch Spinoza

IT WASN'T UNTIL I WENT OVER THE DETAILS OF MY OWN FAMILY HIS-
TORY THAT I LEARNED THAT MY MOTHER HAD MISCARRIED A CHILD IN
the latter months of pregnancy prior to my own birth. While not exactly a secret, this fact had never been discussed openly in our family.
For my parents, however, it represented a terrible loss. While according
to custom, the child had to be named and buried with the same rituals associated with any other death, the emotional impact on them was
buried with the unborn child. This information provided a missing
link in a pattern of intense reactions to loss that made my own birth
especially important in my family, and gave me a special status that had
been previously hard to explain.

This significant event was uncovered while I was working on a
genogram—a "family map" of the life of a family over time. Adapted
from tools used by genealogists and geneticists, the genogram is the
best tool for graphically displaying and simplifying complex family
relationships.

In it, we can view the structure of the family on a single page, including not only how each person is related to the others, but also
how patterns that might eventually turn into a feud echo from one

generation to the next, becoming more and more intense until a feud erupts.

If you are currently involved in a family feud, mapping your family's history in the form of a genogram is the first step to understanding the factors that went into the feud's erupting how and when it did. The more you learn about your family, the better you'll understand how you got to the place you're in, and this understanding is the foundation of any reconciliation or working through of the feud that is likely to happen. If your access to information is limited or the attention to details hard to manage, I would recommend scratching out something rough and simple in genogram form regardless of how detailed you decide to get. Even a little information is better than none at all, and the format of a genogram can make things easier to understand.

BASIC SYMBOLS

Each person on a genogram is represented by a simple symbol, depending on gender—males by a box and females by a circle. Key individuals, such as those directly involved in a feud, are often highlighted by drawing two concentric squares or circles. Death is simply and plainly indicated by an "X" drawn through the box or circle.

Information such as miscarriages, abortions, and affairs, when available, along with dates of marriages, deaths, divorces, serious illnesses, and major traumas are also listed on the genogram. Because the information on a genogram can become unwieldy, a rule of thumb is to only put the most essential information on the genogram itself, while other information is noted on separate pages.

The following list shows symbols for many of the elements mentioned so far:

Male: ☐   Female: ◯

Key Male: ▣   Key Female: ◎

Deceased Male: ⊠   Deceased Female: ⊗

Pregnancy: △   Stillbirth: ⊠

Spontaneous Abortion: ●   Induced Abortion: ✕

BASIC RELATIONSHIPS

All family members are connected by lines on the genogram that denote both their biological and legal relationships. Marriage is indicated by lines that go slightly down and then across, connecting the partners, usually with the husband on the left and the wife on the right. The dates of marriages and divorces are written over the line connecting the two (just the year is sufficient for the genogram itself). If you don't know the year of a marriage, you can also place the age at which someone is married somewhere along the marriage line (for example, "m. 53" indicates that Joe was married when he was 53 years old, while "m. 1953" indicates that Joe was married in 1953). A separation is indicated by a single small slash through the marriage line, and a divorce is indicated by a double slash through the marriage line.

Serious relationships other than marriage, such as unmarried partners, affairs, or long-term cohabitation, are represented by dotted or dashed lines.

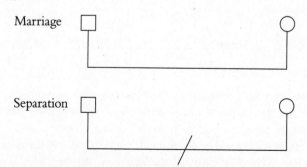

Divorce

Multiple marriages can be difficult to depict, especially when each spouse has remarried several times. There are many ways to indicate multiple marriages, but generally speaking it is best to try to depict marriages chronologically, with the first marriage in the center and the remaining marriages emanating outward. The following diagram shows a husband who's been married and divorced twice:

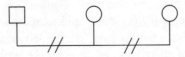

This is how it looks when a woman has had two divorces:

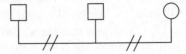

The convention of emanating outward from the center works well when both spouses have been married several times. A couple in which each partner has remarried multiple times:

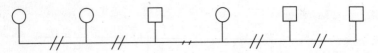

Children are placed underneath their parents, with the oldest child on the left and the youngest on the right. Adopted or foster children are indicated by a broken line with an "A" or an "F" placed in a triangle above the adopted child or foster child. Fraternal twins are indicated by an upside-down vee (still with the oldest on the left), indicating the same birth date, while identical twins are connected by a line between them.

Here's how a nuclear family with three children looks:

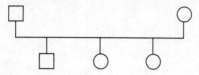

And here's a family with an adopted daughter, a biological daughter, and identical twin sons:

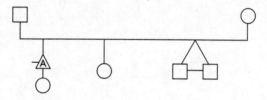

These are the symbols needed to put together a simple genogram depicting the basic biological and legal relationships in a family. Armed with these simple symbols, we can now diagram most family situations. Here, for example, is a genogram of John F. Kennedy's family, using only the symbols discussed so far:

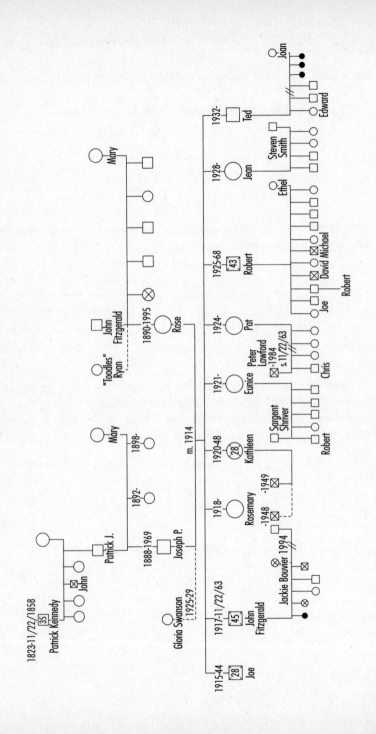

CRITICAL EVENTS

The relationships depicted in the genogram so far tell us very little about the family, only how each person is related to each other. Your family really begins to come alive when some additional information is added to the picture. Basic descriptive information about your family is one set of facts that are listed on the genogram. This includes demographic information about each family member—age, dates of birth and death, occupation, and educational level. The age of each person will serve as an important key to understanding why things happen when they do. Birth dates and dates of death are major transitions, and may hold an important key to understanding your family feud. These dates will help you understand how anniversary reactions such as those discussed in Chapter Four may eventually erupt into a feud. Occupation and educational level give important key information about the people in our family history, helping us to make them a bit more real than merely a collection of circles and squares on a page.

The second set of facts needed includes important data such as serious medical or emotional conditions (including alcoholism), and critical events, such as important geographic moves, losses, achievements, and so on. These represent potentially major factors in the ultimate eruption of a feud. These crucial life events play a big part in understanding why feuds often erupt when they do. Some of the most important of these facts can be written directly on the genogram, or they can be kept on a list or family chronology attached to the genogram. Here is a look at JFK's genogram with some important events added:

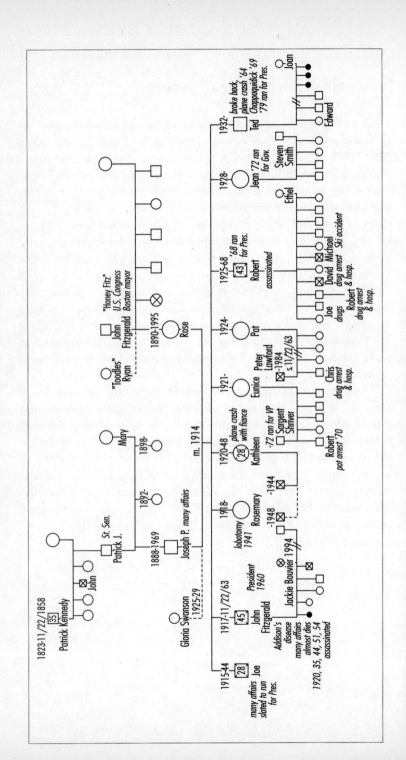

DIAGRAMMING EMOTIONAL CONNECTIONS

So far, we've only used the genogram to portray how people in families are related, and important events in the history of the family. The genogram reaches its fullest potential as a map of the family territory when it's also used to depict the kind of emotional relationships discussed earlier in the book. Enmeshment and triangulation, while often the most subjective observations, are frequently the most powerful keys to understanding family feuds. In order to obtain information about whether such emotional ties existed between particular relatives, it's often necessary to interview other family members, and in doing so you will likely get conflicting information. This has been called the "Rashomon Effect," after the Japanese film in which one event is shown from different perspectives. If you are the one caught in the center of two or more feuding family members, it will be important to get each of their different perspectives, and plot these on the genogram. If you are the one who is locked into battle, your perspective as well as the other family member's perspective will be important. Here are the symbols for showing basic emotional relationships:

Very close or fused:

Fused and conflictual:

Poor or conflictual:

Estranged, disengaged, or cut-off:

Close:

Distant:

In the genogram of Sigmund Freud's family below, it's possible to see at a glance that Sigmund had a distant relationship with his father, while being extremely close with his mother. He was also quite close to his sister-in-law Minna, who enjoyed close relationships with her sister Martha and her brother-in-law Sigmund. Sigmund also had a conflictual relationship with his brother-in-law Eli.

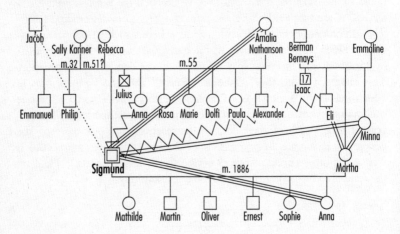

The feud that went on between Harry and his brother Sam discussed earlier became crystallized when Harry took on the task of putting together a genogram of his family. Although there wasn't much information available to him and the resulting genogram was sparse, it still proved helpful by elucidating the feud in his family. His genogram looked like this:

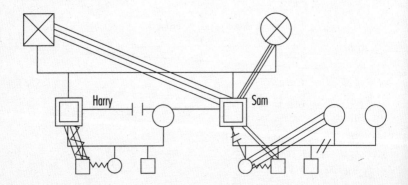

After drawing himself first, and then his brother, Harry marked the feud between them by a line broken in the middle. Harry then depicted his wife and his three children, and then drew Sam's wife and their three children, as well as Sam's current wife whom he married after his divorce from his first wife. Harry also drew his parents, and his estimate of his father's family, which was quite large. He filled it in with a rough picture of his mother's family, about which he remembered little. (For simplicity, I left some of this information out of the genogram.) Moving to a discussion of the quality of the relationships among the siblings, Harry had no trouble remembering that his father had a younger brother with whom his father did not speak. He heard family stories about the jealousy that his father felt about his brother being favored, although Harry wondered out loud if there was more to the stories than just favoritism. It was clear to Harry that both of his parents fawned over Sam, probably due to Sam's polio. Harry felt completely ignored by his mother and father after his brother contracted polio, mentioning that since then they always had a very special relationship with Sam, Sam could "do no wrong" in their eyes, and they acknowledged Sam's talents while ignoring Harry's.

The biggest eye-opener for Harry wasn't just what went on in the generation before him and in his own generation, but the generation that he and his wife bore. When we discussed how his wife's eldest son got very involved in drugs, and how his son's extraordinary talents were wasted, I pointed out that he and his wife seemed to prize their eldest son the same way Harry's brother Sam was prized by his parents. When we diagrammed Harry's children's relationships with each other, Harry noted that while his two youngest children got along well with each other, neither of them got along with their eldest brother. *Harry noticed that in three successive generations, the eldest son and the next eldest sibling did not get along well with each other.* We talked about how the triangulation of a child with special needs had the impact of leaving out the rest of the children, creating a distance between the siblings. In Harry's generation, the result was a feud between him and his brother, a feud that was replicated in the generation before him and might likely erupt in the generation after.

GENOGRAM INTERVIEW FORM

Now that you have an idea of how to create a genogram for your family, there are some tools that can be helpful in gathering the necessary information. This form[1] can help you prepare a genogram. It can be used in interviewing family members, or simply as a guide in creating your own genogram. The form is designed to be used by one person at a time, with the data collected then merged together to create a genogram. The person being interviewed, or the person about whom you are collecting data, is called the "index person."

Index Person:
1. What is your name?

2. When were you born?

3. What have you done for a living?

4. Are you married?

5. Names of spouses:

6. Names and genders of children with each spouse:

7. Include miscarriages, stillbirths, elective abortions, adopted and foster children.

8. Include dates of marriages, separations, and divorces.

9. Include birth and death dates, cause of death, occupations, and education.

10. Who lives in the household now?

11. What is your ethnic and/or religious background?

12. Any major relocations? Why?

Family of Origin:
1. Mother's name:

2. Father's name:

---

1. Adapted from *Genograms in Family Assessment* by Monica McGoldrick and Randy Gerson, New York, Norton, 1985.

3. They were which of how many children?

4. Names and genders of each sibling. Include all miscarriages, still-births, adopted and foster siblings.

5. Include dates of parent's marriages, separations, and divorces.

6. Include birth and death dates, cause of death, occupations and education of the above family members.

7. Who lived in the household when they were growing up?

Mother's Family:
(same information as in "family of origin")

Father's Family:
(same information as in "family of origin")

Ethnicity:
Give ethnic and/or religious background of family members and any languages spoken other than English.

Major Moves:
Any major relocations or migrations in the family?

Significant Others:
List anyone else who lived with the family or who was important to the family.

For all those listed, indicate any of the following:

serious medical or psychiatric problems
drug or alcohol problems
problems with the law or job problems

For all those listed, indicate any who were:

especially close or distant
conflictual
cut off or feuding with each other
overly dependent on each other

INTERPRETING THE GENOGRAM

Once you have managed to successfully put together your own family's genogram, you can use the following guide to help you to understand how the ideas presented in the first half of this book may relate to your own family's feud. I suggest you use a journal to write down some of the answers to the following questions, in order to help organize your thinking about your family.

Structural Issues:

1. Birth order

   What patterns of birth order seem to repeat from one generation to the next? What positive or negative expectations are placed on the oldest, middle, or youngest child?

2. Siblings' gender

   What expectations are placed on women as opposed to men, or vice versa? How do these expectations combine with birth order in a way that repeats from one generation to the next?

3. Distance in age between siblings

   Are there any significant age gaps (six years or more) between siblings in a particular generation? If so, consider the younger grouping as a separate generation.

4. Expectations regarding sibling position and gender

   a) timing of each child's birth in family history

   b) personality characteristics of child

   c) physical features of child (e.g., looks like his dad)

   d) parents' expectations regarding achievement, gender differences

   e) child's position relative to parents' positions in their own families of origin

Patterns Across Generations

1. Enmeshment/ Disengagement

   Who is particularly close to whom? Who is emotionally detached and removed?

2. Triangles

Examine cross-generational triangles (for example, mother and daughter line up against father), and how these might repeat from one generation to the next.

3. Roles

What roles (savior, therapist, helper, sick one, good child, princess, etc.) seem to repeat from one generation to the next?

4. Secrets or myths

What family secrets (your sister has a different father) or myths (no one is an alcoholic in our family) have you discovered that are likely to fuel family feuds?

Life Events

1. Coincidences of life events

Note any coincidences of important events (e.g., I was born right after my grandfather died, and my father recently had moved out of his parents' house).

2. Anniversary dates

Note how particular times of the year may be sensitized or intensified due to traumatic events. Note how certain ages in the lives of people may be sensitized due to the fact that a trauma may have occurred to an ancestor or sibling at the same age (e.g., Tommy's father puts extra pressure on Tommy when Tommy reaches age twelve, which is the same age Tommy's father's brother was when he died in a car accident).

3. Life transitions and traumas

Note when particular life transitions, such as moving, losing a job, or changing a job, take place.

4. Social or political events

Note how certain political or social events may have contributed to the family history and expectations (e.g., holocaust, Soviet downfall, Armenian earthquake, Iranian revolution, Cuban revolution).

WHEN INFORMATION IS DIFFICULT TO FIND

Most of the basic information required for a genogram can be easily constructed from memory, yet there may be times when important information is needed and other people must be relied upon. Unfortunately, when a family is in the midst of a feud it is often difficult to obtain this information because contact is often cut off from key family members. One solution is to utilize "third parties"—outsiders who aren't directly embroiled in the feud. These can include relatives such as aunts, uncles, cousins, or in-laws. Longtime family friends and neighbors can often provide useful information as well. Their stories about your relatives may be distorted by their own motives and history with your family, but outsiders tend to have fewer motives for distorting the truth.

Aunts and uncles often have access to stories about their parents that can shed important light on your family history. They should not only be asked for the details of who married whom when, but also the following specific questions, if applicable:

1. What was going on in my family about the time I was born? Do you remember my parents' reactions to my birth? Do you know if my birth spawned any conflicts between my parents?

2. What was going on in my family about the time my sister or brother was born; do you have any recollections of this?

3. (If the aunt or uncle is older than your parent:) Do you remember Grandma's and Grandpa's reactions when my mother (or father) was born? What was going on in their lives at the time? Where did they live? How was their work going?

4. What do you think were the most significant events in your family's life when you were growing up?

5. What do you remember of your grandparents? How was your parents' relationship with them? Are you aware of any difficulties your parents encountered with them?

The answers to these and whatever other questions you can think of can add rich detail to your family's history, and often hold some welcome or unwelcome surprises. The answers may reveal important information that can be plotted on the genogram, or be kept separately as a way of deepening your understanding of your family and its patterns. Questions such as these and others should not be asked of your relatives as a drill or exercise, but instead as part of a natural information-gathering process. Your task is to make them comfortable enough in your conversation that you get as much material as you can without exhausting them. I often suggest that this process take place slowly, rather than as a sudden quest, which is likely to yield less reliable information.

Aunts and uncles who are less embroiled in a feud may also have direct access to facts that are unavailable to you. If the nature of your own family's feud is such that the information you are after may be intentionally hidden from you by those who have an investment in keeping you out of the information "beltway," aunts and uncles may be willing to act surreptitiously to gather any missing information you might need to fill out your genogram.

Some families have a hidden family "historian," someone who makes it a hobby to chart the background of the family. Besides helping to recreate the details of the genogram, these relatives have a natural curiosity and hunger for information themselves, and can often enlighten a family history with rich family anecdotes from multiple sources. Although these historians may be distant cousins, they may turn out to know more about your family than you might think.

Family Photo Albums

When direct access to family information is difficult to obtain, family photo albums often provide a wealth of information. It's easiest to start with any pictures you might have from your childhood. When these are lacking, siblings or relatives may be willing to drag out their albums, or even present a slide show.

In viewing family photos, the most important task is to find trends or patterns that repeat themselves from one photo to the next, from one year to the next, or from one generation to the next. Occasionally, people discover rather startling evidence that repeats itself in the genogram itself. Look for the following:

a) Repetitive patterns of positioning. Who is sitting next to whom? Who is always between others?

b) Nonverbal communication. Whose arms are always around others? Who looks as though they would rather be elsewhere?

c) Who is always absent? (Be careful here, because while it is common in families for fathers to be peripheral, it was also a gender-related expectation that they would be the picture-takers.)

d) Any family members no longer present?

e) Identify anyone whom you don't recognize. What roles did they play?

f) What new memories do the photos spark?

Archival Sources

Often, a family member will construct a genogram and place it in a family Bible. Old, large Bibles often had a form for this purpose, and are valuable resources. Deceased relatives often kept diaries that were passed on. You may have to inquire among relatives about this. Similarly, letters written by deceased family members may be available. Genealogical libraries, such as those found in the libraries of the Latter-day Saints, are open to the public and can be useful if you wish to transform your genogram into a full-blown genealogical study. Most communities have genealogical societies that often store a wealth of information in various forms. Reference librarians in genealogical libraries are usually very helpful and knowledgeable, and many excellent books are available to instruct the novice. Inexpensive computer software is easily available to assist in this process.

Most people can create three-generation genograms easily from memory. Usually there is enough information available from your memory alone to provide considerable understanding of why a feud has developed in your family. The details that are discovered in a more thorough search can add another level of depth and richness to your understanding of family patterns. Either way, whether you complete the basic genogram or one containing more detailed layers of family information, this tool can enrich your understanding of the historical roots of your family's feud.

From Blame
to Responsibility

Blaming family tragedies on one person's cruelty and neglect is the oversimplification of a society preoccupied with individuality—and of professionals wearing blinders. I see connections and possibilities. I help families search for alternatives. I encourage tolerance of differences and acceptance of limitations. Instead of emphasizing power and weakness—villain and victim—I focus on complementarity and the construction of partnership.

—SALVADOR MINUCHIN

THE CLOSEST I'VE COME TO A HARD AND FAST RULE ABOUT FAMILY FEUDS IS SIMPLY THIS: IT IS ALWAYS SOMEONE ELSE'S FAULT. THE TIDES RISE and fall, the sun sets in the west, none of us come out of this life alive, and a family feud is always the other person's fault. Rarely do people come into my office and describe how they are the fundamental reason why a feud either started or continues. That's because a feud without blaming the other side is not really a feud at all; a feud cannot exist without being fueled by blame.

It might begin as simply as this: "Aunt Harriet forgot to call me on my birthday. I always have to initiate contact with her, and I'm sick of it. She never thinks of me or what I'd like or, heaven forbid, what I might need. I've had it. The last thing I'm going to do is to give her the pleasure of my calling her on her birthday. What goes around comes around—we'll see how *she* likes it."

Or, the stakes may be considerably higher. Consider Karen: "All my life I've been protecting and defending my father, even though he did unspeakable things to me as a child. He's still a jerk, and the truth is, he ruined my life. I should send *him* the therapy bills! I'm through with defending him, and now he's going to have to pay the piper. The way he treated me, he doesn't deserve to have a daughter. As far as I'm concerned, I'm without a father. He can go do those things to someone else, but I'll have nothing to do with him."

And this is a common justification for a feud: Joel's wife Barbara complains that "Joel's mom and stepdad were never really there when we needed them. They've given everything and anything to Joel's sisters, but they've always had conditions on Joel and me. When me and Joel were down and out, and just wanting to spend the night at their house, they made us sleep in the car in the driveway, while Joel's sisters were sleeping comfortably in the house! I don't know how they can live with themselves, but I sure as hell can't take it anymore. If they want to treat us like we don't exist, then it's time we finally get the message and move on. Screw them!"

In each of these situations, blame is deserved and the pain is very real. In fact, nearly every claim I've heard a client make over the years has real hurt and anguish at the bottom of it. But if we stop here, at the stage of blaming someone else for what hurts us, we end up hurting ourselves in the long run. When we blame others, we put a halt to our own emotional growth. We stay paralyzed in our hurt and our blame.

Imagine your family feud through the lens of a camera. If you focus on one person as the "victim," you will certainly take a picture of real hurt. If, however, you have the courage to slowly enlarge the view and take in the bigger picture, you will notice pain on both sides of the feud, you will see similar patterns repeating throughout your family history. You will find your feud is a complex set of interactions that can be understood, challenged, and even resolved.

This process begins and ends with understanding and compassion. We first must understand how it is we came to such an unceasing, burning rage toward others, and we must learn to treat ourselves and our emotional wounds compassionately. Once we've learned how to be compassionate toward ourselves, we have the choice to turn our powers of understanding to those who hurt us and to the world in which we were hurt. We can find the courage to face those who hurt us, if only in our own minds, and to struggle toward making our own world an emotionally safer place in which to relate to our family. We can struggle to understand our own part in our feuds, and how each of us plays a role in a long drama that most likely began to unfold long before we were born. We can then strive toward the ultimate goal of forgiveness, knowing that true forgiveness can never occur without a feeling of safety and justice.

WHY BLAME?

We blame others as a way of keeping ourselves feeling safe. The anger that infuses blame acts like a shield against the crushing weight of our own anguish. I often think of the time back in 1981 when the Israelis attacked an Iraqi nuclear facility based on intelligence reports that linked that facility with the manufacture of warheads that were destined to be aimed at Israel. The term "preemptive strike" was used to indicate striking out against those who you believe will hurt you in the future. Blaming others is a preemptive strike, a way of angrily protesting and attacking those whom we believe will hurt us if we give them a chance.

We blame others and stay angry with them, often to the extent to which we feel hurt by them. Those who hurt us a little anger us a little. We reserve our strongest anger for our deepest hurts. Those people who we feel destroyed our childhood, or our sense of safety in the world by betraying our trust, become the objects of our rage and often the objects of our feuds.

BLAMING OURSELVES UNJUSTLY

It's often easier to blame ourselves than to direct appropriate anger in the direction it belongs. Especially as young children, when we feel powerless to change circumstances, and anger toward our parents may jeopardize our own safety, we often direct blame, however unjustly, toward ourselves.

Over time, this blaming of ourselves turns into depression. Depression, as "anger turned inward," is the result of continually blaming ourselves for the wrongs that have been done *to* us. We believe that if we were just smarter or prettier or more clever, everything would be better. It is our fault for how things have turned out.

Self-blame—whether overt or hidden beneath a veil of rage toward others—is almost always present in a family feud. Here's how Robert, a forty-two-year-old postal carrier who hadn't seen or talked to his father for nearly fifteen years, discussed his blame:

> *It started out simple. I guess everything was simple back then. I knew what he did to my mother. I watched it with my own eyes. He was a bastard through and through. But I knew he loved us kids. I just couldn't have anything to do with anyone who hurt my mother so much. It was like betraying her. But the weirdest thing is that now she forgives him, only I can't. I still think he ruined her life and he totally messed with mine. It's not easy when all your friends have fathers and your own father is off somewhere wining and dining other women. So as long as I avoided him, I knew I was the one who was going to have the last laugh. So I did it, all right, I said 'to hell with him,' and had my own life without him. Now he doesn't know me, or my son, or my wife. But every time I think about what I've done to cut him out of my life, I break up, because now I think I've become just like him. I did to him what he did to us, and I blame myself for hurting him! To think of that, I actually blame myself. I don't even want to talk about it. He's the one who should be suffering, but I'm killing myself over this because I can't let it go. I've got no father, he's off God knows where, and I've hurt him and myself and I feel like shit.*

Myrna's self-blame was clear-cut and direct. After three unsuccessful suicide attempts, this short, corpulent, perennial student in her mid-twenties told me that, although she knew better, she blamed herself for her feud with her family.

> *I don't think I deserve to live, it's that simple. I just don't care. They were cruel to my brother, too, but I was the one who left them. I know*

they treated us bad, and I'm sure they didn't want kids at all, but some-how I know if I only could have done something different they would have wanted me. It's crazy, I know. After all, they're the parents and I'm the kid. But the problem is, for everything they did to me, I turned around and I stabbed them even harder. I did everything I could to hurt them, from sleeping all over town to doing drugs to you name it. I knew what would hurt them, and I went all-out. Now I might as well finish the job.

Many people locked in a family feud have a long history of blaming themselves. They blame themselves for the pain they've caused, *but they also find ways of blaming themselves for the hurt that others inflicted on them.* Some people create a feud as a distraction, a way of avoiding their own painful feelings of self-blame. After some discussion, Gayle, an elementary schoolteacher in her late forties, was able to articulate this well:

Sure, I knew it was my fault. I was the one who told my brothers that I didn't want to have anything to do with them anymore. I even created this ridiculous scene—I feel ashamed of even admitting it—where I invited them over for a barbecue when I knew I didn't have any charcoal. I asked them to go get some, and we started to argue. I told them all to go to hell, and I haven't wanted to talk to them since. The whole thing is that I know I feel guilty and really bad about the way I treated their kids when I baby-sat for them before, and the more I got in touch with how I treated my brothers when we were growing up, I just couldn't take it. I couldn't face them anymore, it was all too painful. It reminded me of my whole childhood, and all the pain I caused everyone in the family. So I created this scene so they'd think I was nuts . . . and boy, it really worked! All that just to avoid having to deal with them and my own feelings . . .

Gayle's feud, like many others, was like a backfire, a fire set by firefighters to entice a more dangerous fire away from populated areas so that it will do the least amount of damage. Unfortunately, these feuds truly do backfire, though, hurting everyone involved.

BLAME AS SELF-RIGHTEOUSNESS

Although it is a less charitable way of looking at blame, at times I've found it helpful in working with family feuds to see blame as a form of self-righteousness. Looked at this way, blame becomes a way of insisting that the "blamer" is right and the "blamee" is wrong. Self-righteously demanding that the world is the way the blamer sees it, and that no other perspective can have merit, the blamer proclaims that she or he is the injured party and the other must pay. The injured party becomes the judge and jury and proclaims herself innocent, while the perpetrator must automatically hang.

Making the assumptions that we each can know the ultimate truth from all perspectives, and that we are in the position to demand that the world be exactly as we want it, is playing God. It ignores the fact that our anger at those who hurt us prevents us from seeing both sides of the story. Our self-righteous anger also keeps us stuck in the uncomfortable but familiar place of being a victim. But as long as we remain victims, we cannot control our lives, and we are bound to remain stuck in our feud.

When Kim, a thirty-five-year-old executive secretary, insisted that her ex-husband was "like all other men," I sympathized with her plight but sensed a deeper rage and self-righteousness in her voice.

Kim: He was just like my current boss. Beneath their polite exterior they're all jerks, out for only one thing, and you know what that is.

Dr. H.: I don't suppose you're talking about acceptance?

Kim: Very funny. You're a man. You know exactly what I'm talking about.

Dr. H.: Sure I do. A lot of men only want one thing, or at least maybe they only know how to go after one thing.

Kim: And I'm sick of it. Life shouldn't be this way.

Dr. H.: Men should be more like . . . what? Like women?

Kim: Yeah, but women are even worse. You really can't trust them, either. Everyone wants a piece of you, one part of you or another.

Dr. H.: That's all there is . . . just people wanting to take advantage?

Kim: Come on now. Give me a break. You know exactly what I'm talking about. Everybody's out for themselves.

Dr. H: You mean you're the only one who's been hurt?

Kim: What do you mean?

Dr. H.: You think these other people are all out to get you, and that they've never been hurt themselves like you've been hurt. I know you've been hurt deeply, and I know I can never be in your shoes. But I know a lot of people who have been hurt badly, and sometimes in turn they go around hurting others, just like when you walked out on your boss last week and your husband three years ago.

Kim: That's not fair.

Dr. H.: Sometimes when we hurt as much as you hurt, it's hard to be fair. But the only way out of your bitterness and your constant battles with other people is to be really fair. That means seeing that other people hurt too, and it means struggling not to see your self and your own pain as the center of the universe.

WHY BLAME DOESN'T WORK

As long as we blame others, it reinforces our beliefs that other people are responsible for the outcome of our lives. If we become stuck in blaming our sister, our brother, our parents, our aunts or uncles, we often become blinded not only to our own role in determining what happens to us, but to the power we have to create the kind of life we want. We lose sight of the fact that there may be others who share in the blame, such as those in our families who may have failed to protect us, or those who previously hurt the people who then hurt us. Occasionally, we lose sight of our own contributions to the feud, ways in which we could have responded differently, or ways in which we acted to fan the flames.

BLAMING IS ADDICTIVE

Blame becomes an addiction, something so entrenched that we automatically seek it when we feel hurt or something goes wrong. "If it wasn't for my brother's constant taunts, I'd feel better about myself and be able to cope when people insult me." The statement may be partly true, but holding on to the blame prevents us from seeking other solutions or learning new ways of coping.

People who get into one feud after another are often "blame addicts." Like Kim, the secretary who blamed all men, and then all women, for making her miserable, people who are addicted to blame simply don't see themselves as responsible for their own behavior. The idea that whatever happens in our lives is someone else's fault comes so quickly and so naturally, and then it feeds on itself. Just like those addicted to chemicals, blame addicts feel like they can't live without it, and often seem to need larger and larger doses to satisfy them.

Steve is just one of many blame addicts who finds himself feuding with everyone. A divorced, immature, awkwardly handsome forty-two-year-old truck driver, he spews blame like smoke from an old diesel engine:

> *Every driver speeds. So why do they always find me? It's the same with women. I don't know. Everyone I meet, all they want is my money. They rob me blind, then they take off with someone else. It's pointless. Now they won't even honor my credit cards. I've got to pay cash for fuel. Nobody does that. But just because I'm on the road a lot and I've got all this alimony and I'm late with my payments on my bills, I mean these people aren't even human. They're all scum.*

BLAME DISTORTS TRUTH

Ultimately, blame distorts the truth, and that becomes the greatest hindrance to moving out of a feud and into a reconciliation. Chronic blamers perceive others as hurtful, so even when those around them try to be loving or try to stop inflicting hurt, chronic blamers still believe they're being attacked. The chronic blamer ends up sabotaging the genuine efforts of others to be loving by misinterpreting their behavior. I see this pattern almost daily in my work with families and couples. Here's how it looked the other day when a feuding husband and wife in their mid-fifties, struggling to revive a relationship torn apart by years of mutual violation, reported to me about how their week went:

Martha: The fact is, doctor, that no matter what I do, it simply doesn't matter, he ridicules me and gets so enraged with me that he completely ruins any attempts I make to make things better between us.

Dr. H.: You made some attempts? That's wonderful. What did you do?

Martha: He just lit into me like he always does. He just tears me down.

Dr. H.: I know both you and Bob feel that way. But you said you did something different, to make things better, and I'm real curious about what it was that you did.

Martha: Well, I have a perfect example. You know we hadn't been sexual, made love, you know it's been over seven years, and well, you know, it's just not right. I talked to my friends and they all say it's just not natural, a woman can't live without sex. It's bad for her health. But I thought, you know, if Bob could only be sexual with me maybe it would help him and me both, so after he ate dinner I just went up to him and I said, "Let's just forget all this fighting and have great sex!"

(After a long pause, I continued.)

Dr. H.: Okay, so then what happened?

Martha: Like I told you, he tore me to pieces, and we got into a huge fight, and it nearly killed me that I finally try to make things better and he puts me down.

Dr. H.: What did he do? How did he react when you asked him to make love?

Martha: He just sat there.

Dr. H.: What did he say?

Martha: Nothing. He just sat there.

Dr. H.: How did it turn into a fight?

Martha: Well, when he didn't tell me he would do it, I knew he was enraged at me and I had to defend myself against his attacks.

Dr. H.: But how did he attack you? (To Bob, who was sitting there quietly, his finger nervously tapping the side of the chair:) Bob, what went through your mind when Martha asked you to make love?

Bob: I don't know, I'm not sure. Mostly, I was shocked. You have to understand that she hasn't wanted to touch me for years now.

Dr. H.: Were you at all frightened, you know, that since it's been so long, maybe you wouldn't be able to perform as well as you would like to?

Bob: That's exactly how I felt. That's exactly what went through my mind. How did you know that?

Dr. H.: Well, after seven years of not being sexual, that's an awful lot of pressure, you know, to snap your fingers and just hop into bed.

Bob: And knowing Martha, I thought it was also probably a trick.

Martha was right. This was a perfect example, but not of her husband trying to sabotage her efforts. It was an example of how Martha genuinely attempted to get closer to her husband. But because of her history of being rejected by her parents and later her husband, Martha misinterpreted his silence as the old rejection and rage, and jumped all over him before he even had a chance to talk about how he really did feel. But Bob wasn't completely innocent either. Because each of them had such a long history of blaming each other, he also assumed that any efforts Martha might make to move closer to him were merely sinister maneuvers to throw him off balance and stab him when he was stumbling. Sadly, this incident was just one example in a vicious cycle of blame that prevented Bob and Martha from trusting one another.

BLAME KEEPS OTHERS IN CONTROL OF US

To forever blame others, without a deeper understanding of the meaning and context of the hurt feelings, is to be doomed to live a life filled with unending and unbounded anger, a life that ironically is dictated by the same people who managed to create the painful feelings to begin with. While many of us claim to want to be rid of the influence and the presence of those who hurt us, our ongoing stream of intense anger actually keeps *them* in control of our lives. As a psychologist in training, I remember telling a supervisor about something one of my clients did during one of our sessions that made me angry. My supervisor responded, "Well, she sure has a way of staying in charge of your relationship." When I looked puzzled, my supervisor explained, "You've been thinking about this all week long. . . . She's been on your mind the whole time. She's certainly managed to make sure that she's always on your mind!"

Our ongoing anger keeps those people who hurt us hauntingly on our minds. Even though they may not seem to be on our minds every waking moment, their influence and the anger caused by the memory of the hurt is always right below the surface, ready to bubble up at the slightest reminder or provocation. To remain stuck in a blaming position requires being stuck in the victim position, keeping others in charge of us and hindering our ability to grow as independent people without being overly influenced by those who hurt us.

BLAME CREATES AN ATMOSPHERE OF DANGER

Another reason why blame is toxic to family harmony is that it wears away any foundation of safety that might exist in a family. As I mentioned earlier, the creation of a physically and emotionally safe environment for children to grow up in is the primary function of a family, and as that foundation becomes worn away by feelings of betrayal, it eventually cracks. If we blame others without first recognizing our own contributions to the family, the blame is experienced by others not as an attempt to be held accountable, but as a dart thrown viciously in their direction, and no one feels safe. As the darts are thrown, each person has to build walls of safety higher and higher to prevent himself or herself from feeling the painful point of the dart. Because the ultimate goal is to take down these walls and rebuild and restore a semblance of safety in a family, any blaming becomes counterproductive.

A seventeen-year-old high school dropout named Megan described what it felt like in her family:

> *My parents constantly fought. They finally broke up, thank goodness. It was the best thing for my mother, but my dad's a wreck. My mom's living with her sister in San Diego, but my parents still fight all the time, only now it's on the phone. It wasn't that I was scared or anything, I just didn't feel anything. Now I have to get out of there, but I have nowhere to live where I can be myself.*

As we talked, Megan let me know how frightened she was of going out on her own. Her feuding family was the only family she knew, and this chaotic, blame-ridden "home" was the home she had to carry inside her when she had to face life on her own. It left her feeling as though there were truly no safe places in the world. Having no internal sense of safety left her feeling unable to face life.

BLAME CREATES A "CONTINGENT FAMILY"

Chronically blaming other people creates a "contingent family," a family in which change or hope for change is always contingent upon the other person changing first. Blame is experienced by most people as someone holding a gun to your head; little genuine change comes when someone feels threatened or manipulated. Sure, when you're standing at an automated teller machine and someone threatens to blow your head off if you don't hand over the money, you best give the person your money. But that is not genuine giving or charity, because it is not a free choice. Likewise, no one will change willingly if told that they are the cause of the problem, that they are being blamed for your grief and therefore must "hand over the change" and act differently. At best, the person will only act the part, instead of willingly struggling to find the courage to change.

While I witness this kind of blaming in nearly all feuds, it comes across most clearly in marriages where two people can't seem to get over their own hurt and self-righteousness. "I'll change only if you change first" is the constant refrain. Here's a typical exchange:

Husband: I can't believe you did it again. How do you expect me to trust you when you continue to stay out late at night and not call me? How do I know you're not seeing someone else?

Wife: Me? What about you? Where were you on Friday?

Husband: There you go again. And what about the dishes? You told me a hundred times you'd do the dishes before you left for work. I come home and once again, dirty dishes!

Wife: I'm not your goddamn servant. There you go again, always finding something to blame me for. You're always accusing me of ruining your life, as if I live just to ruin your life.

Husband: Well, if you wouldn't try so hard to ruin my life, I wouldn't be so angry with you.

These kind of ad nauseum threats leave people convinced not only that there is little hope for the other person, but also that the only way change is going to happen is if the other person changes first. Where there is blame, there is no responsibility, and where there is no responsibility, there's no hope for authentic change.

BLAME DISTORTS HISTORY

When the "bad guy" is identified and anger is boiling over, it becomes nearly impossible to take a step back and look at your own family history rationally. People who blame others see only one side of the story, and their blame acts like blinders to the whole truth. The multigenerational history of the family, and the patterns that repeat from one generation to the next, become obscured by the one-sided nature of blame. There is a haiku that reads: "My storehouse having burnt down, nothing obscures my view of the bright moon." People who carry a storehouse of blame obscure their views of the truth, the longstanding multigenerational patterns that finally erupted into their feud.

TRUTH: THE ANTIDOTE TO BLAME

There is an old Hasidic saying that there are three sides to every story. Blame only allows us to see one side—our own. In that sense, it keeps us from being liberated by the truth. The truth of how our feuds come about is never as simple as blaming someone else leads us to believe. Human lives and the feuds we manage to get ourselves into are never simple. The complex truth may never be known in its entirety, but the more truth we can bring to light, the more panoramic our lens can become, the more likely we are to move from blame to understanding. The only way to ultimately liberate ourselves from the harm done by blaming others (and maintaining the feud) or blaming ourselves (and becoming depressed and hopeless) is to get out of the blame game altogether.

IF NOT BLAME, WHAT THEN?
STEPS TOWARD RESOLUTION

THE MULTIGENERATIONAL CONTEXT

The first step in eliminating blame is to gain a deeper understanding of the multigenerational patterns that have existed in your family. Use the genogram as a starting point for locating the enmeshment, triangulation, role distortion, and other issues that may have plagued your family for generations. Discover if there are patterns that repeat themselves from one generation to the next that may contribute to your feud.

Ask yourself the questions listed at the end of the last chapter. Where in my family has enmeshment occurred, and what has happened in my own feud that might be a repetition of an enmeshed pattern? What significant triangles existed in the family, and what about my own feud has happened as a result of triangulation? What kinds of roles were passed down from one generation to the next, and how does my feud represent people being stuck in their childhood roles? Can my feud be a result of trying to break free of childhood roles? What traumas occurred in my family, and what hidden anniversary dates might be affecting my feud? Are there any myths or secrets that might have exerted a hidden influence on my feud?

Understanding the multigenerational buildup of your feud will help you to challenge assumptions you might have had for many years. For example, in the feud between Nicole and Frank discussed earlier, both had deeply ingrained views about how the feud developed. Frank believed he was "tricked" into having children that he didn't want, and ever since then he hasn't trusted Nicole. Nicole, on the other hand, believed that Frank was a monster who only acted sweetly during their brief courtship, but eventually showed his true colors as an abusive husband.

These assumptions were powerful, and both Frank and Nicole held on to them tightly, no matter how strongly I or the several other therapists they had seen before me objected. It wasn't until both of them were able to see the powerful influence of multigenerational patterns that they were able to challenge these assumptions effectively. Frank learned that Nicole didn't necessarily "trick" him, but that she came from a family that over the years never spoke directly about their most intimate thoughts. Furthermore, Nicole learned from an early age as a girl in her family that she should never outrightly object or say no to a husband, a pattern that existed for many generations. What Frank experienced as being "tricked" actually turned out to be an honest, direct expression of how women were trained to behave in the traditional family Nicole came from.

Nicole learned that Frank wasn't a monster, but that he came from a family in which men were encouraged to dominate and control others, women and other men alike. She learned that he was badly "burned" by his mother, who used to entice Frank with sweets and favors, and then fail to deliver. Frank's pent-up rage at his mother was easily dumped on Nicole, the same way Frank's mother's rage was dumped on Frank's father.

Knowing that these patterns were in effect didn't change anyone's responsibility for their behavior, but what it did was to challenge the assumptions that the feud was really about being "tricked" or being "abused." Frank was able to redefine being "tricked" as a matter of communication style (with major consequences), and Nicole was able to redefine being "abused" as a manifestation of Frank's own pain and his training.

Feuding family members believe that they are still victims, and not in control of their lives. Having been a victim before, we often fall prey to the belief that we are powerless to change the course of our lives. If we are "burned" in childhood, then all we amount to is the charred remains of what could have been. As such, it feels as if there's little hope of moving forward and creating independent lives of our own. Examining the multigenerational context of your family feud, however, allows you to adopt a more realistic perspective and find hope where once there was none.

THE COMMITMENT TO JUSTICE

As you begin to place your feud in a historical context, gaining some knowledge of the influence of the past, you may find it hard to give up blame because you don't know how to protect yourself from the pain in the present, or from any future injustice.

The most effective substitute for blame is a commitment to justice. When I use the word "justice," I don't mean the meting out of punishment to all guilty parties. In this context, justice means that each person in the feud must bear the consequences of his or her actions. Justice is the idea that fair consequences will result from knowledge of the truth. I use "justice" the way Benjamin Disraeli defined it, as "truth in action." One of the keys to moving forward toward reconciliation is to use the energy previously used for blaming for seeking the truth and holding on to it once it becomes clear.

Jackie had a feud going with her eldest daughter Ellen. They had a difficult and troubled relationship as her daughter was growing up, and when Ellen hit adolescence the two of them went at it with a vengeance. Ellen moved out of her mother's house, had little communication with her mother, began getting into trouble with boys, and developed an eating disorder. Their troubles over the years that led up to the feud had been fueled by the secret that Jackie's daughter had a different father from the man who she had believed all her life was her true father. Jackie became pregnant in high school. The father was the rebellious teenage boy from across the tracks whom her parents detested. Jackie chose to please her parents and marry the boy they preferred, the captain of the football team, who turned out in the long run to be a tyrannical, abusive husband. When a second child arrived, Jackie's husband preferred this child, because it was his biological child, and Ellen became the recipient of his tyranny. Despite Jackie's ultimate divorce from her husband, Ellen remained distant and angry with Jackie and actively hostile toward the father who raised her.

When Jackie wondered whether it was better to continue the secret or to ultimately let Ellen know who her real father was, she feared that revealing the truth would only push her daughter away farther. Jackie thought that if she revealed the secret to Ellen, Ellen would see her as a liar, feel ultimately betrayed by the many years of deception, and lose all trust in her mother. Whatever fragment of a relationship the two had left would be lost forever.

The advice I gave Jackie was to take the only path that could possibly end up in reconciliation—the truth—knowing full well that Jackie's fears might come true and that the path was indeed a dangerous one. Jackie also needed to explain to Ellen what she was going through at the time, what her fears were, what she had to deal with as she was growing up, and why she chose to take the path she took at the time. She was to tell Ellen that she regretted the decision she had made (hiding the truth) and to ask for her forgiveness, but Jackie was also told not to expect forgiveness or even understanding. She was warned that the price of telling the truth might be years of pain and hurt feelings, but the deception had already resulted in years of pain and hurt. The truth would allow for the possibility of reconciliation and healing, whereas deception was a road that could only lead to further deception.

The immediate result of Jackie's meeting with Ellen was exactly what Jackie and I had expected. Her daughter was simultaneously shocked at the revelation, and insistent that she had suspected the truth all along. Ellen went into a tailspin that included confusion about her own identity (merely an exaggeration of what she had already experienced), rage, and further detachment from her mother. But after a few months of this behavior, things began to slowly improve. With Jackie's help, her daughter began to see a therapist, whom both Jackie and her daughter visited together for a while. While Jackie and Ellen's relationship improved, none of us expected that Ellen's relationship with the man she called her father would actually get closer, but it did. The road that followed the revelation was rough, but eventually the entire family became closer.

When someone is committed to the "truth, the whole truth, and nothing but the truth," then justice becomes possible. The whole truth means that the person who is responsible will bear the consequences in proportion to the crime that has been committed. You may want to try this exercise:

1. Make a list of all the things that you believe were done to hurt you by the people with whom you are feuding.

2. Make a list of all the patterns in your family that you were able to identify from your genogram.

3. How might the items on your first list, the things that were done to hurt you, have been a result of the patterns on your second list?

4. How were the people who did things to hurt you also victims of the patterns in your family?

5. Make a list of all the things that you have done to fan the flames of your feud. What have you done to hurt others?

6. Make a list of "coconspirators." These are people who may have helped others to hurt you, or who may have helped you hurt others. Do these people share in the pool of responsibility?

7. Once you have completed the above lists and answers, address these final questions:

   a) What are fair and reasonable consequences for each party to the feud, if any?

   b) Have you been acting in accordance with the depth of the crime?

ACCEPTING AND ASSIGNING RESPONSIBILITY

Moving from blame to responsibility starts the slow wheels of justice turning. In a family feud, it is too easy to perceive one side as the victim and the other as a perpetrator—someone harmed and someone who does the harming. It's rare, however, that only one person is hurting in a family feud. Usually, both sides of the feud lay claim to injustices done to them, and as I have said before, they are usually both right. Life and family feuds are rarely as simple as one person doing something to another, and this approach is likely to assign a weighty burden of blame on one side that is a distortion of the truth.

One reason the one-sided approach of seeing one person as the victim and the other as a perpetrator becomes tricky is that it shields the fact that for many perpetrators, their having hurt others is a source of pain. When someone hurts someone else, there are at least two victims, the actual victim and the one who has to bear the burden of guilt, shame, and responsibility for his or her actions. Merely describing a person as a perpetrator often makes it difficult to separate the sin from the sinner, and limits our view of the person beneath the label.

As you read through this chapter, think of how the distinction between victim and perpetrator may or may not be relevant to your own feud. In actuality, this division can be useful if you understand it as only a temporary state. Imagine, for example, a conversation between two people. One person is never only a listener or a talker. In order for it to be considered a conversation as opposed to a lecture, each person fluctuates back and forth between the two roles. At times in a conversation both people can talk simultaneously, and the result is often confusion. Similarly, both people can listen simultaneously, and the result is often an awkward silence. Conversations become most productive and fruitful when one person is a talker and the other a listener at any particular moment in time. As you navigate the rapids of reconciling a family feud, there may be times you will need to see yourself as a victim, and other times as a perpetrator. In a family feud, you *can* be both simultaneously, but in order to help move you through the process, you will get the most mileage out of seeing yourself in one role at a time.

There are some feuds, however, in which the one-sided approach is appropriate: when, for example, a child is horribly abused by an adult who uses the child to work out his or her own emotional problems, or when a spouse is brutally taken advantage of or physically, spiritually, or emotionally abused by another spouse. The fact that the perpetrators of these undeserved injuries may have also been victims in their own families (and most likely were) does not excuse or pardon their injurious behavior to others. While they may have their own forgiving to do, they continue to hold absolute responsibility for their behavior toward others.

In the majority of cases, however, the injuries done in a family feud are circular. Someone feels hurt by the actions of another; this injury might be real or imagined, intended or unintended, and the injuring party may even have no awareness that anything harmful was done. The one who feels injured, however, acts defensively, lashing out in some harmful way toward the perceived perpetrator. The perceived perpetrator now feels as though he or she is the injured party, and the hurt feelings spiral into a tornado of rage or silence that becomes the feud. This circularity of hurt makes it impossible to assign blame in one direction only. When you are seeking the truth, responsibility must be assigned to those who have hurt you and must in turn be accepted by you.

Responsibility is a way of holding people accountable for what they did without the need to turn the knife. It's a way of being clear about who did what and why without self-righteousness or the need to protect oneself. It's a way to stay grounded in reality without becoming both judge and executioner. And it's a way of honoring one's own perceptions, of staying close to the truth of having been hurt without overplaying it for sympathy or attention.

Here is a list of some statements commonly heard at the beginning of a feud, when blame is pervasive. I've paired each sentence with another one that expresses the same thought from a position of responsibility.

Blame: If you hadn't treated me the way you had, I'd be a different person.

Responsibility: *Many things you did hurt me, but the way I responded to those things was my own choice.*

Blame: It's all your fault.

Responsibility: *I did things to hurt you, and you did things to hurt me. We're both victims, and both perpetrators.*

Blame: It's all my fault.

Responsibility: *I know I did some things to hurt you, things that came from my own pain. I'm sorry.*

Blame: I can never forgive you for hurting mother the way you did.

Responsibility: *I can understand how, if I had the same life you did, I might do the same thing you did.*

Blame: I demand that you apologize to me.

Responsibility: *Although what you did hurt me, I can see how I hurt you too, and how you probably did the best you could under the circumstances.*

Blame: I could never have a relationship with someone who treated me the way you did.

Responsibility: *While I'm angry with you for what you did, you're important to me, and I want to try to work things out. We may have a long way to go, but the better I understand you, the more likely I am to find the parts of you I appreciate.*

HONORING YOUR OWN PAIN

At first glance it might seem odd that an important step in eliminating blame is to focus on honoring your own pain. Yet this is where the journey must begin.

One of the most common problems that faces me as a psychologist is when a client, desperately trying to work his way out of a maze of pain, looks at me with anguished eyes and pleadingly tells me that he has no idea where to begin. Most often, people who have no idea how to start out on the road to a less conflicted life suffer from a common malady; they don't know how to begin because they have no idea where they are. They might even have a vague idea of where they're going, but even knowing where you want to go won't help you if you have no idea where you are.

It's easy to get lost when trying to work your way out of a feud. As you've no doubt already seen, family feuds are complex webs spun over generations. In struggling to understand and work your way out of a feud, you might find it easy to get lost in the web. As you confront people whom you may not have spoken with for years, it's easy to fall backward into old ways of thinking. As you struggle to make sense of your place in the family and in the generations of family members who came before you, it's easy to put aside what you already know, altering the truth about your own experience of your life. Knowing who you are, knowing your personal history of hurt, and holding that knowledge inside you is your compass. It is the one thing that, if kept close to your heart and close to your awareness, will keep you from getting lost. No matter how the world treats you, remaining clear about what you stand for, where you've been, and the catalog of hurts and victories that defines you will prevent you from being buffeted by other people's needs and wishes.

The beginning of the journey is always to "know yourself." But self-knowledge is worthless if it is only intellectual. We must understand who we are, where we've been, and then we must be charitable to ourselves as well as to others. Once we fully understand the sources of our pain, we must allow ourselves to have the pain, because it is real and it is an instrumental part of us. We cannot rout the pain out of us because we don't want to pay attention to it. We're too smart for that kind of self-deception.

That is not to say that all we are is the accumulation of all the ghastly things that have happened to us. We are more than that, and it is always a challenge to try to get people to treat themselves fairly and honestly by honoring both their gifts and their pains. When we present ourselves to the world with integrity, we hold out both our strengths and weaknesses for the world to see. To emphasize one over the other would be dishonest. To give more weight to one or the other would be to cheat ourselves and deprive us of the opportunity to be loved and accepted for who we really are, not for the person we pretend to be.

Once we come to grips with the real hurts and the real successes we have managed in our lives, we must make a declaration to ourselves. This "declaration of independence" is a statement of who we are and what we believe in. It doesn't need to be written on paper, but it must be created. It's an honest self-assessment about where we stand and a list of our strengths and our weaknesses. It's a reminder of the work that we've already done to understand ourselves, and a commitment to continue the process despite the difficulty.

Ultimately, it's our task to accept ourselves for who we are. There's an old story about a rabbi named Zusya, who stated that when he gets to the gates of heaven he will not be asked "Why were you not more like Moses?" but instead "Why were you not more like Zusya?" This challenge to be ourselves depends on knowing ourselves, and ultimately accepting ourselves. We write our own declaration, then accept it as if it were a treasured gift.

There is no way to honestly assign responsibility, or alleviate blame, or seek a just understanding, without holding and treasuring our own identity. Any attempt to understand someone else, or to slowly move toward reconciliation, will be damaged if that attempt is made by lessening the intensity of or distorting the truth about one's own pain. When we try to understand someone else by putting our own feelings aside, eventually those feelings resurface and turn into resentment. Genuine change requires genuineness.

Holding and valuing your own pain, your own successes and failures, is the ballast that will always keep you on course, centered in the rough water; it will prevent you from sinking into confusion. If you take this self-knowledge with you wherever you go, if you hold it close to your awareness, it will allow you to take true responsibility for those events that you have created, while at the same time allowing you to honor and know that there are also pains others have created. It will start you on the road to removing blame, because an honest assessment of responsibility will include understanding not only the roles others whom you might have blamed have played in the feud, but also the roles you and relatives in previous generations have played. If you honestly assess the truth about your pain, it will become possible to fairly assign responsibility, rather than blame, to others and yourself.

Mourning and Grief

Nearly all feuds involve losing something in one way or another. People who feud usually feel cheated. In an ongoing feud with a mother, for example, people feel cheated out of having the kind of mother they wish they could have had. "Why couldn't I have had a mother like my neighbor's?" is a familiar refrain. In a feud with a sibling, people feel as though they're cheated out of the positive experiences of having a loving and supportive friend. "Why couldn't I have a sister who really cared about me instead of about herself?" And in cases where there has been emotional or physical abuse, people often feel cheated out of a safe childhood, or of even having a childhood.

Blame can be a way of failing to grieve for these losses. As long as we remain in a blaming position, we are too busy accusing others of hurting us to actually go through the pain and the hurt involved in grieving the loss. When we fail to grieve, we lose the opportunity to ultimately accept the truth of our loss, and we become frozen in a wasteland of "almost feeling," a wasteland of never quite allowing ourselves to move through the pain.

We never completely finish grieving over the losses in our lives; it is an ongoing process. By allowing ourselves to mourn, to feel the pain of our losses, we remain honest and in touch with the truth about our lives, making it harder to let our denial get in the way of attributing responsibility in correct measure to those who have contributed to the feud.

Rational Understanding

Examining the multigenerational context of your feud will help you see it more rationally. In the midst of a feud, the emotions of terror, abandonment, rage, and possibly jealousy, guilt, and shame take over and prevent us from seeing things accurately. These are the same feelings we felt when we were children, when we felt terribly vulnerable to the criticism, abandonment, and attacks of those around us. In response to those feelings and threats, we learned ways of coping. When we were children, we had few choices. We couldn't pack our bags and leave a mother who didn't seem to care for us, we couldn't fight back in the face of physical abuse, we couldn't pick up the phone and make an appointment at a counseling center for a rageful father. We had to develop ways to protect ourselves in the face of danger. We would use these survival skills—denial, detachment, humor, aggression, retreating into our own worlds—as we needed them. They were our strengths, enabling us to feel as safe as possible during the storm of family life.

As adults, sometimes we forget that we are no longer powerless and small, with few options available to us. We use the same protective maneuvers we did when we were children, especially when we find ourselves in a feud. We feel easily threatened, and quick to rage, even when the situation may truly not be dangerous. We protect ourselves when we are afraid that terrible things might happen, we feel small even when we have power, we react as if we must stay even when we are free to walk away.

Although we are better able as adults to keep ourselves truly safe, we rely too much on our protective maneuvers, and we end up using them when we don't need them. We run and hide before we need to, and then we misinterpret the world as dangerous. We react first, then we judge the world based on our reactions, and not on the reality of the situation at hand.

Taking a rational perspective means that we put aside, or at least modulate, our intense feelings in order to see the situation more accurately. A rational understanding helps us move from a defensive, protective stance to a stance in which we can understand that both we and others have strengths and limitations. It helps us to see the difference between those things that we can change and those we can't. Recognizing the choices we have is a necessary step to take before we can finally confront with integrity those who may have hurt us in the past.

Emotional Understanding

Feuds are not rational events. They are based on the very intense feeling of having been deeply wounded by a family member's hurtful behavior. The human instinct for self-preservation rises up inside us with the kind of rage a mother bear feels when her cubs are threatened. We replay the hurtful events ad nauseam in our minds, reinforcing our sense of how terribly we have been treated. Our rage festers until it takes on a life of its own, like a Frankenstein monster pieced together from disparate bits of emotional debris.

In the case of an entrenched family feud, you must move beyond a rational understanding to an emotional understanding. As you look at the genogram, remember that the circles and squares were and are real people. Even though you've never met some of them, imagine something of their lives, of the positions they held in their families, and the burdens they carried. Imagine how each of them may have struggled to manage their own blame. Imagine how if each successive generation continued to blame others there would be little hope for generations to come.

Blame begins to melt away as we gain a deeper understanding of how those who came before us were victims to the same extent as or even a greater extent than ourselves. It was easy for me to blame my father for being emotionally detached from me and my siblings as we were growing up. I blamed him for not being home often, and for ruling the family with such an iron fist that I felt paralyzed with fear as a child. Yet, as an adult I got to know more about his childhood; I learned about the severe beatings he had to withstand at the hands of his parents, and the complete emotional disregard they had for him. I realized that the little I received from my father was more by far than he had received from his parents. I also learned that much of his "neglect" of my emotional needs was a decision on his part not to repeat the same kind of physically abusive environment that plagued his childhood. While his emotional attentiveness to my needs was paltry, his behavior represented his best efforts given the complete disregard of emotional needs that occurred in the family he came from. The more I was able to feel compassionate toward him for the suffering he endured through his own childhood, the more I understood how what he created represented a stretch and a genuine effort on his part to do better. This compassion eased the pain that I felt when I was tempted to blame him for the unhappiness I felt growing up. It is this compassion that is the root of "emotional understanding."

Seeing someone else as a victim doesn't make them less responsible for the injuries they inflicted. Anyone can manipulate their "victim" status to avoid taking responsibility for themselves, such as the classic "Twinkie" defense that lightened the sentence for the man who murdered San Francisco supervisor Harvey Milk. The goal is not to excuse someone for their wrongdoings or the harm they inflicted, or in any way to make them not accountable, but instead to understand the genesis of that harm. To some extent we are all victims and we are all perpetrators. There are no perfect parents, no perfect siblings, and no perfect children, and none of us escapes scrutiny and judgment. Therefore, we must face each other with an eye toward fairness and justice. The problem with blame is that in the midst of a family feud the kind of deep, almost fossilized blame that occurs gets in the way of fairness and justice. We become so emotionally wrapped up in blaming others that we lose sight of the bigger picture. We often fail to see our own responsibility for the feud, and we fail to see how each generation that comes before us managed to set the stage for a feud in the generations to come.

Insight is aimed at knowing how we were hurt, while understanding is aimed at knowing why we were hurt. When we feel victimized, we often turn the victimizer into a monster. By viewing him or her as a monster, there's no hope that we'll ever be able to understand the motivation the other person had for his or her actions because we have trouble identifying with a "monster." To understand someone, we must bring them back to the level of human beings. We must try to see them as fragile, damaged people. If we understand their position in life, their limitations as fallible people, their personal history and their own attempts to overcome their struggles, we may be able to acknowledge that if we were placed in the same situation, given the same circumstances and the same personal history, we might do no better than they did. Understanding is the knowledge that if we were in the other person's shoes, we might cause some of the same hurt and make similar mistakes. As a result of this kind of understanding, we are often able to feel less blame and less self-righteousness. We still hold the other person responsible for the actions that hurt us, but we can exonerate him or her by removing condemnation and blame.

This move from a more rational understanding of how someone might be reasonably and appropriately responsible for his or her actions to an emotional understanding of the situation can be tricky. The difference between the two is, however, not that large. To emotionally understand people simply means to feel for them, or to feel with them as they go through whatever hard times they might encounter. To emotionally understand people doesn't mean you must feel exactly the same way they do; it means you recognize how you might feel if you were in their place. You'll never be able to understand exactly how the other person feels, but what's important is that you allow yourself to feel at least some of the same feelings that might have arisen in you if you were experiencing what the family member with whom you are feuding went through.

Feeling for the other side does not require letting go of your anger, or of your wish to keep yourself safe. Likewise, feeling for the other side does not diminish or dishonor your feelings of having been wounded. Life is too complex for simple solutions such as "I am right and the other person is wrong." In most feuds, all parties have been hurt and are hurting. Going back to the old Hasidic saying that there are three sides to every story, your job is to find the third side—not your side, not the other person's side, but the truth that encompasses both. Understanding the other person's side *with feeling* is a necessary step in getting to the ultimate third side.

There's no question that feeling for the other side can make you feel like you're betraying yourself and joining with the enemy. But it only feels that way if you're unable to hold on to your own hurt, honoring it while simultaneously understanding that you are not the only one who hurts. A feud is a war, and there can be no war without casualties on both sides. You might feel that the other side doesn't suffer as much as you do, and it may be true that the other side may not be as good at expressing, facing, or understanding their own pain. That doesn't mean that compassion for the "enemy" is impossible; in fact, it is this compassion that ultimately will liberate both sides from the feud.

The person with whom you're feuding need not be compassionate toward you. Compassionate understanding can be one-sided, if you understand that as an adult you have learned the necessary survival tactics for keeping yourself safe. Your one-sided compassion will not set you up for further disappointment, sadness, and loss if, in assessing both sides accurately, you don't expect more from others than they are able to give. You might be disappointed that the other person can't be compassionate, but as long as your ability to honor your pain, stay focused on your own integrity, and practice your well-learned survival skills remains intact, that disappointment won't be devastating.

GUILT AND FEUDS

Occasionally, when people begin to assign responsibility for a feud, they get in touch with the things they have done to make life miserable for the other person or people. Looking at one's own contribution to a feud can be eye-opening and painful, so painful that it might spark feelings of deep guilt. At times it's the warding off of guilt that keeps people from looking at their own contribution to a feud. Sensing that the guilt would create emotional pain and anxiety, some people choose to maintain a stalemate rather than confront their own painful feelings of responsibility.

Guilt has gotten a bad reputation as the underhanded weapon supposedly used by Catholic and Jewish mothers to twist the arms of their family members. The hedonistic and troubled sixties attempted to paint guilt as an unnecessary emotion, one that stood in the way of achieving self-acceptance and one's fullest potential. But there is a real danger in looking at only the negative side of something so basic to human functioning as guilt. I prefer to see guilt as a positive emotion, one that when used properly becomes a powerful tool in the quest to do what's right and move through emotionally stormy weather.

Unless we're sadists, most of us don't like to go around hurting others intentionally. We don't revel in their pain, and we genuinely feel bad when we realize we've done something to hurt them. When the hurt we caused is unintentional, we often feel guilty simply for having hurt the other person. The guilt, then, is an acknowledgment that we didn't live up to our own expectations of ourselves, that we weren't considerate or thoughtful enough of someone else's feelings. In this situation, our guilt is a reminder that we didn't do all we could do, or that perhaps we were momentarily too self-involved.

When we don't feel guilty, however, it could be because we truly don't feel inadequate in that situation. We truly believed we were being considerate, and the pain that was felt by the offended party came strictly from their own misperception of our behavior. In these cases, it would be wrong to feign guilt for the sake of reconciliation. We might want to look more closely at our own behavior and motivations, but if after making a genuine attempt to do so we continue not to feel guilty, then we can't take responsibility.

Guilt is a crucial ally in our quest for understanding, especially because we often feel guilty before we know what we're feeling guilty for. It is an ally because if we listen to our guilt, it will teach us that indeed we do feel as though we did something wrong, and lead us to take responsibility for our part in the feud. Guilt is a guiding light that can help us find our way out of a dark tunnel of confused and conflicted family patterns.

The trail that leads to reconciliation begins with blame and ends in responsibility. It starts with a passionate need to stay safe by punishing the other side of the feud with blame, and moves from there toward a deeper and clearer understanding of the elements that combined to create a family feud. It broadens understanding to include the context of the feud, including the generations that came before, the personal histories of the combatants, and the circumstances surrounding the feud.

As you grapple to understand your feud, it's essential not to lose sight of your own pain. Honor it as real. Grieve the loss of the things you hoped for, and challenge yourself to use whatever guilt you might have to spur you to action. As you do these things, you move closer to the stage of forgiveness. In forgiving yourself and forgiving others, you open the door to finally laying your feud to rest.

Forgiving the Family Tree

A man should not act as a judge either for someone he loves or for someone he hates. For no man
can see the guilt of someone he loves or the good
qualities in someone he hates.

—TALMUD

One should despise much, forgive often, and
never forget.

—SARAH BERNHARDT

RECONCILING A FAMILY FEUD CAN FEEL LIKE CLIMBING A MOUNTAIN.
STARTING OUT REQUIRES COURAGE AND PREPARATION. CONTINUING
the journey requires determination. At times reaching the pinnacle feels
impossible, and we wonder why we are trying to do it in the first place.
At other times we can stop at a ledge, rest, enjoy the panoramic vistas,
and be grateful for how far we've come.

For many people whose lives have been altered by the pain of a feud,
forgiveness is like a snowstorm that rolls in during their trek up the
mountain, blocking the view of the summit and threatening the survival of the expedition. It is the place that many of my clients find
themselves feeling stuck, posing questions that beg to be answered:
Must I forgive those who have hurt me so much? Why should I let

them off the hook? Where is the justice in that? How can I ever for-give myself or expect forgiveness after all the hurt I have caused? Should I simply "forgive and forget"? What do I do with all the anger I feel? What is this thing called forgiveness, anyway?

Forgiveness can be greatly misunderstood. Some people mock it as too easy, too mechanistic or too superficial. Others see it as naive or unrealistic—not the stuff of real life or real people. For some, forgive-ness is more relevant to their relationship with God than it is to rela-tionships between people. Most people, however, take the concept seriously, and sincerely struggle with how to translate forgiveness into something personally meaningful.

Sometimes it's easier, when defining a complex concept, to begin by defining what it is not. Here are some common myths about forgive-ness:

"Forgive and Forget." I remember a woman I saw whose life was lit-tle more than a series of feuds. This woman, in her mid-sixties at the time I saw her, insisted that nearly every person who entered her life harmed her deeply. She initiated lawsuits against almost every physician and psychologist who saw her, claiming that each of them wounded her physically or emotionally. She berated her husband constantly, and had no positive relationships with anyone. One of the things I re-member about her the most was her fuming over the phrase "forgive and forget."

"Everyone tells me I'm supposed to forgive and forget. How do you expect me to forgive and forget when those bastards are still out there doing things to other people? How am I supposed to forgive and for-get when I'm still so sick, and they have never paid me for what they did?"

This was her constant refrain, and no matter how insistent or con-frontational I was with her, she sang it over and over again.

Forgiveness and forgetting are clearly two distinct phenomena, re-lated to each other tangentially at best. I prefer an alternate mantra: "Forgiving is divine; forgetting is stupid." It's stupid because forget-ting past injustices, if it were even possible, only sets us up to repeat history. It is our knowledge of the past wrongs that that keeps us safe from repeating the same mistakes twice. But whether we want to do so or not, intentionally "forgetting" a deep hurt does not square with human nature. We can try our hardest to push something out of memory, but doing so only sets us up for surprise visitations of those memories later on in life. It's much healthier not to forget, but instead to accept our past for what it was, and struggle to integrate those hurtful experiences into our lives in a productive and meaningful way.

To Forgive is to Condone. Some people believe that by forgiving we are condoning—"excusing" or tacitly approving the hurtful behavior. When we condone, we decide to "overlook" the offense. After all, the Bible clearly says that when others try to hurt us, we are to "turn the other cheek." The King James translation of Luke's injunction follows right on the heels of the advice to "Love your enemies, do good to them which hate you." The famous cheek-turning phrase actually reads: "And unto him that smiteth thee on the one cheek offer also the other; and him that taketh away thy cloke forbid not to take thy coat also." There is no biblical intent to condone, overlook, or approve of another's hurtful behavior. The phrase "turn the other cheek" in context is a way of describing the importance of loving and giving toward those who hurt us. It's one of hundreds of biblical examples of the concept of turning toward our enemies with love, but not with ignorance or the deception that comes with overlooking or approving of their behavior. In fact, the final sentence in this famous verse is: "And as ye would that men should do to you, do ye also to them likewise." This model of forgiveness is not one of condoning or approval, but instead it is a model of justice.

To Forgive is to Absolve. Some people connect forgiveness with a form of absolution. If viewed as an automatic release of responsibility from punishment for wrongdoing, then absolution can only lead to denial of the hurt we have suffered. If we automatically release ourselves or others, without some form of reparation, then there are no consequences for the hurtful behavior. This can only make us vulnerable to more hurt, because in this model of forgiveness those who have been hurtful to others have only learned that they could get away with their malicious behavior.

To Forgive is to Sacrifice. In this definition of forgiveness, one side martyrs himself or herself, saying that things are really okay when they aren't. The belief goes something like this: If I sacrifice myself, give up what I want and need, everything will smooth over. This is a setup for more hurt. It's a one-sided solution that perpetuates the problem.

Forgiveness is a One-time Act. Forgiveness, in fact, is a slow process, in which trust that has been fractured must be rebuilt over time. Forgiveness that is forced to meet a certain deadline usually is ingenuine, at least, and short-lived at best.

Forgiveness is Excusing In fact, excusing might best be considered the opposite of forgiving. When someone is excused for something, he or she is no longer held accountable. This essentially invalidates the pain that has occurred. If someone's behavior is excusable, there is no need for forgiveness.

Forgiveness is Tolerance. Tolerating something, like condoning or excusing it, is a way of allowing unacceptable behavior to occur repeatedly. In fact, forgiveness ultimately depends on a refusal to tolerate harmful behavior, allowing both sides to move on to more constructive and healthier relationships.

Forgiveness is Minimizing A graduate student of mine once described her own problematic view of forgiveness. She assumed that forgiveness involved measuring your own hurt against the suffering of others. If your hurt didn't stack up, then you were supposed to forgive those who hurt you. She told me that she used to tell herself, "Well, at least my parents didn't lock me in closets and deny me food for days." As a result, she denied her feelings as unworthy, and minimized her painful childhood experiences. Her benevolent gratitude that her childhood was not worse than some others was not a path toward forgiveness, but instead a side road of denial.

So what is forgiveness?

Forgiveness essentially has two components: It is an attitude and a process. The attitude of forgiveness is more a perspective on life than it is a series of specific behaviors. The process of forgiveness, on the other hand, is more a sequence of steps that can be taken than an attitude. The process of forgiveness involves the following steps:

- Exoneration. This is when you lift the burden of guilt off someone who has hurt you, and end your condemnation of them. It doesn't require anyone else's active participation.

- Outright Forgiveness. This step involves a dialogue with others, and requires others to make amends for the hurt they caused. It includes actual overt acts that can be done to set the scales even, and may involve particular forgiveness rituals.

FORGIVING ATTITUDE

An attitude of forgiveness is the culmination of all the work you have done so far. It requires the ability to place the hurts that you feel and the hurts that you have caused in the light of understanding and compassion. It is the realization that there is always a larger context, a context in which we are all victims and all perpetrators. It is the ability to embrace the pain inside us as well as the pain inside others, even if the others aren't completely able to do it for themselves. Forgiveness is NOT a nonjudgmental stance that lets us off the hook, but instead it is an attitude more akin to that of a compassionate judge, a judge who requires that the proper justice be carried out, while struggling to understand the root causes behind the criminal act. Punishment, if it is to be meaningful, must be administered based not only on the crime, but on the motivations for and the context in which the crime was committed.

An attitude of forgiveness is the ability to separate out the sin from the sinner, the ability to judge those wrongs that have been done while understanding that there are people who exist apart from the hurtful behavior. It is the ability to understand that all people have the potential for both good and evil, and those of us who are capable of hurting others are also capable of helping them. An attitude of forgiveness requires a commitment to turning toward those who have hurt us and those whom we have hurt, and seeing each of us as fallible. It is an attitude of charity in which we give to ourselves and to others a special gift—the opportunity to right the wrongs that have been done.

The statement made recently by a female client of mine is a statement I have heard often from many others:

I realized that although I forgave my father a hundred times, I never really meant it. I knew I was supposed to forgive him, that if I did forgive him, then things were supposed to get better. But I never felt like forgiving him. I don't think I ever understood my own pain and his pain well enough to see the big picture. I was still so obsessed with licking my own wounds that I couldn't really see how I could hurt people the same way he did if I lived the life he did. That doesn't mean it was okay for him to do the things he did, and it doesn't mean that it was okay for me to not talk to him or give him a chance to make it better. It's just that now that I really understand as much as I do, I can begin to feel like forgiving. I've got a ways to go, and so does he, but at least I feel like forgiving him now.

Having a forgiving attitude is the first step in the ongoing process of forgiveness. It allows forgiveness to occur genuinely and effectively. The attitude of forgiveness and the process of forgiveness go hand in hand, and neither occurs overnight. We forgive as part of an ongoing search for understanding and truth in a relationship.

EXONERATION

Another aspect in the process of forgiveness is exoneration. When we exonerate someone, we use the depth of our insight and understanding to "lift the load of culpability" from the person who has caused the hurt. Having an attitude of forgiveness is a necessary component in exonerating someone. Yet exoneration goes a bit farther.

When we exonerate someone, we do more than demonstrate compassion. We put an end to condemnation. We still hold people responsible for their actions, yet our attitude of forgiveness enables us to stop complaining about the injustice, stop focusing on the faults or actions of those who have hurt us, and stop obsessing about our lot in life. While we want people to be accountable, to make amends, and to do better than they have done before, we let go of the unending bitterness we feel toward them.

This component of forgiveness requires no participation from those whom we seek to forgive. It's accomplished privately, solely through the efforts of one person. Because of this, exoneration itself cannot repair a relationship with someone else, for without the other party's active participation in balancing the scales of justice, there can be no trust and therefore no new and improved relationship.

If you were hurt by someone who is clearly unable or unwilling to take responsibility for his or her actions, and he or she is likely to continue to hurt you in the future, you can free yourself of the burden of past injustice by exonerating the person, but it would be foolish to go farther down the road of forgiveness by stepping back into a relationship that will only create further harm. On the other hand, if in your heart you know someone is capable of taking responsibility for past behavior, it behooves you to move toward the next component of forgiveness.

Exoneration is the only kind of forgiveness possible when you are dealing with people who are no longer alive, or who in some way cannot or will not take part in the forgiveness process. Understanding your family history and the patterns that have repeated from one generation to the next is designed specifically to give you the insight and understanding necessary to begin the process of reconciliation. The more able you are to identify the patterns, and the price people in your family have had to pay for them, the easier it will be to exonerate those with whom you are feuding.

We can learn a lot simply by studying the genogram. We may not know how many years of school they completed, or what they looked like, or what kind of work they did, but we can often tell where they stood in relationship to their sibling position, or what tragedies they might have had to live through in their family. We might learn that they were married and divorced several times, or that one of their children or siblings died of scarlet fever. Even if the information we have is minimal, we can still use that information productively.

When forgiving our ancestors, we don't step into the role of God and grant them pardons for their lives or behavior. What we can do, though, is use our understanding of forgiveness to move toward them in a conciliatory way, to symbolically release them from guilt or blame, and to accept and understand their role in our lives and in our history. By releasing them, we may discover that we will be released ourselves.

OUTRIGHT FORGIVENESS

The final aspect of the process of forgiveness can be referred to as outright forgiveness, in which both sides must play crucial roles. In order to achieve outright forgiveness, the one who has been hurt should reasonably expect the other person to take responsibility for causing the hurt. Because trust in the relationship has been damaged, legitimate reasons must be given for having created hurt in the first place. Stating these reasons demonstrates that responsibility for actions and behaviors has truly been taken. Furthermore, both sides must promise to refrain from doing further harm although it is never foolproof. When each person demonstrates that he or she is now trustworthy by making amends, or by consistently demonstrating trustworthiness with current actions, the scales of justice become more balanced and a more trusting relationship can develop. This restoration of a trusting relationship leads to the possibility of renewed love and compassion.

Part of outright forgiveness is giving each other the opportunity for restitution, or "making amends."

THE OPPORTUNITY FOR RESTITUTION

In a family feud, when you confront the truth as you see it, you give each side of the feud a chance to demonstrate honesty, love, and trustworthiness. To ensure emotional safety, however, you regulate the amount of trust you give to those who have proven unworthy of your trust in the past. You give them a little bit at a time, and watch to make sure they honor your trust in them. As they earn back your trust, you give them a little more. The more the person who has hurt you demonstrates an ability to act in a responsible, trustworthy way, the more able you will be to once again become vulnerable and enter into a loving, accepting relationship. Because real trust takes time to develop, the process of giving the opportunity for restitution is slow, occurring in piecemeal fashion rather than in a giant leap.

This is a very tricky step to take for many people locked in a family feud, because it requires making yourself vulnerable to someone who might hurt you again. You should refrain from asking for restitution specifically. You don't say, "You hurt me so badly I expect you to pay punitive damages in the amount of twenty thousand dollars." Instead, you extend yourself in such a way that you provide opportunities for the other person to redeem himself or herself over time. If you feel hurt or cheated because your sister stole the love of your life away from you, you can give her the opportunity to be entrusted with someone or something precious to you. When she handles that with love and care, and returns it to you, she earns a bit of her trustworthiness back.

If you blame your father for beating you severely as a child, you slowly and in small increments allow him to take care of your own child, perhaps initially with someone else present, with the articulated caveat that there be no physical discipline. As he engages with your child in a more respectful, loving way, he begins to slowly earn his way back into a trusting relationship.

The more specific you can be in determining what is expected, the more able you will be to judge whether or not you have earned each other's trust. If you simply say to your family member, "I want you to be more respectful of my feelings," it may be difficult for the family member to know just what to do. If you add something more specific, such as, "I'd like you to watch my son once a week," or "I'd like you to call me on the phone at least once a month," or "I'd like you to ask me questions about how my life is going," there can be no doubt about what you expect to see happen and to what extent each of you has met the other's expectations.

In a family feud, both sides of the feud are well aware that there have been hurts and usually a long separation. Regardless of what specific events may have sparked the feud in the past, the reconciliation and the healing of these old wounds always occurs in the present. For the most part, the healing occurs as both sides of the feud engage each other in different ways, continually testing the water to make sure it is safe to go in. As both parties succeed in creating trust over time, the old hurts and feelings of being taken advantage of or being violated diminish.

THE OVERT ACT OF FORGIVENESS

This last component of forgiveness differs from the others in that it is not a process that is drawn out over time. Instead, the overt act of forgiveness consists of an act or ritual that the two parties go through together. It is through this ritual that the two parties agree to begin their relationship anew. Each side "cancels out any claim to the injustice," and the two parties align themselves together in trust and love. In order to achieve this new covenant, three prerequisites must be met: agreement that a severe and meaningful violation transpired between them (although exact agreement on the specific details need not occur); an acknowledgment of responsibility by each person for the violation that resulted in the hurt; and an apology from each person, demonstrating regret for the wrongs that were done. This genuine apology requires a willingness on the part of the other person to accept the apology; otherwise the apologetic gesture will fail to achieve a re-balancing of the relationship. Furthermore, each person needs to offer genuine forgiveness, and the other person must accept the forgiveness, or they will not have reached the point where they can begin again.

Overt acts of forgiveness are usually helpful to both parties, regardless of whether you see yourself at any moment in time as a victim or a perpetrator. As a victim, you can feel justified in your perceptions of who did what to whom, and begin to lay to rest self-doubts and confusion. As a victim, you may feel some guilt at having not dealt with these issues sooner, and holding a guillotine blade over the other person's head, finger poised steadfastly over the blade's trigger. As a perpetrator, you may also feel guilty for having caused another person pain, and even for having "gotten away with it" for so many years without having been called to task. Overt acts of forgiveness allow both sides to release some of their guilt and begin to move on.

Overt acts of forgiveness are usually accomplished through a ritual prescribed by a therapist, although they can be devised by any two or more people who want to move forward toward reconciliation. Rituals usually take the form of symbolic acts or routines in which important messages are exchanged, and are excellent ways of formalizing the forgiveness process. They can also serve as milestones in the transformation of a relationship. Like anything that can have powerful positive effects, rituals have risks and dangers as well.

On the positive side, rituals serve as powerful statements. They validate a victim's experience, making it very clear that one's perceptions are accurate. When rituals are performed in the presence of others, it's difficult to "take back" what is accomplished through symbolically representing what you're trying to say. Rituals create a marker in the life span of a family, because they are out of the ordinary and serve as a way of saying, "What once was is no longer. We are closing one chapter and opening another." Similar to a funeral, rituals also provide a sense of closure, allowing emotions to be expressed in a contained fashion. And rituals create a lasting memory that can be referred back to at times when things seem to take a turn for the worse, reminding people of the vows they may have taken or the positive step they took.

It is essential, however, that people be ready for rituals. Done prematurely, they can be ingenuine and accomplish nothing. Rituals require the active involvement of both parties in the feud, so they can only be performed when both parties are willing. Often, one side of the feud may not remember (or choose not to remember) the details of what occurred in the past, so an apology may appear to be false. Rituals can also give the illusion that everything is now better, when in fact genuine, meaningful forgiveness remains a process that occurs over a long period of time.

In order for rituals to be effective, it's necessary that both parties come to some agreement beforehand on what happened in the past. While the details are often difficult to remember, there must be consensus that harm has been done, and each person must take responsibility for the harm. Each person must be willing to make a commitment to work toward forgiveness, and must agree to perform the ritual as a beginning step in healing old wounds.

Here are descriptions of some rituals used by therapists that can be adapted for use by you and your family.

Burial ritual. This ritual requires that an object that symbolizes the harm done by the perpetrator be brought to the other party. That object is then buried and laid to rest. One wife who had a history of violently beating her husband brought in a lock of her hair, a reference to Samson's source of power. She took this lock of her hair, apologized to her husband for her violence, and promised to do everything in her power not to repeat her destructive behavior. She then proceeded to bury the lock of her hair in her backyard, telling her husband that if she felt like her assaultive behavior was coming on, she would go to the backyard, sit down next to the grave of her hair, and remember her promise.

One man who had an affair with a woman had kept a watch she had given him as a gift. Despite having told his wife about the affair, and ending it, he had never told her that the watch was a gift from his paramour, instead saying he bought it himself. As a way of reassuring his wife that he was remaining faithful to her, he brought the watch in along with a hammer. He explained that he had lied, and that the watch was actually a gift from his ex-lover. He apologized once again for having hurt her by his actions and by his deception, committed himself to being faithful, smashed the watch with the hammer, and threw the pieces in the trash.

Contriteness rituals. It's not uncommon for the perpetrator to have difficulty remembering the details of events that he or she might prefer to forget. Because of the lack of trust that emanated from the original betrayal, the victim is often skeptical about whether or not the perpetrator is truly sorry and remorseful. Rituals designed to deal with this problem involve having the perpetrator perform a symbolic act demonstrating contriteness. This can include tearing a piece of clothing, wearing a sackcloth beneath one's clothes, shaving one's head, or making some important sacrifice. One verbally abusive husband agreed to deposit one hundred dollars in his wife's checking account every time he raised his voice in anger.

A common act of contriteness is for the perpetrator to get on his knees in front of the victim and simply ask for forgiveness. In some cases, when others in the family have been hurt by this person's actions, it's important that this action is done in front of them. This technique has been used by some family therapists specifically in cases of sexual abuse, in order to demonstrate publicly to the victim who is really at fault. While it may be humiliating, some humiliation as the cost of having hurt someone else may help to balance the scales, allowing old wounds to be buried and a new relationship to begin.

FORGIVING YOURSELF

When you move from blame to responsibility and you understand your own contributions to the feud, you must forgive yourself as well. That forgiveness can come in the form of exoneration, in which you understand yourself deeply and release yourself from culpability. As discussed previously, this process involves recognizing and honoring your own pain as legitimate, being compassionate with yourself, and putting an end to self-condemnation.

MAKING AMENDS

When the goal is the healing of the relationship, exoneration of yourself is only the beginning, although an important one. The kind of forgiveness that heals the hurt between two feuding parties occurs when you actually make amends and ask for forgiveness directly. Begin by talking to those whom you have hurt, letting them know your part in the feud. Tell them what you did to spark the feud. Tell them about the pain you felt, and what motivated you to do the things you did, *without making excuses.* Let them know that what you did was a result of your own pain, and that you don't hold them responsible for your pain or for your behavior. The more responsibility you can take, the more likely you will be to move toward reconciliation.

Forgiveness requires taking responsibility for what you did by performing some action to make up for the pain that was caused. You might feel uncomfortable doing this, especially in light of the fact that you have also suffered as a result of what the other person has done. Once again, though, you must hold your hand out to the person, even at the risk of being burned. You should be prepared for rejection, prepared for the same kind of response you have gotten in the past that may have ignited the feud.

Twelve-step programs, such as Alcoholics Anonymous, have a step that is referred to as "making amends." It's one of the most profound steps in the process of recovering from an addiction. It's a step that addresses the fact that one of the consequences of addiction to alcohol or other drugs is that many people have been hurt by it. When people make amends, they compensate for the harm they have done to others by doing something to repair the damage. Sometimes, amends are made without the person on the receiving end even knowing who the amends-maker is. The purpose of the anonymous gift is to make certain that the person who is making amends is not doing it in order to be liked or to receive anything in return. It also prevents the other person from feeling shame.

Making amends is a way of acknowledging that you've hurt someone, or of performing some action that you hope will balance the scales of justice. Even if you believe that the person may have hurt you as well, you are doing what you need to do to clear your own responsibility, to lift the burden of guilt from yourself.

Making amends can start with saying you are sorry, but it shouldn't end there. You must also ask if there is anything you can do to make up for the harm that you have caused. If you failed to pay someone to whom you owe money, you pay him or her what you owe and add reasonable interest—even if the lender tells you that he or she prefers not to receive it. If you failed to be emotionally or physically present or available to someone, you must offer to help him or her in some way that is meaningful to that person. If the person refuses to accept your offer, you need to find some way of unilaterally helping him or her. If he or she outright refuses to accept money, donate the money to charity, and inform the other person that you've done so. You might also perform some sort of community service, enabling you to work at least symbolically toward making amends.

Once you have made amends, the other person may see fit to forgive you for your part in the feud. Often, the other person sees no reason to forgive, because he or she doesn't feel that it is necessary. In that case, you can rest assured that you have done what you can do to be forgiven by the other person. Sometimes, the other party to the feud will spontaneously offer verbal forgiveness. And quite often, the amends that you make may be just the beginning of a long process in which both of you slowly recover your trust of one another, and slowly forgive each other, making amends as you go.

HEALING THE FAMILY TREE

Throughout this book, a link has been described between our family feuds today and the patterns of behavior our families inherited over the past generations. In a very real sense, who we are today, the way our families functioned when we were growing up, and the way the families that we have created function now are all determined by the patterns handed down to us from prior generations.

Several biblical passages emphasize this point. In one of them, we are told that the Lord visits "the iniquity of the fathers upon the children, and upon the children's children, to the third and to the fourth generation" (Exodus 34), and in another we are told that the Lord forgives "iniquity and transgression, but he will by no means clear the guilty, visiting the iniquity of fathers upon children, upon the third and upon the fourth generation" (Numbers 14). Throughout the Bible, and in the key documents of other major religions, the link between the behavior of one person and that person's progeny is clear; we are all in some way impacted by the behavior of those who came before us.

A recent political debate highlighted this issue. President Clinton declared that he personally apologized for the actions of his ancestors toward African-Americans who were enslaved in the United States. Furthermore, he wanted the American Congress to do the same. This action posed a dilemma: Is each of us today responsible for the behavior of his or her ancestors? Those on one end of the debate declared, with the rugged individualism that is embedded into the national character, that no individual is responsible for those who came before, for people who we don't know or whose behavior we might not have even condoned at the time. One cannot apologize "by proxy." Others believed that all of us are linked together in a more profound way and share the accomplishments as well as the burdens of those who came before us. If we suffer as a result of the behavior of our ancestors, or benefit from their behavior, then we must also be responsible for their behavior. One cannot reap someone else's harvest without sharing in the responsibility for how that harvest was sown. In that sense, an apology for the behavior of our ancestors is perfectly reasonable.

From the perspective of a family therapist, it's clear that the behavior and actions of those who came before us affect us deeply. That is not the same thing, however, as saying that each of us is ultimately responsible for something someone else in our family has done. As is so often true in political debates, there is a tendency to take complex issues with much gray in them and make them black and white. While it is true that we are genetically and behaviorally linked to those who came before us, and that we usually share in their wealth when they become wealthy and suffer when they are poor, it is also true that as individuals we can squander their wealth with our own ineptitude, immaturity, or bad fortune. We can also make our own wealth when we were given little.

We are not, therefore, merely products of our history. Especially as adults, by choosing to live our lives the way we do, we make our own history. Our children and their children will make of it what they will. Yet there can be no doubt that the family patterns that have existed in our families for generations play a strong role in influencing our families today.

That is why when we forgive ourselves and those with whom we are directly feuding, we are only going part of the way to resolve a family feud. While it may seem odd, forgiving our ancestors is also an important part of healing our family tree.

Because our ancestors are no longer around, we cannot reconcile with them. We cannot perform overt acts of forgiveness; we cannot make amends to them or they to us. In many cases, we may have no idea who these ancestors are. But we can perform the work of exoneration, and in so doing at least symbolically free ourselves from the burden of their past behavior.

What good does it do to exonerate someone who you might not even know, someone who you might not have even heard of until after you've learned something about your family history? Here are some reasons why I believe exonerating your ancestors is an important step in healing your family tree:

1. *Doing so makes it easier to understand the patterns in your family and how powerful those patterns can be.* Exonerating those who came before you requires studying your genogram, doing your best to understand as much as you can about your ancestors (even with very little information), and thinking about the role they played in the long history of your family. As you do that, you increase your understanding of your family patterns, and you better understand the power they have in determining the events that occur in your family. The concepts discussed in this book come to life when they are illustrated by the lives of the real people in your family.

2. *We don't forgive others to change them. We do so because it helps us move forward in our lives.* The goal of exonerating your ancestors is not necessarily to save them from eternal damnation, but to help each of us move forward in our lives. It is an exercise that permits us to take our understanding of our families to new levels, and therefore, to understand ourselves more deeply. Because the feelings of blame that exist prior to exoneration interfere with our current relationships, exonerating our ancestors helps to clean out whatever cobwebs of blame might exist in the corners of our house. In situations where we actually did know the ancestors whom we exonerate, a more direct benefit accrues as we release ourselves from the burden of our own anger toward them.

3. *It creates a catharsis, a release of feelings of anger and guilt.* When we exonerate our ancestors, we let go of whatever residues of anger and

guilt we might be feeling. Negative emotions get washed away as we imagine their lives and let go of the blame.

4. *It symbolically helps you come to terms with your own internal conflicts.* The more we know about our ancestors, the more we get a sense of their unique characters. We get to know Uncle Joe as a "lady's man" and Aunt Elizabeth as a "devoted mother." As we think about how their behavior fits in the puzzle of our complex family tree, we identify with them. We think of the parts of ourselves that may be like them. We might have heard that Uncle Joe got in trouble once for flirting with Aunt Elizabeth's best friend, and that may remind ourselves of our own flirtatiousness. We can see on our genogram how Aunt Elizabeth lost two children at a young age, and it might remind us of our own grief over similar losses. As we meditate about the impact these discoveries had on our families, we meditate about our own conflicts and our own pain. When we exonerate those who came before us, we often experience a mirroring of that exoneration within ourselves. We let go of the suffering we might hold our ancestors accountable for, while simultaneously feeling a relief from our own.

5. *It helps you to focus on the link between prior generations and present generations, making it easier for you to see how you might be repeating these patterns with your own children—therefore helping the generations to come.* As you exonerate your ancestors, you focus on the linkages between their behavior, their position in the family, and the same patterns in the current generation. As you do this, the ways in which patterns may be repeating themselves among you and your children become clearer. You can then use this knowledge to prevent these patterns from taking root in your children's generation, helping to heal your family tree for generations to come.

When we exonerate our ancestors, we use the tools discussed earlier in this chapter to free them of the burden of our blame. We make every effort to understand their lives, the patterns that they inherited, and the patterns they may have passed on. We think about the struggles they had to bear, and imagine how they might have tried to cope with them. Once we come to the fullest knowledge we have of their lives and their position in the family, we simply attempt to release them. We can do it in words, out loud, or we can say it in our minds. We can write about them in journals, or write them letters. Ultimately, we tell them that although there is much that we don't and cannot know about them, we take what we do know, relate what we know about them to our own lives, and find in ourselves a way to be compassionate. With our compassion, we symbolically reach out to them, embrace them, and tell them that to the extent to which we can, we release them from blame.

What follows is the story of how Ashley, a twenty-six-year-old graduate student in chemistry, went about exonerating her ancestors. The process took place over a period of about nine months. Originally, Ashley sought help because she was feeling depressed, unhappy about her life in general and particularly unhappy about her relationships with men. Although she saw herself as a "good catch," bright and attractive, she managed to end up with men whom she described as "uninspiring." Shortly after beginning to see her, I learned about a feud she had with her father. She hadn't spoken to him for over a year after she visited him once and he was "drunk, stoned and rude to me."

Ashley was familiar with doing genograms from college courses she had taken in genetics, and took to the exercise with gusto and a scientist's passion for precision. She researched her family thoroughly, and proudly handed me a rather complex chart. It turned out that her family was riddled with enmeshment, triangulation, and secrets, and that a serious feud had been present in at least the three generations that came before her. Ashley recognized the enmeshment that existed between her and her father, and saw similar enmeshment between daughters and fathers for several generations. Ashley also was able to make the insightful connection between her feud with her father and her difficulty accepting his own inadequacies. As an enmeshed daughter, it was too painful for her to see how his alcoholism and drug addiction was ruining his life and the lives of many of those around him. As a child, Ashley refused to acknowledge that her father was anything but a saint, even though his behavior didn't warrant such a generous view.

In the first few months of our work together, Ashley realized that she needed to find a way of reconciling with her father. She courageously telephoned him, and set up a meeting on her terms. She insisted that he appear sober at a restaurant near her school. When he did,

Ashley shared with him her disappointment, and prompted him to discuss his own life and his own pain. While he was able only to do this a bit, Ashley began to see him more as a pathetic character, someone whom she loved dearly, but who wasn't the same person she thought he was. As she understood his life more, and was able to put it into the larger context of the multigenerational family history, Ashley became less angry and more accepting. She was able to forgive him, while setting the terms for their future relationship and accepting his limitations.

This was an important process for Ashley; afterward she felt greatly relieved, and felt as though she had "grown up" considerably. She also saw how her relationships with other men were repetitions of her relationship with her father, and how she chose men who, like her father, could not meet her needs. But seeing the pervasive feuds in her family tree concerned Ashley. Afraid that she would be passing on these patterns to her yet unborn children, she gathered as much information as she could about the rest of her family.

At my recommendation, Ashley kept a "reconciliation journal." This was a journal in which she was to write short biographies of the key players in her family history. Her stories read like a novel, a collection of intriguing vignettes that included scoundrels, murderers, adulterers who seemed like the rule rather than the exception, and a smattering of heroes whose model lives were stark contrasts to the others. Most relevant to Ashley was the fact that there was enmeshment and triangular betrayal galore in her family.

I also suggested that Ashley attempt to find photographs of the characters who populated her family tree. A visual image often makes people come alive in ways that stories cannot. With the help of her mother, Ashley was able to find pictures of about half of the twenty or so family members she felt played pivotal roles in the family history. For those she found pictures of, she taped a picture to the short biographical sketch she had written of that family member.

I asked Ashley to take a week to think about each key family member, shuttling back and forth between their biographical sketch and their position in the family as represented on her genogram. Ashley was to think about the kinds of things each family member had to contend with in their lives: their educational level, their occupation, their relationships with their parents and their siblings, the traumas that were going on around them, and the pressures and roles they lived with. At the end of each week, she was to recount what she thought.

Ashley brought in the following description of one of her family members:

> *Uncle Jeff. (machinist, married to Katherine Lee, 2 sons, 1 daughter, died of bone cancer) I understand just some of what you had to contend with in your life. I know your older sister died when you were only three, and I imagine your mother went through hell trying to survive that devastating loss. It must have been hard for her to pay much attention to you when she was grieving so much. She might have put tremendous pressure on you to be a success, to take the place of her precious daughter. I know your father was a tyrant. He apparently beat you and your mother terribly. That must have been terribly hard on you too.*
>
> *You must have inherited the family curse, because I know you got into a lot of trouble with the law, that you were caught stealing. Your father must have beaten you to a pulp when he found out, but you kept on doing it. You must have been incredibly angry, and unbelievably hurt to do those things.*
>
> *As part of a long line of Johnsons, I felt a lot of the same pressures you did. Like you, I had a father who was a tyrant to my mother, although he was usually good to me. Recently, though, I've learned that he was a lot more like your father than I ever knew. My dad didn't beat my mother with his fists, but he abused her with his words. Unlike you, I tried to be a good girl, to make everyone in my family happy, especially my dad. You went the other way, but I think both of us suffered a great deal.*
>
> *You died even before I was born, so you had no way of knowing how your life and the choices you made would affect me. For all I know, you did the best you could, given how you were treated. I accept you and accept you as part of my history, and I won't blame you or hold you responsible for my life.*

After a few months of writing and reviewing her reconciliation journal, Ashley felt a tremendous relief. She said that she felt as though she was able to get rid of a lot of "emotional baggage," but most importantly she felt a renewed sense of her own identity. Remembering who she was helped her to remember what she wanted in life, and she realized that she didn't have to "settle" for men who didn't challenge her. This is how she described her experience of exonerating her ancestors:

I felt an incredible sense of belonging. It was weird. I moved so far away from the family, to be away from all that craziness. Yet I discovered that in a strange way I really belong to that family. I'm a Johnson through and through. I feel lucky that I didn't go in some of the same directions a lot of my relatives went, but sometimes now I think of how easy it would be to do something really crazy, something that would really get me in a lot of trouble. There's a much thinner line there than I thought.

I'm grateful for them, though. Because I understand now that I'm a lot more than I thought I was. I'm not just a good girl from a crazy family. They're a part of me too, and there's a lot of craziness in me too. And it's not exactly that I'm proud of it, it just makes me more interesting. It kind of gives me permission to be more than just a proper, perfect angel. For years I felt trapped in that role, and I think it's made me more boring than I really am. So it's kind of special to come from this family, and I'm kind of special to be in it.

Forgiveness, whether it takes the form of an attitude, an overt act, or exoneration, is the most powerful tool we have in reconciling with our family members. When we're able to forgive, we've come far along the path of reconciliation. With forgiveness firmly in place, we're ready to turn toward those who we believe may have hurt us in the past, and begin a relationship in which renewed love and mutual support may once again be possible.

ten

The Courage to Confront

Courage is the price that life exacts for granting peace.

—AMELIA EARHART

RESOLVING A FAMILY FEUD CAN BE ONE OF THE MOST DIFFICULT TASKS IN YOUR LIFE. MANY PEOPLE I'VE KNOWN WOULD RATHER WALK OVER a bed of hot coals than to be caught in the same room (or city, for that matter) as the person with whom they are feuding.

For some, the pain of revisiting old conflicts is just too great. We fear the feelings that might emerge, we worry about rocking the boat and making the situation even worse. Powerful feelings contained in the silence make the proverbial can of worms too daunting to open, too laced with dangerous, sharp edges.

Yet the need to resolve a family feud is often equal to or greater than the fears. Many people know that resolving their feuds is a necessary step in their own growth; they know that not resolving their feuds is a stumbling block that stands in the way of all attempts at intimacy with others, not just with those with whom they are feuding. During the course of my work, I've been inspired by people whose pain and anguish seemed insurmountable, yet they managed to accomplish meaningful and lasting reconciliations. Having been honored to be allowed on the sidelines to coach these remarkable people, I find their stories difficult to forget. What stands out most is their courage.

Reaching back to about twelve years ago, I remember being called in to consult on a family in which one brother cut himself off from the other siblings, after learning of their sister's brutal murder by her cocaine-driven husband. This brother, Darrell, blamed his siblings for not doing enough to protect their sister from her husband. After two years of grieving for her loss, the family was torn in half. The rest of the siblings not only lost their sister, but they lost their brother as well, and in so doing also lost the integrity and support of a loving, tight-knit family. When a few of the remaining family members first appeared at my office, I succeeded in convincing the mother of all the siblings that it was necessary to bring all the surviving family members together in a room. A week later, six remaining family members sat in a lopsided circle—a sister, two brothers, their mother, and two young boys (the children of the sister who was shot, now living with the surviving sister). Darrell sat with his chair set apart from the rest of the circle, off to the side and slightly behind them. The gap in the circle next to Darrell reminded me of a space for their murdered sister. After I commented that Darrell's positioning of himself away from the rest of the family might partly be a respectful way of making room in the family for his sister, several family members began to cry. When their mother commented that she believed her daughter was with them all the time, Darrell's agitation turned into anger. He turned to the rest of the family and, seething with anger, told them that his life was not the same, and that it never would be. The other siblings gently confronted him, telling him that their lives had not been the same either. They talked about their difficulties dealing with their loss, and talked about the blessing that now their sister's two young children, although without a mother, can be brought up in a loving home without drugs.

The turning point came when Darrell's remaining sister met Darrell's outrage with an equal measure of her own intense emotion. She turned to him and, with a mixture of anger and sadness, told him how enraged she was that his cutting himself off from the family was forcing her to lose two siblings. She couldn't save her sister, although she had tried on many occasions to help her, but she didn't want to lose him as well. Although the isolated, brooding, and feuding brother had barely spoken with his siblings in two years, instead making his feelings known through his mother, he was now being forcefully but lovingly prodded to share his discontent directly with his siblings. When they reacted with kindness, reaching out to meet his pain with their own, he slowly came to realize that his blame of them was merely a cover for his own guilt that he didn't do enough, and he was able to regain the support and comfort of a family who cared for him deeply. Facing his family meant facing his own pain; and I'll never forget the courage that Darrell mustered in order to expose his grief and his vulnerabilities to those from whom he sought to hide.

Susan was an actress in her late twenties, separated from the rest of her family by about twelve hundred miles of road and nearly seven years of silence. She came to me in a deep depression, after making several suicide attempts. Susan told me, softly and with embarrassment, that she felt numb most of the time, so every few months she would take a razor and slice away at her wrists; it wasn't until she felt the cold steel and saw blood oozing that she felt alive again. The pain and the bleeding helped her to remember who she was and from where she came, and it gave her the "relief" she needed from having to hold in her feelings.

Her ongoing feud with her mother was a constant source of pain. She had a desperate wish to feel loved and cared for by a mother who could see her for who she really was, instead of the cardboard character Susan believed her mother actually saw. The source of Susan's pain—years of sexual abuse beginning when she was five years old—was no mystery to Susan. She had been in treatment groups and had read plenty of books. Over the years Susan had come to grips with the rage she felt toward her father and stepfather, who both molested her. Reconciling with the mother who betrayed her years ago by not believing that she was molested, and continued to betray her by refusing to see and acknowledge Susan's pain, was another story. The fact that Susan's mother remained in a comfortable relationship with Susan's stepfather, one of the men who molested Susan, didn't help matters. Yet, through three years of on-and-off coaching, helping Susan to understand her mother while honoring her own pain, Susan was able to establish contact with her mother. Susan reached into the part of herself that was most difficult to find—her desire to be a mother herself, and her wish to heal the hurt that drove her to the brink of death—and found the courage to confront her mother. Using a series of carefully planned phone calls, and then eventually meeting with her mother, Susan was able to deal directly with the ghosts that chilled the nights of her second decade of life.

Sam, a fifty-year-old psychologist, despite a silent feud with his younger and only brother that stemmed from an ongoing dislike and distrust going back more than thirty years, got in touch with an aching loneliness. As he looked back over his life, he realized that although he was close to his wife and children, Sam felt terribly alone. Both his parents had died, and his only brother Mike lived three thousand miles away. The two brothers had spoken only twice in the past twenty years, an emotional distance arising from what Sam called "two completely different views of the world." They were two brothers who grew up in complete opposition to one another. Sam was primarily intuitive, Mike was basically rational. Sam was a Democrat, Mike a staunch Republican. Sam committed his life to helping others, Mike was focused completely on himself. Yet they shared the same bedroom as children, and the same parents. They heard the same arguments, and ate dinner at the same table.

Sam resented his brother, because he felt all their lives that he was the one who initiated any contact. The last thing Sam wanted to do was to reach out once again, trying to make contact with someone who "wasn't home." Yet Sam's loneliness couldn't be soothed.

After initially resisting, Sam looked more closely at his family history. He looked at his genogram and discovered patterns he had never seen or given much thought to. When he understood his relationship with Mike as the culmination of a long history of divisiveness between siblings, it eased Sam's blame of his brother. Sam understood that the two of them were playing out a script that had been written before the two of them were born.

Feeling guilty himself about not having tried to contact Mike earlier, and fully expecting to be rejected, Sam mustered the courage to begin a series of contacts with his "long-lost" brother. As Sam said to me once: "Understanding what went on and why was easy. Picking up the phone and calling my brother, I just couldn't do it. That's the hardest thing of all. I really miss him, even though I don't really like him! I just found it hard to think that he'd see me as this bleeding-heart liberal wanting to make a connection when he wouldn't have the least bit of interest in me. It was like walking out on a gangplank, waiting for someone to push me from behind. But I knew I had to do it. I had to give it another try."

Just as Darrell and Susan found the courage they needed to face themselves and their families, Sam found the courage to make the initial phone call. To his surprise, Mike turned out to be more than interested in his brother Sam, and the two of them planned a reunion between both of their families. Their silent feud began to fade away as Sam found the courage to make the initial phone call.

The desire to move toward reconciliation is often the easiest part of the process; it's starting out on the journey that's the hardest. It takes courage to begin the journey in the first place. Many people will claim that it is a lack of understanding, not having a road map of the territory and the directions to the destination that is the problem. Yet once those directions are firmly in hand, these same people often fail to budge. It's not the lack of knowledge that prevents most people from moving, but instead the lack of courage.

Although I've become a great believer in the idea that many traits or temperamental characteristics are genetically inherited, I'm thoroughly convinced that courage is not one of them. Ultimately, courage must be learned. I remember once watching the brilliant family therapist Carl Whitaker having a conversation with a very depressed and suicidal man. The man asked Whitaker what the secret of life was, and in his characteristic way Whitaker unhesitatingly shot back three words: "Take more risks." Life was certainly a riskier proposition than death for this man, death being a certainty. And the only way we learn how to be courageous is to take risks. The more risks we take, the more we learn that we can survive them, and the more able we feel to face future risks.

For most people I talk with, being courageous means shunting fear and blindly moving forward. It means going back in the family, pretending everything is all right, and forging ahead. Attempting to resolve a family feud that way is foolish; it's merely a setup for a repetition of the same dance the family knows so well. We are afraid of facing those with whom we feud, because on some level we know well that to do so is fraught with danger. The danger might be that the person will do again the very things you felt hurt by, or that the person might even do something else to take advantage of you. These "familiar enemies" on the other side of the feud might deny that they ever did anything hurtful, and as a result we might feel injured further. We know that people change over time, but we also know that they don't change that much.

It is our fear that tells us that there is danger. It is the emotion that guides us through treacherous waters. Without our fear, we simply lose our way—as though our guidance mechanism is broken. A fascinating study was done at the end of World War II, in which the Rorschach inkblot tests of American fighter pilots who survived the war were compared with those pilots who were shot down and killed. It was discovered that of the many variables studied, the only thing that differentiated those who survived from those who didn't was that the ones who survived went into the war with more fear and anxiety. It appeared that it was their fear that led them to be less cocky, more vigilant, and better able to master the rigors of war. The other example that comes to mind is the one that most people think of when they think of courage—what to do when a building catches fire and there are people inside who need to be rescued. It has been persuasively argued that the person who blindly runs in to rescue those inside has very little chance of coming out alive. As the burning timbers fall, and smoke fills the house, it is the fear of being hurt that keeps a person aroused and vigilant enough to keep from making stupid mistakes.

Courage is the ability to combine our fears with action toward the very thing we fear. Too little fear leads to losing sight of the real dangers, acting foolishly and in ways in which we are likely to continue to be hurt. It's often been said that too much fear can be crippling as well, but it can only be crippling if we fail to act. Having tremendous fear only means that we need to think more, plan better, and from there begin to take action toward the thing we fear.

Understanding the multigenerational roots of your family feud is one of your most powerful tools. Hopefully, by completing your genogram you have isolated those patterns that have replayed themselves from one generation to the next and that have combined to create your feud. Simplified to two or three main points, you carry that understanding back into the family, and hold onto it firmly. With a sense of who's responsible for doing what, and less of a blaming attitude, you are now equipped with both an understanding of why the feud erupted and an attitude conducive to reconciliation. Now you must create the courage it takes to reenter the family, and move to the next step in creating a new family history.

CREATING CONTACT

In some families, merely understanding the roots of their feuds is enough to motivate family members to put their swords down and begin to make peace. But in most families, peace is more difficult to attain, especially if the feud has run for a long time. If the family member on the other side of the feud is still living, some form of contact must be made. The word "confrontation" is often used to describe this contact; it's a difficult word because it implies a hostile and aggressive stance. Rather than think of confrontation as hostile, think of it instead as strong, rigorous, or committed. We can confront sweetly, we can even confront gently and kindly; we just do it in a committed way. Confrontation also implies coming face to face with not only the darkness of the other side of the feud, but with one's own fears as well. When we confront others, we are confronting ourselves to an even greater extent. The challenge lies not only in picking up the telephone or writing a letter, but in confronting our own responsibility, our own ability to hold tightly to the truth, our ability to refuse to fall into the same patterns that have plagued us for many years. Successful confrontation of others depends exquisitely on successful confrontation of ourselves.

How contact is made with the other party can be important. For many people, establishing direct, face-to-face contact is too threatening and difficult a first step. For others, anything short of face-to-face contact is considered an "easy way out." There is no single "correct" way of making contact. You should honor and pursue whatever form of contact makes you most comfortable at the outset.

THE TELEPHONE

If you choose to make a phone call, often a simple "get acquainted" call works best as a place to start. This is simply an icebreaker, a phone call in which you expect little else than to say hello, to set the stage for future discussions. It may seem phony not to address the circumstances of the feud, or the reasons why twenty years have passed with no contact, but there are two things to remember. First, the call need not be phony. You can simply make a statement to the effect that "I know it's been a long time since we've talked, and I know there's a lot of history between us. I also know that there's a lot to talk about, but I don't think now is the time and place. I just wanted to let you know that I'm interested in working things out, and possibly setting up another time or place to talk more about those things."

The second thing to remember is that the other person obviously hasn't called you in twenty years either, so he or she has a stake in the feud as well. It may be just as much a relief to the other person not to go into a deeper discussion on the telephone, especially if the other person had no warning or indication that you were going to call. The timing is more likely to be bad for the other person than it is for you.

Remember that in the early stages of reconciling, you're not trying to change the other person. You must come from a place of accepting the other person as he or she is. Expect that he or she will behave the same as always toward you; you may have come a long way, but that doesn't mean the other person has. Be careful not to set yourself up for disappointment by expecting him or her to have changed.

In the unlikely event that the other person can't resist and begins to blame you for the feud, even to the point of berating you, it's important that you listen to what the other person has to say. If you find yourself getting too upset to continue without a blow-up between the two of you, simply say that it's hard for you to hear the other person when he or she talks to you that way, that you'd like to have a more civil conversation, and that when the other person calms down you'll be happy to continue the conversation. Even if the initial contact turns out to be a blame-fest, if you are able to end the conversation with an understanding that you would like to have more contact in the future, you have been remarkably successful in breaking the silence of many years duration.

THE LETTER

On the other hand, if the feud you are engaged in is one of continual rageful barrages, and you already have contact (it's just not the kind of contact you'd like), then the challenge is a different one. In this kind of feud, you must struggle to deintensify the feud, to take the transgenerational wind out of its sails. Writing letters is often a better approach than phone calls with these kind of feuds, because the lack of direct contact will prevent each of you from pressing each other's non-verbal buttons. Things that may be signals to set either of you off, such as "that whine in your voice that sounds like Mom," or "that sarcastic tone that makes me feel like shit" will be less apparent in a letter.

In general, letters are excellent ways to begin the process of healing. They offer many advantages over other forms of contact, and only a few disadvantages. One of the biggest advantages of a letter is that you have plenty of time to craft exactly what you want to say and how you want to say it. You can show it to other people to get their feedback and suggestions, helping you to discern where you might be unduly blaming, where your thinking gets muddy and confused, and where you might fail to say what needs to be said. With a letter, you can hold on to what you've written for a while, returning to it a week or so later in order to read it afresh and think about how it might feel to receive it.

As discussed in the last chapter, letters are also excellent ways of healing the family tree. The act of writing helps you clarify your thoughts. By putting your thoughts on paper, you no longer have to hold them in your mind, and you are free from trying to hold on to too many ideas at once. Knowing that you've put your ideas onto paper makes them permanent, with no risk of losing them to memory.

The biggest disadvantage of letters is that they are often written but never sent. In the case of writing to those who are no longer alive, this is obviously not an issue. It's often helpful to begin the letter-writing process by assuming that the letter won't be sent, so that you can say whatever you like without having to worry about the consequences. You are writing a first draft to be honed later. But when trying to reconcile with someone who is still living, it can be tempting to write a draft letter and stop there. Because so much emotional energy is spent on just getting something on paper, there is little emotional energy left to find the courage to take the letter to the mailbox. At some point, in order to be an effective method of making contact, the letter must be sent.

In writing letters, there are a few guidelines I recommend.

- The letter should be written without anger.

- Summarize what you've learned about the family, and what you think are the real underlying issues beneath the feud.

- Tell the other person what *you* are willing to do to make things better between you. If you don't know, ask what the other person would need to see happen in order to begin the process of healing old wounds. Don't insist or demand that the other person do anything differently.

- Do not make the letter too long.

Here are two "introductory" letters that were successful at reestablishing contact between people who had been feuding for some time. In both cases, I worked with the authors to edit these down from their original lengths.

Dear Mom:

I know we haven't spoken in many years, and I'm not even sure you really want to speak to me. I thought it would be a good idea to write to you because I didn't want to put you off guard with a phone call when you weren't expecting it. I know there's a lot that happened between us, and I have been working hard to understand it. There's a lot that I still don't understand. I know there were a lot of decisions I made in my life that you didn't approve of. Marrying Bill against your advice I know was really a blow to you and the rest of the family. I've been doing a lot of thinking and I know there's plenty of other things I've done that have hurt you. I know you know that I have felt hurt by you many times also, and have stayed distant to avoid fighting.

I know that by trying to understand things I've really blamed you for a lot of what went wrong in my life. You probably blame me as well for not being a good enough daughter. One of the things I've really come to understand is that you worked hard at being the best parent you could be, and that you did what you thought was right based on what happened to you in your life. The things you did that I still don't understand I think I would be able to understand if I knew more about you and what happened to you in your childhood. I do know that we've both made some of the same mistakes. As a mother that must have been hard for you to watch.

I guess I'm trying to say that while we have blamed each other for many years, maybe we all did the best we could under the circumstances. I think that there's a long history of people not really knowing how to get along in

*our family. It didn't just start with us. I'd like us to stop blaming each other
and try to begin to make things better between us.*

*If you'd be willing, maybe a good place to start is to talk on the phone
and catch up with each other. That may be hard for both of us, but I think
it would be worth it. I'd like to hear more about your life, and I'd like to
listen to you without getting angry. That's what I've always done, and I
want to change that. Please call or write me if you want.*

Your daughter,
Laura

This letter elicited an immediate telephone call from Laura's mother,
who tearfully told Laura how painful it had been for her to endure their
years of distance from each other. It was the beginning of a new dialogue between the two of them that eventually led to Laura's discov-
ery of several generations of detached feuding in her family.

Jeff's letter to his father took him about three months to write. After
being told by his father that Jeff was a "flake," Jeff was informed that
his portion of his father's inheritance would be held in a trust, and
doled out as an "allowance," despite the fact that Jeff was now fifty
years old and maintained a respectable job as a house painter. The
process of writing this letter was a frequently frustrating exercise for
Jeff, because each time he brought me a draft I would point out the
bitterness and anger that remained. While the goal was to remain genuine, it was clear that until Jeff understood his father's point of view,
and the reasons for it, Jeff's anger would dominate any efforts made toward reconciliation. Jeff wasn't ready to reconcile his relationship with
his father until he was able to better understand, emotionally, his father's point of view, as well as the powerful patterns in his family that
led up to the feud. Once he was able to accomplish this, his anger
would be considerably less intense, and he would be able to approach
his father in a way more likely to succeed. This is how Jeff's final letter looked:

Dear Dad:

*It's been a long time since we've talked to each other. Many things have
happened in my life, just like they have in yours. From our talks I know
you're not happy about what I've done with my life.*

I want you to know that I've worked very hard at trying to understand our relationship and our family. I learned that I've spent a great deal of my life rebelling against you. That must have been hard for you, because I know you really believed in me and wanted me to succeed the way you did. I know that my experimenting with drugs, my lifestyle, and my choices about the kind of work I do were all hard for you. As you always used to say, you pulled yourself up by your bootstraps, and I'm proud of you for it.

In looking at our family I realize that I wasn't the only rebellious one. I learned more about Uncle Nate, and how unhappy your father was with him. I learned that I'm a lot like Uncle Nate, and I know you were very disappointed in him too. I know that Uncle Nate was a gambler, and wasted all his money, and I'm sure you're worried that I would do the same.

One of the things you always preached was that anybody can start all over and bounce back even from the worst situations. My life is going good right now, and I'd like to try to bounce back from the bad place our relationship is in. I'd like to get together with you to try to start out on a new foot. I'd like to meet over lunch, just to try to get to know each other better, and talk about some of the things I've learned about our family. It's also really important to me to get your opinions about our family, so that I can understand things from your position too.

Love,
Jeff

Jeff's father responded with a phone call, and the two of them arranged to have lunch together. After a carefully planned lunch, in which Jeff did nothing but share the results of his genogram and get more information, the two developed a common interest and eventually worked their way out of a feud that had lasted for almost a decade.

WHAT SHOULD I TALK ABOUT?

Many people who attempt to establish contact with someone in the family with whom they have not spoken in many years find themselves wondering what to talk about. The first thing to keep in mind is that typically people like to talk about themselves more than they like to talk about anything else. Be inquisitive; ask people to talk about their lives, their ups and downs, struggles with their children, accomplishments, interests, work, and so forth. If the person with whom you're reestablishing contact is not a "talker," you might be better off listening as much as you can, and then talking about yourself. In a friendly manner, open up as you would with anyone who you're just beginning to have a relationship with. Tell the other person what your life has been about, what you've been doing all these years. Just as people typically love talking about themselves, most people are voyeuristic at heart, as the popularity of soap operas suggests. The more comfortable and at ease you are talking about your life, the more it sets the other person at ease as well.

I REALLY DON'T LIKE THIS PERSON

A common rationalization for avoiding making contact is to take the stance that "I really don't like this person. Why should I establish contact with someone I don't like? Isn't this ingenuine?" You already understand that reestablishing contact with someone with whom you've been feuding will not only help you to heal other relationships in your own life, but it will also help you to prevent a continuation or recurrence of the same patterns in your family in future generations. Remember, the work you do now to free yourself from the patterns that created the feud to begin with will pay off in generations to come; future generations will be less likely to "inherit" the damaging patterns that came before them.

As for the fact that you don't like the person with whom you've been feuding, it's important to examine this a bit closer. So often we have no way of really knowing whether we like someone or not if our views of that person are colored by years of anger and resentment. It's easy to recognize how distorted our views of the truth become when we have an axe to grind with someone. Similarly, if we have spent years avoiding someone, we have lost the ability to see who he or she is now. What we dislike about people is often what we believe they've done to us, what they've done to others (stories that we may not know the other side of), where they came from (no choice of their own), or whom they associated with. Knowledge of the person himself or herself is often obscured by these observations. Frequently when people do end up getting to know their "familiar enemies," they feel a sense of surprise at how much they are alike. Getting to know a person better is often the surest antidote to hating that person.

Even if the truth turns out to be that there is so much about the other person you don't like that your overall impression is negative, for the sake of your own reconciliation and for the sake of your family it's often helpful to struggle to find at least one thing about this person that is likable. Find one positive attribute or quality and, without discounting the rest of the truth, keep this one quality in mind when dealing with this person.

EXPECTATIONS FOR CHANGE

Another frequently heard statement from those who have difficulty finding the courage to face other family members is this: "I know nothing will change, so why put out the effort?" The effort you put forth to resolve a feud is not made in order to change another person, but instead to change yourself in relation to the other person, and to set an example for your own offspring of how to deal with other people whether you like them or not.

Change does happen in reconciling family feuds, and the change is often dramatic, rewarding, and exciting. I have had many family members who have confronted difficult feuds tell me that they feel as though they are gaining a family they never had, and it is a rich and rewarding experience. But you have to keep in mind that most change is slow to take root. Expecting that change will occur slowly is often the best medicine for preventing disappointment. Most people who struggle to overcome feuds will tell you that in the early stages they often feel like Don Quixote, tilting at windmills. But as the feud begins to break down, the payoffs begin to sink in. Give yourself time to make small changes; in the long run these are the kinds of changes that last. Be patient. Even if the reconciliation takes years, you will feel better knowing that you are on the right track, and not continuing to avoid the work that needs to be done.

At the beginning of this chapter, I mentioned the feud between

Susan, the suicidal actress in her late twenties, and her mother. During the three years of working together, there were times when Susan worked very hard on facing her pain and working up the courage to face her mother. She constantly struggled with the fear that when she finally got in touch with her mother, she would once again have to face her mother's denial and disbelief that her husband had molested her daughter. When Susan finally did make contact with her mother, they initially established a friendly, superficial connection—the kind they had many years before the feud. Susan was prepared to face the fact that her mother was no different from what she had been a long time ago—still the same conservative, Bible-wielding woman filled with denial of what was going on around her. But rather than being devastated by this, Susan slowly, patiently, and compassionately pursued her mother's understanding, until her mother finally was able to face the truth. As Susan related it to me not long ago:

> *Of course I'll never have the mother I want, but Ira, at least now I have a mother. Who has a perfect mother anyway? Who is a perfect mother? The important thing is that she believes me, and I think she knows who I am as much as she could ever know who anybody is. I can talk "girl talk" with her on the phone, and I have a place I can call home. It sounds stupid, but I really love getting cards from her—it's just the way I was brought up. I love sending cards to everyone else, it's nice to get them from your mother. And she knows the truth about Bill [her stepfather] and at least for a while she made him go to therapy. She still lives with him, but that's her life. She's got to put up with the guilt, not me. So she may not be everything, but having a relationship with her means everything to me.*

Susan's words reflect a more realistic view of her mother than her earlier fantasy. She was able to do for her mother what she hoped her mother would do for her: accept her for who she really was. Just as her mother had harbored a fantasy of her daughter that was different than the reality, Susan harbored a fantasy of her mother as better able to deal with the truth than in fact she was. Once Susan was able to gauge her expectations of her mother to the truth, accepting her mother for who she was, her mother was able to do the same with Susan.

SEEKING THE RIGHT MOMENTS

While it's important to make an effort to create the right circumstances, often change occurs by looking for the right opportunities and "seizing the moment." Steve was a thirty-two-year-old firefighter who complained that his mother was so intrusive that he had to do everything in his power to avoid her. When I saw him, he wasn't in a feud with his mother, although he told me that when he was in his late teens he left home and hadn't spoken to his mother for several years because he just "needed his space." After reconciling with her, he continuously fought with her, and it was nearing the point where he was going to tell her that he no longer wanted to have anything to do with her again.

Running his fingers through his short-cropped blond hair, Steve smiled as he told me that his answering machine was his best friend, because it forced distance between him and his mother, who refused to leave messages on it. Every time he heard a dial tone emanating from his answering machine he assumed it was his mother, and he felt a sigh of relief.

Despite my coaching Steve that he needed to learn how to "put out the fires" created by his mother's intrusiveness by calling her and setting limits on her behavior, this was very difficult for him to do. It wasn't until one Sunday morning, after Steve had been working for three days straight, that he found the right moment to confront his mother. The phone rang three times within a half-hour period, and each time his answering machine blared a loud dial tone. The tone that had come to be more annoying than a fire engine's siren was the wake-up call that Steve needed to confront his mother. He called her, confirmed that it was indeed she who had called three times, and he used his anger as the spark he needed to ignite the fuse of his own ability to set limits with his mother. In no uncertain terms, he recited some of the same language he and I used together to proclaim his limits. "I'm no longer a child," he told his mother, "and I expect the same kind of respect and consideration you'd show your friends. From now on, either leave a message on my machine or don't call at all. And all I need is one message to know that you've called. Once you've left a message, I'll call you back when I'm able to." Steve's sternness with his mother prevented an uncomfortable situation from turning into a feud.

Committing yourself to working on reconciliation means that you should keep your eyes open for opportunities to present themselves to you. These opportunities often drive home the points you are trying to make better than talking about them later. In my office I know that whatever message I try to give sinks in much more deeply if I'm able to say, "You're doing this right now with me." Whether it's confronting someone's denial, or demonstrating how words don't necessarily match actions, the ability to point out the activity as it's happening makes it much more difficult to refute or deny.

Family events. Often, seizing the right moment involves learning of a family event in which the member on the other side of the feud is going to be present. It may be a wedding, funeral, bar or bat mitzvah, graduation ceremony, or confirmation. If this occurs, you might find yourself "rushed into action," needing to prepare for the event emotionally or deciding not to go at all. This is a common conundrum, and in fact it's often news of the upcoming event that brings people into therapy to see me. A new client will say, "I've been avoiding my brother for years, and now I know he's going to be at my parents' fiftieth wedding anniversary. I can't let my parents down by not going, but I'm afraid of what's going to happen between me and my brother if I do go. One of us might make a scene, or at the least it will be uncomfortable for both of us."

This common situation forces people to do some quick work, or to avoid the family event altogether. It's usually better to do whatever work can be done before the event, understanding as well as possible the multigenerational roots of the feud, and planning some strategies for how to handle situations that might come up. Even though it is wise to *expect* as little as possible, the more preparation that can be done ahead of time, the more likely the event will not only go well, but can be a watershed for healing deep divisions.

PLANNING THE CONFRONTATION

While seeking the right moment to put your new best foot forward is important, there is really no substitute for planned change. It's difficult to seize the moment if you have no idea what you want to say or how you want to act differently. Spontaneity is undoubtedly a wonderful gift, but "planned spontaneity" is divine. Planning involves figuring out ahead of time just how, when, and where you are going to act differently.

Considering how and what you are going to say, even to the point of writing down key phrases and rehearsing them, makes for a feeling of empowerment. An important tool in planning is the "worst-case scenario." Knowing how to deal with a worst-case scenario offers a layer of protection against falling into the same powerful patterns that predominated in your family life.

The worst-case scenario is a picture of the worst possible way a situation can play itself out. It not only refers to a person reacting the opposite way you hoped and planned for, but it also refers to your own failure to say what you want and to recover from difficult situations. A truly worst-case scenario assumes not only that terrible things will happen, but that you will fail to respond appropriately.

In struggling with worst-case scenarios, remember Murphy's Law: "Anything that can go wrong will go wrong." Plan as well as you can for anything that can go wrong. When something does go wrong, plan for your inability to carry out your own plan. In other words, plan to fail, and prepare yourself for your own failure. In that way, you can come to grips with an essential component of reconciliation—the idea that everything that happens is grist for the mill, and that in a family, the mill never stops turning. Everything that happens during the reconciliation process is in fact part of an ongoing process that can be talked about with people you love and who care for you. Every battle fought in a war is not won, and the process leading to peace can be as treacherous and laden with land mines as war itself. I comfort myself when working with difficult family feuds by thinking of the Middle East peace process, or the Irish quest for independence from British colonization. I think of the lives lost and the years spent, the backstabbing and always precarious negotiations, and I remember to remain patient and be grateful for slow progress, regardless of how many setbacks occur.

Here's how one male client in his mid-forties worked up the courage to reconcile with his sister using a "worst-case scenario":

> *My brother Jack was having a get-together at his apartment. He called me and told me my sister Selma was gonna be there. Now you know about*

*me and Selma. She's the one who gained twenty pounds, and when I
asked her if she was pregnant, she stopped talking to me. Not until after
she read me the riot act about how I screwed up her whole life by constantly torturing her when she was a child. I told her that's what kids do,
and you know I'm a cracker jack, cracking jokes all the time, trying to
make light of it, but she wasn't too interested in listening to anything I had
to say. Anyway, it was all this triangle stuff going on that we talked about.
Like we said, Selma was Daddy's little girl and me and my brother were
on my mother's side. We were sort of locked out of everything, and Selma
always blamed me anyway, cause that's what Dad wanted her to do. You
know Dad had it out for Mom, and the rest of us except Selma were on
Mom's side. So I figured I could stay away from the party, and screw myself out of a good time, or I could go and have to deal with Selma. What
I wanted to do was to talk to Selma, you know, serious, and explain all
this stuff and try to start over, but instead I thought, no way. It's all gonna
explode. I'm gonna go to the party, she'll be there, she'll see me and then
she'll walk out. Okay, so I figured I'd call her first, let her know I was
gonna be there, and promise no jokes at her expense. Then I thought,
okay, I'm there and she's gonna get me back. She's gonna start telling
everybody at the party what a jerk I am and try to turn everybody against
me. Then I thought I could just ignore it, make it into a joke. But then I
thought, wait a minute, what if she really does get to me and I lose it?
What if I lose my temper and start to scream at her? I mean I'd never hit
her or anything, and you know I never have more than one or two beers,
so I'm not gonna lose control. . . .*

This client of mine went on for several more minutes, describing in
excruciating detail all the things that could possibly go wrong if he attended his brother's party. For each disaster, he had a comeback plan.
He even had a plan for failing to do what he wanted to do.

PLANNING FOR THE FALLOUT

One often overlooked fact in dealing with family feuds is that
change in the family system will reverberate throughout the whole
family, and as a result many people might end up being affected by your
reconciliation. If there was a history of triangulation in your family,
and as a result you became distant from one member of the family,

then another family member might feel threatened by your newfound closeness. A mother who needed you to be close to her and distant from your father might feel frightened by your closeness to him, because it threatens to disrupt the equilibrium, the exquisite balancing act that might have gone on for generations in your family.

Or if you always played the role of family caretaker, and as a result you rebelled and distanced yourself from your family, then coming back into the family as a caretaker again might threaten whoever may have stepped in to fill the caretaker role in your absence.

Any feud that has gone on for longer than a year or so usually results in a rebalancing of the family system, such that each family member finds some way of accommodating or adjusting for the feud. To reconcile the feud means good things for most family members, but if anyone did any substantial rebalancing acts, it might be hard for him or her to welcome you back into the fold. When planning how you would like to reconcile, consider others in your family who might be affected by these changes, and plan for the best ways of dealing with them as well.

A thirty-four-year-old grocery store manager, who worked hard on planning his reconciliation with his mother, sensitively told me:

> I was thinking about my younger brother Terry. Ever since me and Mom had this feud going, he's kind of stepped in to take my place. I knew that would happen, because he was always on the fringe of the family and mad at me for how close me and Mom have been. I think part of the reason I ended up leaving Mom was because I knew Terry was going to be there for her, and in a way it was like a gift to Terry. Now what's he going to think when I try to get back in the family? I know I can eventually work things out with my mom, but I realize I have to find a way of not alienating Terry. I want him to still be close to Mom, and I don't want him to be angry at me for pushing him out of the family again. Maybe I should talk to him first. But no matter what I do, I guess I have to be real watchful about how he reacts, and real sensitive and considerate to his feelings. If I do that, I think it'll be okay.

There is another type of fallout, which in its own strange way can be disconcerting. This is the fallout that occurs when people get what they want. It's similar to the "buyer's remorse" that comes shortly after purchasing the home of your dreams. It's the reason one of my favorite sayings is "Be careful of what you dream," because usually when people commit or dedicate themselves to reconciling a feud, they succeed. Success has its rewards, but the victor also gets the spoils. Once you reenter the family, things will not automatically and quickly change. There is always a need to stay vigilant, on guard for anything that might set the old patterns into motion.

Also, many people are not prepared for the positive things that may lie ahead of them. So used to not getting what they want, they don't know how to be thankful and nurturant of healthy relationships. I can think of several family feuds in which people who were so alienated from their families reconciled only to feel pressured in a positive way. Now that I'm getting called on my birthday, I have to remember *their* birthdays! Now that my sister cares about me, she doesn't stop calling! Now that my ex-husband is no longer enraged with me, I can get in touch with all those loving feelings I used to have for him, and now I feel so lonely without him!

Think of the "cost of success" and work it into your plans. Imagine not only the worst-case scenarios, but also the best-case scenarios, and plan for both.

AUTHENTICITY

Many people, in their efforts to muster the courage to engage their disenfranchised family members, and out of fear that they will only make matters worse, sugarcoat their attempts to reconcile—a strategy that is likely to backfire.

I met Rachel, a thirty-two-year-old housewife, when she came to my office after having felt depressed and confused for some time. After I learned of her family situation, it became clear that her confusion and depression were linked to a complex feud going on in her family. Rachel believed that her older sister Helen had had an affair with Rachel's husband, and had been instrumental in causing the breakup of Rachel's marriage five years earlier. While both Helen and Rachel's ex-husband denied having had the affair, Rachel harbored deep feelings of betrayal and anger toward Helen.

After working together on her genogram, Rachel and I unveiled a pattern of triangulation and sibling wars in her family that had lasted at least three generations. But when Rachel thought she was finally ready to bridge the deep rift with her sister, she decided that no good would come from "opening up a can of worms" by delving into their family history. Instead, she would merely recontact Helen and try to make amends, without discussing her residual feelings of anger.

Rachel's effort was well-intended, but it suffered from a crucial flaw: Her anger was still noticeable, and so was her attempt to conceal it. Helen, who for nearly a decade had been on the receiving end of Rachel's indignant condemnation, was keenly sensitized to her sister's hostility. She could see through the inauthentic language Rachel used, and this made her even more angry.

Rachel recounted her telephone conversation with Helen as follows. I have left the words and phrases that might have upset Helen the most in regular type.

> *I wanted to tell her,* let's let bygones be bygones, *but I'd told her that a hundred times before, and I knew she never believed me. So this time I tried to tell her I loved her and that she was important to me. But what came out was that,* yes, I was still *a little* annoyed *about what may or may not have happened between her and my ex.* I told her it still *bugs me a little,* but that no matter what happened or didn't happen, I forgave her *for everything she might have done. For some reason, as soon as I said the word "forgive,"* Helen exploded. *It was a nightmare, the whole argument started up again and we ended up in a yelling match. I couldn't take it, and I hung up.*

Although Rachel's intent was genuine, her words were not, and Helen responded with mistrust and rage. Helen was still seething about being falsely blamed for breaking up Rachel's marriage. In Helen's mind, the feud was the result of Rachel's jumping to erroneous conclusions. Helen had merely tried to console both her sister and her brother-in-law, in the hope that their marriage would be saved. And what had she gotten for her well-intentioned efforts? Rachel accused her of getting "too close" to her husband, blamed her for the breakup, and tore apart their relationship as sisters. What Helen needed to hear first was an apology from Rachel for Rachel's contribution to the feud, and she also needed to hear Rachel fully express the anger both of them knew was there. Only then would she have been able to believe that Rachel was ready for a genuine reconciliation.

I knew from my previous discussions with Rachel that she could take responsibility for what she had done to create this feud. She also understood the multigenerational patterns of triangulation and intense sibling conflict that were at play beneath the surface of her sister's defensive behavior. But with all her understanding, she remained angry with Helen.

Both sisters felt betrayed, and both wished things had been different. But while each had a right to her anger, neither took responsibility for it. The problem in Rachel's reconciliation attempt was that she tried to bury her anger, and therefore her conciliatory remarks seemed disingenuous. Helen, on the other hand, felt as she had throughout the long, simmering feud: that Rachel could not acknowledge or speak the truth.

Authenticity is never easy to achieve. It requires the courage to deeply examine your own feelings at every turn in the conversation and to honestly state them. If you are asked whether or not you are angry, you must look inside yourself and take responsibility for even the slightest bit of anger. Whether you feel anger, regret, guilt, or shame, it's important to share your feelings with those people with whom you're trying to reconcile.

All parties in the feud tend to respond to each other with extreme sensitivity. A slight indication of anger will be experienced by the other party as rage; a slight indication of sadness will be assumed to be an indication of deep grief. When everyone involved in the feud is so sensitized, attempts to cover up feelings with artificially sweetened language will be perceived either as a failure to take responsibility or as a form of deception.

Achieving genuineness is not always easy, especially when those in the family are not used to communicating honestly. But this behavior can be learned through practice. Here is an exercise to help you become more authentic in your communication with family members with whom you're feuding:

Imagine that you are speaking to a trusted friend, someone with whom you could share your most intimate thoughts. Perhaps it's a spouse, a therapist, or a family

member you feel close to. Talk to that person. Write down what you would say to the relative you're feuding with *as if that relative were the trusted person you've just imagined*. Read it repeatedly, until the words feel natural. Don't attempt to contact the family member with whom you're feuding until you feel comfortable speaking in this manner.

Don't expect that the person you're feuding with will respond with the same level of honesty. He or she doesn't need to. The most important thing is that you begin the reconciliation process with a greater level of genuineness than you have before. If you don't succeed, or find yourself lapsing into a more familiar, less vulnerable, and less open mode of interacting, don't give up hope. Remember that a feud is the culmination of a long series of events, and healing it may entail a series of partial successes and partial failures before an authentic reconciliation can take place.

THE LANGUAGE OF CHANGE

Rachel's story exemplifies how "everyday language" doesn't suffice in the midst of a family feud. That's because family feuds do not operate the same way everyday life operates. Emotions are much more heightened and require more potent words to reflect that heightened state. Words designed to express more refined emotions, such as frustration, annoyance, or nervousness, fall terribly short of their mark. When Rachel used such tame phrases as "a little annoyed," "bugs me a little," and "let's let bygones be bygones" to describe to her sister how she felt and how much she wanted to make things right between them, Helen didn't buy it. Since these words failed to mirror Rachel's true feelings, there was no way Helen could.

Feuds speak their own language—the "language of the unconscious." In this language, people don't feel sad, they feel devastated. They don't feel annoyed or angry, they feel enraged. They don't get frightened, they become terrified. These words can be found in the lexicon of the unconscious. Because these are the words the feuding parties understand, these are also the words needed to reconcile feuds.

In the context of reconciliation, the language of the unconscious becomes the language of change. A fascinating event occurs when someone begins to speak the language of change in the middle of a feud. Rather than fanning the flames of the feud, speaking the language of change often has a calming, normalizing effect. This occurs because tension builds up between people not when the two face their deepest feelings, but rather when they sense that their deepest feelings are being cloaked, disguised, or somehow altered.

People use "everyday language" in order to avoid a heightening of emotional intensity, but doing so when attempting to reconcile a feud nearly always backfires. "I guess I felt a little annoyed at you when you didn't return my phone calls for two years" may be easier to say, but it smacks of inauthenticity and sarcasm. Feuding family members who feel terrified and enraged are already hypersensitive when talking to each other, so trying to use nice words to describe intense feelings leaves the listener feeling puzzled at best and lied to at worst.

In order to avoid using everyday language when approaching a family member with whom you are feuding, practice using words such as *rage, terror, despair, horror,* and *hopelessness* in describing your feelings toward that person. Replace "two-bit" words such as *annoyed, angry, worried,* or *bothered* with more accurate descriptions of how you really feel. For example, "When you didn't return my phone calls for two years, I was so enraged I wanted to kill you. When you finally called me, it all came to the surface. When we began to talk to each other again, I was ecstatic and hopeful, but then I remembered how you ignored me and cut me out of your life, and I was terrified that it might happen again." These words, spoken in a calm, self-assured voice, are more likely to open up true channels of communication than well-intended attempts to soften the blow with "nice words."

There is also a tendency for people to minimize their feelings by qualifying their statements with the word "just." "I guess I just felt a little bothered." "I think I was just annoyed with you." In these cases, "just" is used as a way to say "I only feel things a little bit," or "My feelings aren't really too important." Again, few listeners who hear other people diminish their feelings really believe it; as a result, they feel a lack of trust in the speaker's genuineness.

In talking to Rachel about her attempt to reconcile the feud between her and her sister, I reminded her that, although it was difficult, it was crucial that she speak from her heart no matter how strong the words sounded. We practiced a more genuine approach, and the following message is what Rachel eventually was able to deliver to her sister. I have left the words that were particularly powerful in communicating the depth of Rachel's feelings in regular type.

> *First, I want to apologize for my last phone call. I realize I was still blaming you and not admitting both* my anger and self-righteousness. *I just couldn't express* how terrible I felt. *With all the suffering and resentment we've both experienced over the last few years, the truth is that I love you very much, and I've been* grieving *and* terribly troubled *about losing you as my friend and sister. I know I've blamed you for my husband leaving me, and I've been struggling really hard to figure out what happened and why. In my heart I couldn't tolerate all the pain in my marriage, so I blamed you and others. Now I know I didn't have what it takes to make that marriage work.*
>
> *As for you and me, I think we were both caught up in a pattern that's been going on for a long time in our family.* It's been traumatic for me *to take responsibility for how I set all this up, because I'm still so angry about it all, and I know how* you must be enraged *at me too. But I really think I understand more about things now, and I want to tell you that I'm very sorry for what I did to hurt you so badly. I want to get together with you to talk about it, to try to see if together we could understand each other better. I want to look at what I did to hurt you, and I want to talk about the things Mom and Dad did with their brothers and sisters, because I think that had a powerful role in making things happen the way they did between us. . . .*

This conversation was the beginning of a new relationship between Rachel and her sister. Helen was receptive to Rachel's apologies, and the two of them finally met in person to discuss their feud. Rachel brought with her the family history that she and I worked on together, and Helen was fascinated to learn the pattern that the two of them had played out together had been going on for generations. When Helen finally was able to see her role in the feud, she too could reveal strong feelings of competitiveness and deep enmity that she harbored toward Rachel and hid throughout their teenage years. Most important, Rachel and Helen were able to start down the road of reconciliation, opening up lines of communication that had been closed for years.

No family feud can be resolved without the courage to face your own fears, and ultimately, no reconciliation with other family members can occur without your having the courage to eventually face those family members directly. When you are courageous, you use your fear to guide you to do the very things that you're frightened of. The initial confrontation, whether in person, on the telephone, or in a letter, should be one in which expectations for change are kept small.

While spontaneity is important, most feuds need to be combatted with careful planning. When making contact, do your best to be genuine, and take as much responsibility as you can for your part in the feud. Use your understanding of the multigenerational repetition of family patterns to guide you toward compassion.

eleven

Creating the Climate for Change

There is a time for departure even when there's no certain place to go.

—TENNESSE WILLIAMS

A MAN DRESSED IN COMBAT FATIGUES, STANDING AT A BUSY DOWN-TOWN INTERSECTION, OPENS FIRE WITH AN M-16 RIFLE ON A LUNCH-hour crowd of people. He is arrested, carted off to jail and is judged insane. That same man, merely twenty years earlier, wearing the same fatigues, may have stood in the middle of a rice paddy in Southeast Asia, firing the same rifle wildly at all those around him. For that same behavior, he might have been awarded medals and hailed as a hero.

Our actions alone do not determine whether we are perceived as heroes or villains, or whether we succeed or fail. In order to be mean-ingful, our actions must be placed in context. In the case of family feuds, the context of our attempts at reconciliation has a powerful im-pact on whether our efforts pay off.

When most people think of context, they think of the surrounding behavior. They think of the setting, the players, and factors such as tim-ing. There is also an *internal* context to our behavior, which consists of our attitudes and beliefs about what we are doing and saying. Both are important to consider as you move toward reconciliation.

INTERNAL CONTEXT

While some internal aspects of resolving feuds have already been discussed in earlier chapters, such as an attitude of forgiveness, the need for genuineness, and authenticity, other aspects can also be critical in determining the ultimate success or failure of our actions.

How often have you heard that it's not *what* someone says, but instead *how* it is said that's important? The verbal message often gives us one meaning, while the nonverbal message gives us another. I used to demonstrate this in my classrooms by asking a student to come to the door. I would open up the door, hold the doorknob in my right hand, make a sweeping motion toward the corridor with my other hand, and say the words, "After me." Inevitably, the student walked through the door, choosing to "hear" the nonverbal message while ignoring the verbal statement that I was instructing the student to pass through the door "after me." In this, as in most situations, the nonverbal message, how a message is a sent, is the context that takes precedence over the content, the actual verbal message.

When moving toward those with whom you have been feuding, it is not only important to be very clear about how you feel about what you are saying and doing, but your success in communicating those feelings may depend on your awareness of the nonverbal messages you are sending as well. If the verbal and nonverbal messages are conflicting, you are likely to be misunderstood. Consider the common situation in which mixed messages are communicated. With the best of intentions, the words spoken are "I want to stop fighting," but this is said with folded arms over the chest (as if creating a protective armor) and with a frown on the face. The message most clearly communicated is not one of genuine reconciliation, but one of fear at best, and most likely anger.

COMPASSIONATE DETACHMENT

Family feuds are tornadoes of emotion. Like other tornadoes, they will pick up the garbage around them, twist them into knots, and leave destruction in their wake. For feuds to continue, they depend on you and your emotions getting sucked up into them. You will need to do everything in your power to avoid getting caught up in what is inevitably a destructive maelstrom of intense emotion.

In light of this, an important contextual factor to consider is how to keep your emotional distance. This means being able to recognize a family's emotional "traps," the things that happen in your family that are likely to press your buttons and get you tied up into behaving the way you wish you wouldn't. Once you see this happening, you need to find ways of calming down and becoming less emotionally reactive. Remind yourself that no matter how well you understand what is going on, you are likely to get upset, and that these upset feelings will only bring you further into a feud. Instead of allowing yourself to give in to these feelings, take deep breaths, relax the muscles in your body, and take some time to calm yourself down. Remind yourself of your own part in the feud, as well as the long family history and patterns that led up to this "button-pressing" behavior. You might want to gently point out how what is going on at the moment is upsetting to you, but in doing so it's important to eradicate blame from the situation. Instead of blaming others, understand it as a dance everyone in the family dances, and that you are determined to learn new ways of dancing.

Rochelle had been successful in reconciling with her mother to a large extent. Several years ago, the forty-four-year-old dentist had completely cut herself off from her mother, because, as she put it:

> *There wasn't room in this world for the two of us. I spent so much of my life hating her, trying to be as different as possible from her, and after having my own children I had to wake up in the morning, look at myself in the mirror, and see that I was just like her. It wasn't just that I looked like her, but I was critical of my children the same way she always criticized me. I hated her, and when I looked at myself, I hated me. Every time I saw her, every time I talked to her, I heard the same silent criticism. It was something she did with her voice. I knew she hated me, she hated everything I stood for, and she hated my kids.*

So Rochelle concocted a feud as an excuse to have no more contact with her mother, so that she could "breathe, and feel like myself again." But after realizing that her feud with her mother would never get her to a place where she could accept herself, or could grow out of her feelings of being tied to her mother by virtue of her rebelliousness,

Rochelle did everything she could to reinstate their relationship. Rochelle succeeded, and the two of them continued a civil, if not deeply rewarding, relationship. But on one occasion Rochelle explained:

> I felt like all the progress I made was about to go down the drain. Mom was over for Easter, and we were just sitting around dyeing Easter eggs with the kids. It was pleasant, for about five minutes, and then there it was. Her expression, the tone of voice, I can't tell you exactly, but I knew she was upset with the kids. They didn't do it good enough for her, or they spilled some of the dye, it didn't matter what. It just brought back all the old memories in seconds, and I remembered how I felt with her all those years. I wasn't good enough for her, never good enough for her. But I wasn't going to let the work I did go down the drain. Instead of freaking out, I took about five or six deep breaths. I just told myself over and over again that this was her, this was all about her life, and this had nothing to do with me or my kids. I calmed myself down and never let on that I was feeling devastated by her. I really let it go, I let it fly out the window. I did so good that I even felt a little sorry for her.

Developing this "arm's length" attitude toward your family is a necessary tool in combatting the tendency to get caught up in a whirlpool of emotion. One preventive measure that has been helpful to many families is to "externalize" the feud by giving it a name. While that seems silly and awkward at first, the results of this strategy can be powerful.

Think of your family feud as having a life of its own. Imagine that it developed and grew up over several generations in your family. You can think of it as a disease, like a cancer that spread through your family. You can think of it as a monster, or as a ghost that has haunted your family for generations. Or, if you wish, you can be more neutral about it, and simply think of it as an acquaintance, a noisome neighbor whom you haven't been able to get distance from. Regardless of how you see it, give it a name, any name you like. It could be Elmer, LouAnn, Fred, Sally, or whatever appeals to you. (Avoid using the name of someone you know!)

As you think about your family's feud, call it by its name. You can do this silently to yourself, or if you are bold and shameless enough, you can jokingly refer to it by its name to other family members. The joke may catch on—after all, everyone in the family has been victimized by Elmer at some time or another.

Naming your family feud helps in two ways. First and foremost, it creates a needed sense of distance between you and the feud. If the feud has a name of its own, it's easier to understand that the feud is something other than you. It's easy to see that it has a life of its own. As something "outside of yourself," it becomes easier to control, because it is not seen as an inescapable fact of your existence. You can live without it. At the same time, it also creates a sense of distance between other family members and the feud. This makes it easier to avoid the pitfall of blaming them, by seeing them as victims of Elmer as well.

The second thing that naming your feud accomplishes is that it casts a less serious, more humorous light on something that's been painful and even devastating to the family over the years. Taking yourself, your family, and its feuding ways less seriously is one way to detach yourself from the family's entangled web.

Be careful not to go to extremes with this detached attitude, becoming an automaton and acting like a cold, callous person. Usually, this means that your detachment is really a cover for your rage, or that you are working too hard to cover your feelings in order not to allow some vulnerability to overtake you. When you sense you might be going too far, imagine that you have a solid core that cannot be shaken. At the same time that you realize that you have a solid core, you have a periphery around that core that is flexible, being willing to share your feelings, willing to allow some vulnerability. This is a periphery of openness to others' points of view, an openness to empathy for others' feelings. This solid core, combined with a more flexible periphery, allows you the balance you need to face difficult emotional strains. It gives you the ability to be more neutral on a deep level, yet compassionate with others. "Compassionate detachment" is the attitude to strive for when facing family situations that you fear might shake you up. Your ability to do this is important to assess as you attempt to resolve your family feud. It provides the context that is more likely to bring success.

ACCEPTANCE OF THE SMALLEST IMPROVEMENT

One of the dangers found on the road to reconciling family feuds is the expectation that massive change in the family will occur. We will be led out of the dark caverns of family unrest and into the sunlit beaches of peaceful and enlightened family interaction. We will finally have the father, mother, sister, or brother we always wanted.

The expectation of grand changes often backfires. When the family doesn't change as quickly as is hoped, the result can be feelings of hopelessness, loss, and depression. As a temperamentally impatient person, I've had to harness my impatience with advice from Buddha to "Expect nothing and the world will be at your feet."

In my earlier days of working with families, I used to wonder to myself why the family members with whom I worked so often seemed satisfied with the results of family therapy, despite the fact that it often appeared to me as though there wasn't much difference between how the family looked when I first met them and at the end of our time together. So why were the family members so pleased?

As I looked deeper, I began to understand that for most family members, a small change in the way a family interacts can yield a significant difference in the way people feel about being in their family. I developed a principle that "small change is significant change," and when I applied the principle to my work I realized that this in fact is how families operate. This simple exercise demonstrates the principle well:

Think of the things your family does that set you off. List your family members and their annoying behaviors. Then, make a "wish list" of all the things you'd like to see change in the family. Now, of all the things on the list, choose one item on the list that is small, simple, and specific. *This item should represent the smallest change you would like to see take place in your family that would let you know that things are beginning to get better.* It can be something as simple as "I would like my mother to call me once a week,"

or "I'd like my sister to initiate a telephone contact once a year." Imagine how you would feel if this one change were to take place. What would need to happen, and what could you do, to help make this change take place?

Focusing specifically on small family changes can go a long way toward preventing the frustration that might occur because things are taking too long to happen differently in the family. It also enables you to see that things actually are going better, and that leads to a greater feeling of hope for the future.

Lenny, a forty-eight-year-old architect and contractor, told me how one small change in his family made all the difference to him:

My relationship with my sister goes way back. We were always close, but we always fought like cats and dogs. Actually, she was the cat and I was the dog. I did a lot of barking, but she used to use her sharp claws to scratch at me. When we were teenagers, it was all words, but I used to criticize the boys she dated and she used to give me a hard time about everything I did. A few years ago we had a big fight, and it was like years of built-up anger was unloaded on me. I thought she was totally out of line, and I just had it with her. I told her we didn't need to have anything to do with each other, and I refused to call her. I thought there would never be any way of getting over it. When I had to see her last Thanksgiving, I didn't talk to her and refused to sit near her. Then, out of nowhere, she came over to me and touched my arm. I tensed up, like I was going to hit her, but she was just gentle, and she looked at me and told me she loved me. I just melted away. That was all it took, and now it's like we're best friends.

INTEGRITY

Along with an understanding of nonverbal cues, an attitude shift that emphasizes emotional distance, and an appreciation that families move in small steps, another aspect of internal context is important to mention. While I've already discussed the importance of genuineness in all respects, this can also be understood as an attitude shift as well. Feuds are often fueled by a lack of integrity, each person in the feud often being motivated by his or her own covert agenda. I like to think of an attitude of integrity as a fortress against the backstabbing and dishonesty that can run rampant in a feud. In this context, I understand integrity to mean an uncompromising allegiance to accurate, honest self-expression. As you become the model of integrity in the family, over time other family members begin to feel safer. As each family member feels safer, an atmosphere of trust develops, and each person works in his or her own way to make the covert agendas overt, ultimately making true reconciliation possible.

I remember thirty-four-year-old Dawn's words after she got back from a family get-together:

> When I went back home, I felt the family magnet pull me back in. I had to be different, I had to be so careful to not hurt anyone's feelings. I was afraid that no matter what I said, I was going to hurt someone, and I'd start a war. I realized that if I said things softly, that if I wasn't hiding my anger, and just told the truth, they could deal with what I had to say. Every once in a while I could see my mom wince. It was amazing, actually. She'd literally wince when I said what I felt. I knew I was breaking a family rule, but it was a riot. At one point my dad starting saying things to me that I never knew he felt. It was like a domino thing. It was great.

EXTERNAL CONTEXT

The external context, or logistical variables that enter into resolving family feuds, include timing and the use of family events, as well as the location of confrontations.

TIMING AND FAMILY EVENTS

Most people use timing as a way of avoiding reconciliation. "My mother's in the hospital, so I don't want to burden her with family talk" or "It seems inappropriate to bring up old wounds at my dad's birthday party" are common concerns, but they can also be self-deceptive mechanisms designed to avoid the fact that someone doesn't feel emotionally ready or prepared to begin to reconcile. We want to wait for the right moment, when things are calm enough or rational enough or ordinary enough. Most likely, that time will never come. In a family feud, when things settle down, usually the motivation to do anything settles down too. It is, in fact, the emotionally intense times, often times of family transition or gatherings, that are ideal times to begin the process of reconciliation.

Holidays and milestones in the ongoing life of a family are natural avenues for working through the process of reconciling family feuds. Holidays are times that bring back memories of the family all together, and as such they are often rife with both painful memories and opportunities to create new memories of healthier family interaction. As discussed earlier in this book, many family feuds erupt during or around holidays, and because holidays create opportunities for family members to reconvene as a family, they are often the best times for resolving feuds.

Holidays such as Thanksgiving, Christmas, Easter, Jewish High Holy Days, and Passover are ideal for beginning the healing process for two reasons. First, they are holidays that are known about well in advance, leaving plenty of preparation time. Second, the holidays themselves symbolize a "rebirth" of one kind or another, and they often carry with them the message of new beginnings and starting anew.

Knowing that the family was to be together for Christmas, a forty-five-year-old engineer named Murray decided that this Christmas he was going to take the initiative to bring the family together in a way it had not been brought together in the past. After working for some time on his genogram, and studying the history of the family, he stumbled upon some fascinating family secrets. In studying the generation that came before him, he learned about an ongoing family feud between his father and one of his father's brothers that continued until his father's brother died. That feud, which had not been discussed publicly, created a deep chasm in the family and explained the mysterious absence of one side of his family during most family holidays. Murray also discovered several "love triangles," including competition for boyfriends and girlfriends that ended up creating great pain. Most of this information had been kept secret, and on one occasion Murray told me that he felt like a priest hearing confessions as he gathered the family's information. Fortunately, Murray told me with a sly grin, he had no obligation to keep the information quiet.

Murray believed that revealing his family's secrets would start the family on the road to closeness. As the one who had always been shunted by the family, he felt that his attempts to help bring the family together didn't carry much risk. If he failed, he would only be pushed back into the dusty corner he already occupied in the family. Since most of the more provocative secrets concerned family members who already had passed away, he would not be breaking anyone's confidence.

Murray decided that about two weeks before the family was to get together for Christmas, he would write to his siblings. In each letter that he wrote, Murray revealed carefully selected information, designed specifically to incite and inflame the passions of the family members. His hope was that if he could upset certain family members before they arrived for Christmas, the family would be less likely to fall into a passive position of merely repeating timeworn patterns. Murray wanted to upset the apple cart, so that once the apples fell he could orchestrate putting them back into the cart in a neater, "healthier" way. He tried to first console and then upset the brother with whom he was feuding, first by revealing that many of the things he had been angry toward his brother about were things that Murray had done himself. Murray apologized for calling the kettle black. But Murray made sure to combine that bit of consolation with the new revelation that their father had once told Murray that he resented Murray's brother because Murray's brother looked and acted like their father's mother (Murray's grandmother), whom Murray's father detested.

To his sister, Murray revealed that their brother had once offered him five dollars to follow her on a date and take pictures of her kissing her boyfriend. While Murray declined the offer, he never did tell his sister just how jealous and possessive their brother was about her dating. And to his mother, Murray revealed that all of her children had disobeyed her injunctions against dating, sneaking away and lying about their behavior.

While Murray knew that these petty disclosures would do nothing to help the family resolve their conflicts, he was hoping that it would inflame them just enough to "throw them off balance." When he arrived for Christmas, he found that at first no one even acknowledged receiving any letters. Murray discovered that the conspiracy of silence that is so common in some families ran deep in his family. Yet, after they had been together for a full day, squabbles began to break out. Other issues emerged, and Murray asked them to sit together in the living room with the television off. He then proceeded to talk about his family research, and explained how some of the patterns in the family worked and how they seemed to repeat from one generation to the next. Despite an initially hostile remark made by his brother, the family was fascinated by the stories Murray uncovered. Murray ended his lecture with a plea for breaking the patterns that had existed in the family. He apologized to his brother for his own anger and emotional distance. Without any prompting, Murray's sister then apologized to her mother for the trouble she had given her, and their mother then broke down into tears. Their mother described some of the difficulties she had growing up, and validated much of the research Murray had done. She said that while she had done her best as a mother, she knew she had made big mistakes for which she hoped she would be forgiven.

Murray felt that his planned confrontation was successful. He became a bit closer to his brother, and he saw his sister and mother together begin to heal certain wounds. As an engineer, he was used to solving different kinds of problems, but when it came to his family, he felt as though he had engineered a beginning step in changing long-standing family patterns.

Family milestones such as weddings, funerals, family reunions, birthdays, and bar and bat mitzvahs also provide good opportunities for conciliatory confrontations. These milestones are often intense moments in the life span of a family member, and as such often function as magnifying glasses for the family's functional and dysfunctional patterns. A family in which secrets run rampant will create new secrets, a family in which there are entrenched roles will find people sinking deeper into their roles, families in which enmeshment exists will enmesh further, and family members who triangulate with each other will intensify their triangulation. Weddings, funerals, and other events in which emotions run high provide a caricature of the family patterns, making them easier to see.

Some of these family milestones can be predicted well in advance, leaving you with time to prepare for how you would like to proceed with your conciliatory efforts. But others, such as funerals, give short notice. Whether or not you will choose to use the short notice to prepare for making conciliatory gestures will depend on how emotionally ready you are at the time. When there is short notice, the more you can use the deadline to push you toward beginning the process of healing family wounds, the better. Remembering that it is best to expect the least amount of change, you can use the short notice to at least come up with one goal that will move you closer to your long-term goal. If you feel so rushed into action that you are fairly certain that you will be unable to act with compassionate detachment, or that you suspect that you will be unable to stop yourself from blaming others, then it is best to instead commit yourself to making another opportunity for reconciliation at a different time.

Some people are concerned, and rightly so, that using a wedding, funeral, or bar mitzvah as a forum for resolving a family feud can be seen as selfish by moving the spotlight away from the person who is being honored or grieved. Unlike what happened when Murray sat his family down in a living room to discuss the family history, these events rarely provide the time for a relaxed discussion. Yet working toward resolving a family feud doesn't necessarily require long, drawn-out discussions or explanations. It can mean simply sitting down at a dinner table for twenty minutes with someone you haven't spoken to in a long time, breaking the ice and making a date to speak again later. It can mean sharing a few carefully selected words with specific people with whom you have unfinished business. It can even mean standing next to people with whom you've feuded in the past, reaching over and gently supporting them as they sob at a funeral. This small gesture can be more powerful than many words, and need only take a few seconds to accomplish.

Working toward resolving a family feud at a milestone event often involves coming equipped with a new understanding of where the family has been and how the feud developed in the first place. Holding this new understanding close to your heart allows you to commit yourself to acting differently toward key family members and toward those with whom you've feuded.

When you're ready to begin to reconcile, your understanding of the multigenerational roots of the family feud, your ability to take responsibility, and your attitude of "compassionate detachment" will be a welcome relief and a preferred stance over the feuding stance that preceded it, whether that shift takes place next to a hospital bed or at a birthday party.

LOCATION OF CONFRONTATION

When you decide to have a face-to-face meeting with a family member, it's often best to have that meeting on neutral territory. If you meet a person with whom you've been feuding in his or her home, there is an automatic power imbalance, and an imbalance of comfort level as well. This imbalance is even greater when you are confronting a parent; the childhood message that says "When you're under my roof, you do as I say" operates in the background no matter how old you are. Similarly, when the meeting takes place in your own home, it often puts the other family member at a disadvantage, feeling that he or she can be kicked out of your house at any moment if things don't go your way. You might feel comforted by the additional safety this gives you, yet you might not want the burden of guilt for having thrown a family member out of your own house.

Similarly, when there is a choice about whether the meeting should take place publicly or privately, there is a significant advantage in having the meeting in a public or semipublic place. While a private home might feel more cozy and conducive to intimate expressions of feeling, that same conduciveness might be threatening as well. The added level of safety and constraint that a public place offers is not available in private places. Meeting in a public park or a restaurant allows for a certain amount of privacy, yet there are built-in limits to how much emotion can be expressed appropriately. Wild, unleashed fits of rage are less likely to occur as the waiter asks if you would like more water, and the public park allows each of you the freedom to stand up, walk around, calm yourselves down and return to the discussion.

Michelle's feud with her father and brother seemed at first to stem directly from having been molested by her father as a child; her brother sided with her father while her two sisters, who also were molested by their father, sided with Michelle. When I met Michelle, she had already been in a group therapy sexual abuse recovery program for some time, and as part of the program she had been strongly encouraged to confront her father. In my individual work with her, it became clear that while Michelle's molestation was a definitive experience in her life, she suffered more from her father's ongoing emotional abandonment than from his inappropriate sexual advances. (Michelle's mother died when Michelle was eleven.) This pattern of fathers abandoning daughters had existed for generations in the family.

For many years Michelle had tried to tell her father about how angry she was that he had made sexual advances toward her. Michelle was concerned, as are so many who have been sexually abused, that her father would deny his inappropriate sexual behavior. Michelle and I agreed that he would be more likely to hear her if she were able to broaden the scope of her confrontation to include her feelings of continual emotional abandonment. She needed to be careful not to discount her anger about his sexual advances, nor did she want to give him an "out" by allowing him to focus on other issues. But we both agreed that as long as she was forthright about the facts of his sexual misconduct, her father would be more likely to hear her if she discussed that behavior in the context of his overall abandoning behavior: his unfulfilled promises to call her, his denigrating comments about her appearance, his greater attention to her siblings. Confronting him in this way would make it more difficult for Michelle's father to deny his ill treatment of her.

Michelle's father lived about two hundred miles away, in the northern part of the state, while she lived in the south. She knew that if she called and asked to see him, his curiosity, and perhaps his fear of being exposed, would lead to an affirmative, if not welcoming response. Michelle didn't want to invite him to come down to visit her, because she only wanted to spend the few moments it might take to have a discussion with him and then leave. She also didn't want to visit him at his home, because she felt he would have the advantage of feeling "at home" while she felt like an outsider. She decided that the best venue for their meeting would be the airport restaurant. From prior experience, she knew the restaurant was rarely crowded. There, she could meet him when her plane arrived, spend a limited amount of time, and take a return flight home. Michelle also felt comforted by the fact that the restaurant atmosphere would prevent either of them from engaging in a huge display of emotion; they both would be constrained by the social demands of being in public.

Her plan worked beautifully. The two of them met in the restaurant, and they spent about forty-five minutes talking. Michelle prepared the important points that she wanted to get across ahead of time, and went through them one by one. Her father listened attentively, his facial expression alternating between anger and sadness. As Michelle had predicted, he denied the sexual abuse with the statement "I don't remember having done any of the things you mentioned, but whatever I did, I didn't mean to hurt you." He could not deny, however, the pattern of neglect and abandonment that Michelle (and her two sisters) experienced, especially when it was put in the context of Michelle's current feeling of being neglected. He promised to try to do better, made a meager attempt to explain how miserable he had been during the years when Michelle had been abused, and the conversation ended on a polite, and somewhat emotionally detached, note.

Michelle's choice of an airport restaurant as a place to try to begin to repair her feud with her father was perfect, for all the reasons already mentioned. Michelle knew that bridging the deep chasm that existed between her and her father was not going to occur in one meeting; she knew that the "journey of a thousand miles begins with a single step." Her first step was to "come clean" with her father, to tell him all the things she had been too frightened to tell him in the past. Yet she knew that if she were to do it on the telephone, it would be too easy for him to deny his part and turn it all back on Michelle. She wanted a face-to-face encounter so that he could see the earnestness and pain in her facial expression, and so that she could see his nonverbal responses. She wanted to limit the time spent, so that it didn't turn into an open-ended battleground. She wanted the feeling of safety provided by being in public, to prevent the discussion from deteriorating into a shouting match. She knew her father wouldn't lose his temper or make a scene in front of other people. And she wanted the meeting to occur on neutral territory, so that neither of them felt at a disadvantage.

When discussions take place on neutral turf, neither party feels trapped by the environment. If the discussion had taken place in Michelle's father's home, it would have been difficult for him to say, "I've had enough of this, I've got to leave." If her father had been the one to end the discussion, he would have had to kick his daughter out of his house. Likewise, Michelle would have had to kick her father out of her house if the situation had been reversed. This would turn an act of separation (the desire to leave), into an act of aggression and hostility (kicking the other party out).

•   •   •

The chance of successfully reconciling a family feud depends to a large extent on the context. Internal variables include an attitude of forgiveness, the ability to accept small improvement, awareness of nonverbal cues, genuineness, and integrity. External variables include issues such as timing and the location you choose. The following case illustrates some of the contextual factors discussed in this chapter:

Many years ago, I remember working with a woman in her midforties who suffered from severe pain due to an injury she received on her job as a set designer. She endured severe pain not only as a result of her injury, but also from the unsuccessful surgeries that followed. The depression that accompanied the pain didn't seem to remit, despite a considerable amount of physical and emotional therapy. In exploring her life, I discovered that she had not spoken with her mother for over fifteen years. Sandra felt deeply betrayed by her mother's lack of support for her educational efforts, and she also held her mother responsible for not being around to save her father, who died from a heart attack. Sandra was enraged at her mother for spending the money her father had left for Sandra on herself, and refusing to support Sandra's desire to attend law school. Sandra felt that her mother had always competed with her, and that her mother had never felt any real love or appreciation of her. Her anger came to a head a few years after her father died, and Sandra left for California from the South without ever letting her mother know where she was living or how to get ahold of her.

While I recognized that Sandra's depression stemmed in large part from the pain she was unable to overcome, her anger over the botched surgeries, and her inability to work, I also believed that she could get little relief from her depression without resolving her feud with her mother. My belief was underscored when I discovered how adamantly Sandra objected to doing this. I argued repeatedly and eventually persuasively that she needed to deal with her feelings toward her mother before she could ever be freed from her depression.

Sandra did keep in touch with an aunt—her father's sister. Sandra knew that her aunt was a confidante for her father while her father was alive, and despite some reluctance to open old wounds Sandra contacted the aunt for more information. It turned out that there was to be a huge family reunion in their hometown, and that both Sandra and her mother were invited to attend. At first Sandra insisted that she would only go to the reunion if she could be somehow assured that she wouldn't see or have anything to do with her mother.

With the assistance of Sandra's aunt, who provided considerable information about both sides of the family, Sandra learned a lot more about her mother than she initially cared to know. She saw a pattern of triangulation that permeated each generation of her family history. As I learned more about the circumstances of her father's death, I learned that after his heart attack, Sandra had tried to resuscitate him unsuccessfully. The anger and blame she felt toward herself for not being able to bring him back to life was too much for Sandra to bear, and she transferred this anger onto her mother, who she felt was never there for her father to begin with. This view that her mother was never present for her father was part of a multigenerational pattern of triangulation. In fact, people being pulled toward each other and pushing a third party out had infected Sandra's family tree from the roots up to the branches. When Sandra saw herself as part of a larger pattern, she began to understand herself less as a victim of her mother's faults and more as a victim of a timeless tale of triangulation. Her anger eased toward her mother, and the two of us together began to plan for the reunion.

Sandra's long history of rage at her mother made conciliatory efforts difficult. Even facing her mother was a huge challenge for Sandra. Although we prepared a rough script of statements that she hoped to deliver to her mother, it was clear that Sandra remained ambivalent up to the very moment she saw her mother. When Sandra returned from the reunion, she reported to me that she did indeed see her mother there, that she spoke to her briefly, and even sat next to her during dinner. She did not deliver any of the messages in our prepared script, yet Sandra felt that the mere fact that the two had made contact was a huge step. While I didn't see Sandra for much longer after that, I do know that not long after the reunion she felt relief from both her depression and her physical pain. In a recent phone call from Sandra, she told me that she now talks to her mother regularly. She still feels angry at her from time to time, and she has yet to forgive her, but she remains guardedly hopeful that over time the two of them will grow increasingly closer.

twelve

Acceptance and Letting Go

Rose is a rose is a rose is a rose, is a rose.

—GERTRUDE STEIN

NOT ALL FAMILY FEUDS CAN BE RESOLVED. NO MATTER HOW HARD A PARTICULAR FAMILY MEMBER TRIES, OTHER FAMILY MEMBERS MAY NOT be operating on the same emotional schedule. Those who attempt to resolve a family feud must eventually face the limitations of other family members, as well as their own. While you may be ready to move toward reconciliation, others simply may not be able to meet that challenge. Sometimes it is wiser not even to try.

With three groups of people, achieving a closer, more rewarding and nurturing relationship is nearly impossible. These groups are sociopaths, addicts, and the severely disturbed.

THE SOCIOPATH

Sociopaths are people who use their feelings primarily to manipulate other people. The single most important characteristic that separates sociopaths from the rest of the population is that they have no capacity to feel guilt. If this characteristic were easy for people to see, sociopaths wouldn't be dangerous. Unfortunately, because they are often smooth-talking, charming, and socially adept, it's difficult to see their lack of remorse or guilt. In fact, the more devious sociopaths can easily feign guilt, making them even more deceptive.

For a sociopath, society's rules are there only to see how far they can be bent in order to accomplish whatever it is that he or she needs or wants. They are often the ones who get involved in criminal activity; our prisons are filled to the brim with sociopaths. They are the bad seeds who, growing up as a child of the sixties, I didn't believe really existed. They are the ones whom my young liberal mind saw as victims of poverty, drug abuse, a system gone bad, or severe beating or torture at the hands of cruel parents. Having spent two decades as a psychologist, I have come to believe that those assumptions were—for the most part—wrong. These are the people whom I thought the correctional system was supposed to correct, instead of warehouse. Now I believe that these are people who are best separated from the rest of society, people whom psychology, medicine, or so-called correctional institutions cannot correct.

Trying to resolve a feud, or reconciling a relationship to the point of achieving a sense of closeness or mutuality, can be an illusion at best when the other person is a sociopath. Without the ability to feel guilt, any act of forgiveness is likely to be feigned. More deeply troubling is the fact that any vulnerability you might exhibit, or any amends you make, is likely to be seen by a sociopath as something to be taken advantage of, something that can open up the opportunity for a future emotional injury.

Beth, a forty-six-year-old attorney, knew that she chose her profession in part to prove to her father that she was competent. Recently, she told me that she realized that she chose her profession because she secretly felt that by honing her skills at thinking and arguing, she could stay safe in the world.

As a child, I always knew I was pretty. Everyone told me that. But they also knew I was smart, and that scared them away. I learned that I could handle most men easily. To this day most men are a breeze. They really are a fragile bunch of misfits, you know. I don't know too many who seem like they even fit in their skin.

But my father was different. He was clever, and there was nothing I could do to impress him. He was a master at everything he did. He was a carpenter, an engineer, he could do almost anything. And no matter what I did, I couldn't seem to get to him. Neither could my mother. I think we were all afraid of him. There was something cold and sneaky about him. No matter what anyone did, he never showed much emotion. Frankly, he was a cold bastard. At some point I realized he was married to Mom only because it was convenient for him. He used to travel a lot; none of us really knew why he did, or what he was up to. And when he was gone there'd never be a way of contacting him. So when I was about seventeen I decided I had it with him, I had enough of his crap. So that's when I left home, and I've never looked back. He's never called me. I don't even ask about him when I talk to my mother. She even hates him. God knows why she stays married to him, but that's her problem.

The more we talked about Beth's father, the more clear it became that he seemed unable to feel guilt. When we talked about some of the business dealings he had, as well as rumors of him having a series of women on the side, it seemed that Beth's feelings of hopelessness about him were based on the fact that he truly was unable to give what is required of a real relationship to anyone.

Attempting to reconcile with her father would not bring Beth any closer to him, but instead would likely expose her once again to his callous manipulation and control. Instead of moving toward reconciliation, we worked on grieving for the father she never had, and replacing the stilted and stereotyped view she had of all men with one that was more charitable.

Here are some clues to the kind of person with whom you might have difficulty reconciling:

1. *Lack of empathy.* If someone simply doesn't care about the feelings of others, you are unlikely to achieve a satisfying relationship.

2. *Arrogant, inflated sense of themselves.* When someone maintains an arrogant, superior attitude, he or she is not likely to enter into a mutually rewarding relationship.

3. *Pervasive disregard for the rights of others.* This goes beyond the lack of empathy, into a realm in which you are seen only as an instrument for the other person's needs. You are not recognized as someone with rights of your own.

4. *Consistent irresponsibility.* Someone who doesn't care about the feelings or rights of others usually has no need for responsibility.

5. *Superficial charm.* Sociopaths are often charming; it is a learned routine designed to get the sociopath what he wants from a relationship. Rarely, however, does that charm extend beyond superficial banter.

6. *Deceitful and manipulative.* The truth is an irrelevant concept; the sociopath uses whatever manipulative means he has at his disposal in order to get what he wants.

7. *Irritability and aggressiveness.* Usually, the traits mentioned above are combined with a general irritability and tendency to get into fights.

These qualities are pervasive in sociopaths, characterizing all their relationships, including personal, social, and work relationships. They are attributes that have nearly always existed from childhood on. Given their lack of a capacity to form deep, meaningful relationships, or even to see other people as anything more than objects to be manipulated, it is futile to expend effort reconciling with people who meet these criteria. You would be better off struggling to make sure you populate your life with those with whom you can achieve a mutual, loving relationship.

THE ADDICT

Another group of people with whom true reconciliation is near impossible is the group of people whose lives have been taken over by an addiction to drugs or alcohol. This group includes some people who are addicted to gambling, or to other compulsive behavior that severely impacts their ability to function in relationships. Most addictions work similarly from a psychological point of view, so for simplicity I'll use the example of people who are addicted to drugs. While some people who are addicted to drugs are capable of making deep, meaningful attachments to others, the use of drugs often interferes directly with any attempt to reconcile.

People who are addicted to drugs stop their emotional development at the age they first started using drugs. If someone starts abusing alcohol, marijuana, cocaine, or certain other drugs at the age of fourteen, and uses those drugs to her present age of forty-two, then interacting with that person is like interacting with someone whose emotional age is fourteen. The drug freezes emotional development, for the same reason that it makes reconciliation difficult.

Most drugs work because they are powerful anesthetics. They shield the person who takes them from feeling the effects of painful life experiences. They are also very powerful anti-anxiety agents; they virtually eliminate the feeling of anxiety. Because emotional growth is dependent on using the anxiety and tension of a difficult life experience or conflict to overcome or resolve the conflict, eliminating the anxiety and pain of the experience prevents emotional growth.

Resolving a family feud often requires reliving difficult and emotionally painful life experiences. In order to resolve a feud, you need to grow emotionally. You need to use the anxiety and emotional discomfort of facing someone whom you may have avoided, someone who has caused you great hurt, or someone whom you have caused great hurt, to find the courage to move forward. It requires courage, and, as I mentioned before, courage requires feeling fear. Someone who takes drugs in order to reduce or eliminate feelings of tension, anxiety, or fear is robbed of the basic ingredients needed to move genuinely out of a family feud.

Erica, a fifty-two-year-old writer, recounted to me with a mixture of disgust and resentment her ongoing feud with her brother Patrick, who is two years older. From her earliest memories on, the two of them fought wildly. Erica told me about the abuse she suffered at his hands, but admitted that she found ways of sabotaging him and getting him back. Although they still see each other on holidays, Erica goes out of her way to avoid him. She has harbored deep anger toward him for years, even blaming him for robbing much of her childhood.

As we examined the patterns that existed in her family, it became clear to Erica that she was caught in a multigenerational pattern of intense, enmeshed sibling rivalry. Her father had not spoken to his only brother in many years, after a falling-out that followed a lifelong rivalry between the two. Similarly, her parents fought constantly with each other, and although her mother and father now seemed very close, the two of them seemed near divorce many times as Erica was growing up.

Erica understood clearly the roots of her feud with her brother, and she understood even how she and her brother unconsciously mimicked the constant fighting between her parents as they were growing up.

Despite feeling burned by her brother throughout her life, Erica felt a void where she had always wished her brother could be. She had tried to forgive him on several occasions, and once she apologized to him for the pain she had caused him. Patrick seemed pleased to hear her apology, but at the same time, Erica felt that he "didn't seem to get it."

When Erica mentioned that Patrick was addicted to marijuana, everything came into focus. I asked her how old he was when he started, and she told me that he started when he was about sixteen. She described him further as someone who didn't really understand social cues, someone who made a fool of himself frequently at family gatherings. While he was once intelligent and charming, he now doesn't know when to stop talking. He doesn't seem to feel anything deeply, and *doesn't seem to let anything bother him.* It was no coincidence that Patrick had no meaningful relationships in his life.

When I asked Erica if it felt as though speaking to Patrick was like talking to a sixteen-year-old, she said that that was giving him too much credit. Patrick didn't need to let anything bother him; his daily use of marijuana shunted the pain. There was no possibility of a meaningful reconciliation, because Patrick could never allow himself to feel deeply enough to take it in, and to grow emotionally as a result. Patrick's addiction kept him emotionally frozen in time, and emotionally unavailable.

If someone has a history of taking drugs or abusing alcohol, and with or without the help of a twelve-step program or some sort of therapy has been able to stop using for some length of time, then hope remains for a reconciliation. Usually, someone who was once addicted and has managed to face the addiction has had to work hard. This hard work bodes well for his or her chances of successfully dealing with the emotionally taxing work of reconciliation.

THE SEVERELY DISTURBED

There is one other group of people with whom reconciling a family feud is near impossible. These are people who are so entrenched in their rage that they simply refuse to take part in anything. They usually are so caught up in the multigenerational web of intense rage that they simply can't see where they are and seem to have no ability to see a way out. At times, they are people who suffer from some sort of intractable psychiatric illness. This might include a very deep depression that doesn't respond to treatment, a severe disorder that might cause unpredictable outbursts of rage, or a deeply embedded, long-term paranoia. They often see themselves as life's victims, and have difficulty sustaining relationships with people their own age.

Sean, a shy, handsome thirty-six-year-old graphic artist, complained to me constantly about his older sister. She "destroyed the family," as Sean expressed it, with her constant need for attention. Whenever she entered the room, she insisted that all eyes be on her. She had a remarkable talent for pressing everyone's buttons.

> *There hasn't been a single family get-together that she hasn't ruined. It got to the point that I refused to see her, or even to go home if I knew she was going to be there. No matter what she does, she gets on my nerves. I don't know how she does it. I used to think I was crazy, but everyone else in the family and everyone who's met her says the same thing about her. We've all tried to talk to her, but nothing helps. She's been in and out of therapy for years, but nobody's been able to help her. I don't know what it is about her, but she manages to walk into a peaceful, quiet gathering and within five minutes there's some sort of fight going on. There's something about her that's impossible to describe—she demands that no matter where she is, she's the center of attention. She has this gleam in her eye, and out of nowhere she'll explode, she'll just go off and nobody has any idea why. People are terrified of her. She paralyzes everyone she comes in contact with. I couldn't take it anymore, and I finally told her that I couldn't have her in my life. I couldn't take the stress.*

The fact that Sean's sister has the same effect on everyone in her life, along with the fact that she seemed deeply troubled for much of her life, led me to believe that she was suffering from some sort of intractable psychiatric disorder. While Sean could learn about the disorder, understand the role that his sister plays in the family, and even feel great compassion for her, the chance of his being able to establish a rewarding, close relationship with her is poor. Instead, I suggested to Sean that he strive to understand her, while continuing to set the limits he needed for his own peace of mind. Reconciling with her would likely be futile.

Even if the family member is someone with whom you can't establish a meaningful or intimate relationship, it might be valuable to establish limited contact anyway. For many people who have cut themselves off from family members, civil if not intimate contact has given them a feeling of self-respect. They no longer have to go out of their way to avoid the family member, and they know that they have done everything in their power to repair the damage that was done. This can often be done by setting clear limits for what kind of behavior is acceptable to you and what isn't. It means preparing yourself for more of the same sort of behavior, and using your understanding to deal with the behavior with a newfound equanimity. On the other hand, if establishing contact means putting yourself or others at even greater risk of harm, then it is wise to avoid contact altogether.

The fact that you may be unable to reconcile with your family members should not, however, deter you from doing the work of forgiveness and eliminating blame. While you will not be able to reach the ultimate goal of establishing a healthier, nurturant relationship with the other family member, you can do the work of exoneration. You can go a long way toward relieving yourself of the burden of blame by understanding the multigenerational patterns that may have damaged your family, letting go of the anger and condemnation and breaking the cycle of destructive family patterns in future generations.

One ultimate goal of reconciliation is to learn how to accept your family members for who they are. Inevitably, as you become healthier and more open to trusting, mutual relationships, you may find yourself bumping up against the limits of what other family members can achieve. In many family feud situations, I have found that the reconciliation process has brought other family members, ones you might least expect, into a professional therapeutic relationship as part of their healing. This welcome step usually facilitates the positive emotional growth of the whole family.

Yet there is often a limit to how much any particular family member might achieve or want to achieve in his or her own emotional growth. As you move through the reconciliation process, you'll often find yourself wishing other family members could do more. You might be tempted to be their therapist, and to push them to go further than they may feel able to go. While gentle prodding might be helpful, forcefully insisting on people doing more than they are able always backfires. It is usually based less on a desire to help the other person than it is on your own wish that your family could be something other than it is.

RELINQUISHING THE FANTASY FAMILY

One obstacle to accepting your family members for who they are is the attachment you may have to the belief or fantasy that they are something else. Giving up your fantasy family may not be easy. For many of us, our fantasies of what a family should be like have sustained us through very troubling experiences in our lives. Realizing that we may never have the kind of family we dreamed of can be like losing an old friend.

Melissa, a thirty-eight-year-old banker, told me that she rarely cried. Speaking in measured tones, as was her style, she told me:

I always get what I want. I've made sure of it. I may not get it right away, but I taught myself that there was nothing I couldn't do. The only thing that has ever kept me awake at night was having to face the fact that I didn't have the kind of family I wanted. Every once in a while it still gets to me. Frankly, I'm angry about it. I used to think they were wonderful, the best family on the block. My parents even stayed together—they're still together! They even love each other, I guess, although I never heard them say it. I don't think I actually ever saw them touch each other. I thought they were perfect, until I saw what other kids had. Then I still refused to admit that they couldn't teach me a thing about affection, until I was in college. I had to face the fact that they weren't the best thing since sliced bread, and well, it really made me upset.

Ed, an energetic electrician, was even more direct:

When I finally realized my brother could never be the person I always wished he could be, I just broke down. I fell apart and cried off and on for about a week. I always thought I could count on him, I always thought he

was sensitive and cared about people. When I realized what he was about,
that he was willing to take anybody for what they had, I couldn't bear it.
I tried real hard to let go of my fantasy brother—the good guy who would
always protect me. It was hard, and every once in a while I still start to cry
over it.

Here is an exercise that may be helpful.

Fold a piece of paper in half lengthwise. On one side of the paper write a list or a short description of your "ideal family." On the other side make a list or describe what your family is actually like. There may be some similarities, but you are bound to note some differences. Now, after reviewing both sides of the page, on a separate sheet of paper write a description of what you think your family realistically might become. Decide what changes are reasonable, given your increased knowledge of your family members' personalities and the choices they made and wedded themselves to.

By doing this exercise, you are forcing yourself to face the truth about who your family is and what the members of the family might be expected to accomplish. For some, the results of this exercise can be depressing, because it requires giving up the hope for achieving something that you once might have felt was possible. It feels like giving up the hope that we will get what we need—what we've always wanted. That realization may bring you face to face with loneliness, fear, and sadness. Yet, refusing to face the loss of your fantasy family keeps you stuck as an angry victim.

As a result of not healing the wounds in the family, many people I have met and have worked with are reluctant to have children. When I see couples who have decided to not have children, the single most common reason for this choice that I hear them voice is that they would not want to do to their children what was done to them. These are people who are keenly aware and sensitive to the influence of prior generations on their current relationships, and they know well that not repeating the destructive patterns of the past is a continuous struggle.

While those who choose not to have children keep themselves safe from the burden of repeating the past, they also lose the opportunity to repair the damage done in the past through future generations. Instead, they often work hard in their own lives and in their own relationships to steer a clear course away from the patterns that yielded divisiveness and feuds.

REPAIRING THE NEXT GENERATION

When it is impossible to find a way to forgive or to reconcile with certain family members, there are ways of addressing the pain of an irreconcilable feud. One way is to make every effort not to repeat the multigenerational patterns that have existed in your family. We use all the strategies discussed in this book as tools to consciously monitor our own parenting. We struggle to understand the patterns in our family, keeping a keen eye out for them. If triangulation or enmeshment or entrenched roles have been at the root of your family's feud, carefully examine your own relationships and your own family's patterns for a repetition of the ones that plagued your family history. If there are significant anniversary dates, or ages at which significant traumas occurred in prior generations, carefully watch for the tendency to over-intensify relationships at those key points in time. By going out of your way to insure that the next generation will not repeat the same patterns, you are doing "reconciliation by proxy," essentially working through your children and your children's children as the medium through which you can heal yourself.

Whether or not you have children of your own, another helpful strategy is to "adopt a family." Many people find the family they never had in the family of their spouses. In-laws can be extremely nurturant and kind, and can help give you some of what you may have lost, or never had, with your original family.

For some, the key to healing is to develop close friends. Close friends can often function in similar roles to other family members. They can help you through difficult parenting decisions and help you avoid familiar emotional traps. They can support your forging new territory as you create your own family. When you look to friends to replace some of the functions of the family, it's important that they understand as much about your family history as possible (making sure, of course, that this is a two-way street). They should know the patterns in your family, and you should specifically ask for their help in noticing when you might slip into familiar but destructive patterns with your own children. The better the friend, the more likely he or she is to confront you when you find yourself violating your own principles.

Too many friends may make you feel confused and weak as a parent. Asking five different people for advice and guidance will often yield five different answers. Ultimately, as you would have to do with your own parents anyway, your job is to find your own way, by taking your own risks and remaining responsible for your choices. Find just a few friends whose lives and whose depth of compassion and understanding you respect and trust, talk to them often, share your children with them, listen to their advice and criticism, and then ultimately do the thing you believe in your own heart is right.

REPAIRING SOCIETY

Another way of coping with an irreconcilable feud is to shift the focus from the microcosm of family to the larger family of society. Many psychologists have reported, and research efforts have confirmed, that those who have suffered severe emotional, physical, or sexual abuse don't feel completely liberated from the burden of their painful past until they have spent some time helping others. This is true even when those who have been hurt have confronted the perpetrators and have been involved in formal psychotherapy.

To a large extent, those who have been hurt severely in their lives often ask the question "Why me?" When they free themselves from the burden of self-blame, and even when they thoroughly understand those who have hurt them, they are still left with the question of why they were "chosen" for this fate. In essence, when there is no one left to blame, we often turn to blaming God, or whatever it is we believe that gives order to the universe. A sense of aimless anger remains, brought on by the burden of having suffered so greatly.

The only way to lift this "cosmic burden" is to find some sense of meaning or purpose that the abuse served. Often, there is really no deeply felt lesson that suffering abuse gives us. We can say that it ultimately makes us stronger human beings, or that it teaches us not to trust anyone blindly, but the depth of these lessons doesn't match the depth of suffering that we have encountered; these lessons inevitably fall short of the mark.

The only lesson that seems to have a great enough impact to yield peace of mind is the lesson that having suffered greatly gives us the wisdom and compassion to help others in ways that those who didn't suffer as much cannot. Those who have suffered at the hands of others recognize that there is much suffering in the world, and that we are never alone. We remember feeling terribly alone in our own suffering at the time it occurred, and that feeling serves as a wake-up call that others are in the same position, desperately needing but not knowing how to get help. Finding those who suffer as we did, perhaps not in exactly the same way, and then turning our attention toward them, sharing with them the wisdom to find the pathway out of their pain, gives meaning and purpose to our childhood experiences when no other meaning is available.

Giving ourselves and our time over to helping others is not just something that we can or should do if we suffered tremendous abuse. Nearly all religious traditions require acts of charity or giving, perhaps because of a universal sense that none of us are complete without doing what we can to help others. When a feud with a family member cannot be healed, for whatever reason, then some form of helping others can keep you firmly on the path of your own healing.

FACING YOUR OWN LIMITATIONS

Over the years as I work with families and individuals who struggle to find or create a family that can be a safe harbor, I'm often struck by the intense self-criticism of those on the journey. People often tell me that they worry that they're not doing all they can as quickly as they can. They feel hopelessly stuck in their rage, not able to find the courage to take the next step. Or they simply feel mired in self-doubt and self-criticism, continuing to punish themselves for somehow not being worthy of the family that they wish for.

As I end this book, I'd like to try to put the process in the right perspective. One of my favorite book titles was written by the noted psychologist Paul Watzlawick. The title of the book summed up its contents well: "The Situation Is Hopeless, but Not Serious." His message in part was that even when we face the things we fear the most, we often feel relieved that those things are not as bad as we initially feared. Our hopelessness comes not from truly facing our fears, but from avoiding them, thinking instead that we will be devastated should we face them. Yet, if our families were truly "hopeless," if they could never be what we want them to be, where would we be at that point? When we come to grips with feeling hopeless, we are often able to accept the truth, and the truth is often not nearly as bad as we fear it will be.

The truth may be that our families may only be able to give us a little of what we want from them. In that case, we'll have to face those limitations and turn to ourselves and others to fill the holes where we would have preferred our family members to have been. But a more difficult truth to face might be that we, ourselves, are limited. We can only give, understand, or do so much. Facing what we can't change in ourselves may let in a flood of emotions that we'd prefer not to face, but it also enables us to see what we have accomplished, and how strong we have been. So while the situation we are in might be hopeless, it isn't necessarily that serious, or that awful.

There is no time schedule for healing deep divisions. Resolving a family feud is not like ordering french fries at a fast-food restaurant; you need not judge yourself or be judged by how long it takes to deliver the goods. If along your journey you are faced with a feuding relative who is dying and has only a short time to live, you can do your best under those circumstances to understand and offer the level of forgiveness and reconciliation that feels genuine for you at the time. True reconciliation takes time, and the work may need to continue after the person with whom you are feuding is gone. Be patient, and take the time that's needed to do it right. Small steps tend to work better and prove to last longer than giant leaps.

Committing yourself to resolving a family feud is the first step. It's a step that lasts throughout the entire process, and in fact may last a lifetime. I believe strongly that once that commitment is in place, you can relax. You don't need to punish yourself for every small mistake you make, or even for going slowly along the road. Over time, the commitment you have to making things better will guide you in the right direction.

Index

absolution (distinguished from forgiveness),
    205
abuse
  of children, 89–94, 116–118, 153–155,
    192–193
  healing effects of, 282–283
  spousal, 192–193
  See also sexual molestation and family
    dynamics
accepting limitations of family members,
    271–284
accountability. *See* justice; responsibility
addiction
  blame, 181–182
  and reconciliation, 274–276
  as triangulation, 43–44, 74–75
adopting a family, 281
affairs (extramarital), 69–73
  causes of, 70–72
  children resulting from, 120–121
  effects of, 70, 73, 118–120
age (chronological), role in triggering
    trauma memories, 14, 80
age differences between siblings, 147
alcohol abuse
  myths about, 103–104
  and reconciliation, 274–276
  as triangulation, 43–44, 75
amends, 210–211, 214–26

ancestors
  forgiving, 216–223
  See also multigenerational family history;
    multigenerational patterns
anger. *See* rage
anniversary dates of traumatic events, 14,
    78–80, 85–89
  anniversary depression, 85–89
  in multigenerational family history, 19–21
anniversary depression, 85–89
apologies, 211–212
  contriteness rituals, 214
archival sources for family history, 174
assignment of family roles, 133–135
authenticity in confrontations, 245–248
  integrity, 259–260
  language, 248–251, 254
  See also responsibility
avoiding reconciliation, 260–261

"baby of the family" role, 129–131, 149–150
  See also youngest children
basic relationships in genograms, 159–161
basic symbols for genograms, 158–159
behavior patterns and family history, 14–15
  See also multigenerational patterns
benefits of exonerating ancestors, 218–219
birth circumstances and family history,
    17–18, 19, 120–121

birthdays
  significance of, 78–80
  See also family events
birth order, 19, 87–88
  and family roles, 130–131, 146–150
  and gender expectations, 147
  middle children, 148–149
  and new children, 150
  oldest children, 147–148
  only children, 149
  youngest children, 148
blame, 175–202
  antidotes to, 189–191, 194–201, 282–283
  between couples, 72–73, 182–184, 186, 188–189
  distortion in, 182–184, 186–187
  and guilt, 201–202
  justifiable, 175–176
  moving beyond, 154–155, 187–202, 218–219, 226–227
  multigenerational patterns, 187–189
  and perspective, 180–181, 197–201
  problems of, 176–177, 181–187
  as a protective device, 177, 197–198
  purposes of, 177–181, 196–197
  responsibility differentiated from, 193–194
  self-blame, 177–179
  as self-righteousness, 180–181
  as threat, 185–186
  victim role reinforced by, 181, 184–185, 189, 198–200
  See also forgiveness
burial rituals, *213–214*
business. *See* careers
button-pressing behavior, 255

careers
  family influence on career choices, 105–107, 132, 272–273
  as triangulation, 73–74
causes of feuds. *See* origins of feuds
change, 254–269
  expectations of, 238–239, 258–259
  integrity in, 259–260
  language of, 248–251, 254
  over time, 238–239, 242, 258–259, 284
  small changes, 258–259, 264, 278–279
changing family roles, 128–131, 140–146, 149–150, 222–223
child abuse, 89–94, 116–118, 153–155, 192–193
  See also enmeshment; sexual molestation and family dynamics; triangulation
children

abuse by parents, 89–94, 116–118, 153–155, 192–193
birth circumstances, 17–18, 19, 120–121
child-focused triangles, 57–63
child-stepparent feuding, 65–66, 136
dartboard children, 59–60
disabled children and family dynamics, 47, 50–51
and extramarital affairs, 70, 73
fatherhood of children (biological), 120–121, 189–191
father's jealousy of, 46–47
football children, 60–61
gender expectations, 86–87, 137–140, 144–146, 147
genogram symbols for, 160–161
as marital partner substitutes, 58–59
mental illness in, 107–108
as parents, 61–63, 143–144, 147
role assignments, 134–144
sexual molestation of, 89–94, 116–118
tasks of, 2–3
therapy for, 2, 153–155
  See also birth order; parenting
co-dependency and healthy dependency, 32–33
commitment to justice, 189–191
communication
  authentic, 245–248
  exercise, 247–248
  language for reconciliation, 248–251
  nonverbal, 254
compassion
  from abuse, 282–283
  and detachment, 254–258
  and forgiveness, 207–208
  lack of, 273–274
  and reconciliation, 176–177, 180–181, 198–201, 207–208, 239
compulsive behavior and the capacity for reconciliation, 274–276
concealing rage in confrontations, 245–247
conflicts
  among siblings, 48–53
  creating common enemies to resolve, 68
  enmeshment as cause, 26–27
  internal conflicts, 219
  and parent-child triangulation, 59–60, 128–131
  unresolved, 12–13
confrontations, 225–251
  authenticity, 245–248
  best-case scenarios, 244–245
  contacting family members, 228–229, 231–237, 240

emotional intensity of, 226–227, 245–247,
260–264, 265, 268–269
fallout, 243–245
language for, 248–251, 254
locations for, 265–267
of myths, 104
peaceful confrontations, 231
planning, 241–245
of secrets, 261–263
timing, 240–241, 260–264
worst-case scenarios, 242–243
confusion stemming from family myths,
99–100
contacting family members, 228–229,
231–237
and dislike of family members, 237–238
expectations of change, 238–239,
258–259
letters, 232–236
limited contact, 278–279
subjects to discuss, 236–237
telephone calls, 231–232, 240, 267
context for reconciliation, 254–269
external context, 260–268
internal context, 254–260
"contingent family" created by blame,
185–186
contriteness rituals, 214
couples
blame between, 72–73, 182–184, 186,
188–189
childless couples, 280–281
enmeshment, 26–28, 29–32, 34, 36–41
extramarital affairs, 69–73
gender expectations between, 145–146
genogram symbols for, 159–160
in-law triangles, 54–57, 65
mate selection, 92
rage between, 69–74
secrets between, 111
spousal abuse, 192–193
workaholism's effect on, 73–74
See also children; divorce; parenting;
triangulation
courage as an element of reconciliation,
225, 229–231, 275
cultural influences on family roles, 137–138
cutoffs (cutting off family relationships),
5–6, 33–35, 36–37, 226–229, 255–256

damaging properties of blame, 176–177, 185
denial, 93
myths as, 98–99, 100, 103–104, 108

secrets and, 114
of sexual molestation, 93, 227, 239,
266–267
dependency in relationships
healthy dependency, 32–33
See also enmeshment
depression
from avoiding fears, 283–284
from pain and anger, 268–269
from self-blame, 178
from sexual molestation, 227–228
from traumatic event anniversaries,
85–89
detachment
compassionate, 254–258
rage camouflaged as, 257
disease. *See* illness
dislike of family members as a barrier to
contact, 237–238
distance in family relationships, 5–6, 33–35,
36–37, 226–229, 255–256
See also contacting family members
distortions
from anger, 237–238
from blame, 182–184, 186–187
from myths, 97–98
divorce
ex-spouse feuding, 31, 63–65, 67–68
extramarital affairs as fuel for, 69
genogram symbols for, 159–160
in-law triangles as cause, 57
parent-child enmeshment following,
30–31
and sexual abuse, 117
drug abuse
and emotional development, 275–276
myths about, 103–104
and reconciliation, 274–276
as triangulation, 43–44, 75

eldest children, 147–148
See also birth order; siblings
emotional connection symbols in
genograms, 165–167
emotional history. *See* family history
emotional intensity, 12–14
and confrontations, 226–227, 245–247,
260–264, 265, 268–269
detachment from, 254–258
distortions created by, 237–238
language to express, 248–251, 254
from trauma, 78–80
from withheld information, 20–21
See also blame; enmeshment; feelings;
rage; trauma

emotional maturity
    anger as a move toward achieving,
        129–131
    blame as a deterrent to, 176–177
    drug abuse and, 275–276
    in mate selection, 92
emotional traps, 255
emotional understanding, 198–201
emotions. See feelings
enmeshment, 23–41
    and blame, 187–189
    co-dependency, 32–33
    in couples, 26–28, 29–32, 36–39
    cutting off family relationships to relieve,
        33–35, 36–37
    healthy dependency differentiated from,
        32
    independence and, 28–35, 40
    influence on future relationships, 34
    intensity as a hallmark of, 31, 39
    loss of identity, 28–32
    multigenerational influences, 35–41
    parent-child enmeshment, 25–26, 36–39
    rage stemming from, 28–32
    role in conflict, 26–27
exonerating ancestors, 218–223
    goals and benefits, 218–219
    journaling family history, 221–223
exoneration, 206, 208–209, 214, 278
    See also exonerating ancestors
expectations
    of change, 238–239
    See also family expectations; gender
        expectations
expectations in the family, 127–151
    cultural influences, 137–138
    letting go of, 271–284
    See also family roles
expressing emotions. See communication;
    confrontations
ex-spouses and feuding, 31, 63–65, 67–68
external context reconciliation, 260–268
extramarital affairs, 69–73, 118–120

failure in confrontations, planning for,
    242–243
fallback plans for confrontations, 242–243
fallout from confrontations, 243–245
families
    creating, 281–282
    idealized, 279–281
    See also children; couples; family events;
        family expectations; family fights;
        family history; family roles; family

therapy; multigenerational family
    history; parenting; stepfamilies
family events
    and confrontations, 241
    and family roles, 131–132
    and reconciliations, 261–264, 268–269
    See also holidays
family expectations, 127–151
    fantasy families, 279–281
    See also family roles
family feuds. See feuds
family fights
    feuds differentiated from, 11–12
    healthy fighting, 11
family history, 14–21
    archival information sources, 174
    birth circumstances, 17–18
    genograms, 157–174, 209
    interviewing for, 165, 168–169, 171–173
    secrets in, 113
    See also multigenerational family history;
        multigenerational patterns; trauma;
        triangulation
family myths. See myths
family roles, 130–151
    assignment of, 133–136
    birth order and, 146–150
    changing roles, 128–131, 140–146,
        149–150, 222–223
    and confrontation fallout, 244
    cultural influences, 137–138
    gender roles, 139–140, 144–146
    illness, 131–133, 135–136
    multigenerational roles, 135–136
    multiple roles, 142–143, 151
    problems of, 139–143
    purpose of, 132
    at reunions, 131–132
    role reversal, 143–144
    trauma to bring out, 131
    See also victim role
family therapy, 3–4
fantasy families, 279–281
    ideal family exercise, 280
fatherhood of children (biological), 120–121,
    189–191
fathers-in-law, triangles involving, 56–57
fathers. See parenting
fear
    facing up to, 284
    useful aspects of, 230–231
feelings
    diminishing through language use,
        249–250
    emotional understanding, 198–201

forgiving attitude, 207–208
gender expectations about expressing, 145
reluctance to experience, 125
sensitization to, 114
small changes to alter, 258–259, 284
See also emotional intensity; rage
feuds, 4–6, 9–12
circularity of injuries, 192–194
emotional intensity, 12–14
with ex-spouses, 31, 63–65, 67–68
family history, 14–21
feud-naming exercise, 256–257
fights differentiated from, 5, 11–12
healing from, 10
injuries inflicted by, 10, 11–12
See also family history; origins of feuds; reconciliation
fights
feuds differentiated from, 5, 11
healthy fighting, 11
finances as a family secret, 123–124
forceful attitude to reconciliation, 278–279
forgetting (distinguished from forgiveness), 204–205
forgiveness, 203–223
of ancestors, 209, 216–223
apologies, 211–212
attitude of forgiveness, 207–208
authentic forgiveness, 246–247
definition, 205–207
exoneration, 206, 208–209, 214, 218–223, 278
outright forgiveness, 206–207, 209–211
overt forgiveness, 211–214
over time, 206, 210–211, 258–259, 284
rebuilding trust, 209–211
and reconciliation, 154–155, 203–223, 246–247
and responsibility, 205, 208–209
and restitution, 210–211, 214–216
rituals for, 211–214
self-forgiveness, 214–216, 219
forms, interview form for genograms, 168–169
friends as family members, 281–282
funerals. *See* family events

gender expectations, 86–87, 137–140, 144–146
and birth order, 147
going against, 139–140, 145
generational flip-flop, 60–63
genograms, 157–174, *162, 164, 166*
basic relationships, 159–161

basic symbols, 158–159
critical events, 163
emotional connection symbols, 165–167
information sources and methods, 165, 168–169, 171–174
interpreting, 170–171, 191
uses of, 209, 218–223
ghost of former spouse (in remarriage), 67–68
goals of exonerating ancestors, 218–219
"good child" role, 141
grandparent triangles, 68–69
grief
exoneration, 206, 208–209, 214
expressing, 196–197
impact on families, 83–84
See also forgiveness; trauma
guidelines for letters to family members, 233–234
guilt, 201–202

healing from feuds, 10
healthy fighting, 11
healthy relationships as a threat, 244–245
helping others as a way of healing abuse, 282–283
history
of family feuds in society, 4–5
See also family history
holidays
and family role-playing, 131
and reconciliations, 261–264
as a trigger for feuds, 85–86
See also family events
honoring pain, 194–201
See also forgiveness
hopelessness
from avoiding fears, 283–284
See also depression
humor as an element of reconciliation, 257
hurt
honoring, 194–201
See also forgiveness

idealized families, 279–281
identity
gaining through family history research, 222–223
See also family roles; identity loss
identity loss
in enmeshed relationships, 28–32
in feuds, 194–196
in role playing, 140–143
illegitimate children, 120–121

illness
    family role expectations, 131–133,
        135–136
    mental illness, 107–108
    secrets about, 125–126
improvement. See change
incest, 89–94, 116–118, 227–228, 239
independence
    in enmeshed relationships, 28–35, 40
    and healthy dependency, 32–33
    illusory, 33–35
    rage as a means to, 129–130
    self-knowledge as a key to, 195–196
    See also identity loss; victim role
injuries inflicted by feuds, 10, 11–12
in-law triangles, 54–57
    in stepfamilies, 65
insecurity
    from child-parent role reversal, 143–144
    from family myths, 100–101, 103–104
    from family secrets, 113–114
insight differentiated from understanding,
    199–200
integrity, 259–260
    See also authenticity; justice
intensity as an element of feuds. See
    emotional intensity
internal conflicts, 219
internal context of reconciliation, 254–260
interpreting genograms, 170–171, 191
interviewing for genograms, 165, 171–173
    form, 168–169

jealousy. See triangulation
jobs
    family influence on, 105–107, 132,
        272–273
    as triangulation, 73–74
journals as tools for reconciliation, 221–223
justice
    commitment to, 189–191
    and forgiveness, 207–208
    integrity, 259–260
    making amends, 210–211, 214–216
    questionnaire, 191
    responsibility and, 193–194
    See also forgiveness; responsibility

language for reconciliations, 248–251
    exercise, 249
    nonverbal messages, 254
letters to family members, 232–236
    examples, 234–236
    guidelines, 233–234

letting go of expectations for family
    members, 271–284
lies
    blame and, 182–184, 186–187
    secrets as, 110, 121–122
life events in multigenerational family
    history, 171
limitations
    accepting in family members, 271–284
    in ourselves, 283–284
limited contact with family members,
    278–279
locations for confrontations, 265–267
loss of control through blame, 184
loss of identity
    in enmeshed relationships, 28–32
    in feuds, 194–196
    in role playing, 140–143
loss. See trauma

making amends, 210–211, 214–216
marital partners, children substituted for,
    58–59
marriages
    genogram symbols for, 159–160
    See also couples; divorce; parenting;
        stepfamilies
martyrdom (distinguished from
    forgiveness), 205
men's roles. See family roles; gender
    expectations
mental illness
    myths about, 107–108
    reconciliation deterred by, 276–279
    sociopaths, 271–274
middle children, 148–149
    See also birth order; siblings
mismatched family roles, 139–140
mothers-in-law, triangles involving, 54–56
mothers. See parenting
motivation through family myths, 99
mourning, 196–197
    See also grief; trauma
multigenerational family history, 14–15
    anniversary dates of traumatic events, 14,
        19–21, 78–80, 85–89
    enmeshment, 35–41
    and gender expectations, 86–87, 137–140,
        144–146, 147
    journals, 221–223
    life events, 171
    myths, 94
    responsibility of descendants for
        ancestors' actions, 217
    structural issues, 170

traumatic events, 80–84
and triangulation, 51–53
withholding information, 20–21
See also genograms; multigenerational patterns
multigenerational patterns, 14–15, 18–22, 37–41, 170–171, 216–223
birth order, 19, 87–88
blame, 187–189
and childless couples, 280–281
cultural influences, 137–138
exonerating ancestors, 216–223
in extramarital affairs, 69–70
generational flip-flops as, 63
genograms to show, 166–167, 209
myths, 108
parenting, 198–199
physical characteristics, 88–89
and reconciliation, 16–17, 21–22, 157–174, 197–198
repairing, 281–284
role expectations, 135–136
secrets, 261–263
sexual molestation, 89–94
See also multigenerational family history
multiple family roles, 142–143, 151
myths, 94, 97–109
case histories, 103–104, 106–107
"close family" myth, 102
confronting, 104
as denial, 98–99, 100, 103–104, 108
as distortion, 97–98
drug and alcohol abuse myths, 103–104
failure myths, 106–107
fantasy families, 279–281
"happy family" myth, 101–102
insecurity stemming from, 100–101
as legends, 95–97
mental illness, 107–108
as protective devices, 98–99
purposes of, 95–99
secrets differentiated from, 109–110, 121–122
success and wealth myths, 104–107
as teaching tools, 96
and trauma, 101–102
See also secrets

naming family feuds, 256–257
neutral places for confrontations, 265–267

oldest children, 147–148
See also birth order; siblings
only children, 149
opportunities for confrontation, 240–241

origins of feuds, 12
child abuse, 155
enmeshment, 28–32, 187–189
family history research to determine, 17–19
myths and secrets, 97, 100–101, 126
role expectations, 138–143, 151
secrets, 109, 115–116
traumas, 78, 85–86, 94
triangulation, 46–47
outright forgiveness, 206–207, 209–211
overt acts of forgiveness, 211–214

pain
honoring, 194–201
See also forgiveness; grief; rage
parent-child enmeshment, 25–26, 36–39
and divorce, 30–31
parent-child triangulation, 44–53, 57–63
children as dartboards, 59–60
children as footballs, 60–61
children as marital partner substitutes, 58–59
children as parents, 61–63, 143–144, 147
in-law triangles, 54–57, 65
and reconciliation, 268–269
in stepfamilies, 63–69
parenting
abusive, 153–155
arrival of new new children, 150
enmeshed parents, 39–40
enmeshment of parent and child, 25–26, 30–31, 36–40
gender expectations for children, 86–87, 137–140, 144–146, 147
generational flip-flop, 60–63
grandparents as parents, 68–69
multigenerational patterns, 198–199
stepparenting, 66–67
support in, 281–282
See also family roles; multigenerational family history; parent-child triangulation
patterns
family roles, 129–131
repetition compulsion, 89–90
in sibling conflict, 52–53
triangulation as an avoidance pattern, 44
See also multigenerational patterns
peaceful confrontations, 231
perpetrators distinguished from victims, 192–194, 199–200
perspective
as a means to reconciliation, 180–181, 197–201
See also forgiveness; understanding

physical characteristics in family dynamics, 88–89
planning confrontations, 241–245
professional choices stemming from family influence, 104–107, 132, 272–273
protection devices
blame as, 177, 197–198
myths as, 98–99
secrets as, 110–112, 124–125
silence as, 113
psychiatric illness
family myths about, 107–108
reconciliation deterred by, 276–279
sociopaths, 271–274
psychotherapy
for children, 2, 153–155
for families, 3–4
public places for confrontations, 265–267
punishment. *See* justice

rage
as an independence quest, 120–130
between spouses, 69–74
as a bond with others, 31–32, 50
in confrontations, 226–227, 245–247, 268–269
detachment camouflaged as, 257
distortions created by, 237–238
editing out of letters, 235
and emotional understanding, 198–201
enmeshment as cause, 28–32
as loss of control, 184–185
in parent-child triangulation, 59–60, 268–269
physical characteristics provoking, 88–89
and psychiatric disorders, 276–279
self-blame as a substitute for, 177–179
from sexual molestation, 90
and suicidal tendencies, 29
understanding origins of, 176–177
rational understanding, 197–198
rebuilding trust, 209–211, 214–216
reconciliation, 6
with addicts, 274–276
at family events, 261–264, 268–269
authenticity, 245–248
avoiding, 260–261
and blame, 154–155, 175–202
compassion, 176–177, 180–181, 198–201, 207–208, 239, 254–258
confrontations, 225–251
contacting family members, 228–229, 231–237, 278–279
context for, 254–269

courage as an element of, 225, 229–231, 275
difficult or impossible cases, 271–281
dislike of family members, 237–238
exoneration, 218–223, 278
expectations of change, 238–239, 258–259
in family therapy, 3–4
and fantasy families, 279–281
forceful attitudes to, 278–279
forgiveness, 154–155, 203–223
humor as an element of, 257
journals, 221–223
multigenerational patterns as a key to, 16–17, 21–22, 157–174, 197–198
perspective, 180–181, 197–201
with psychologically disturbed people, 271–279
repercussions of, 243–245
restitution, 210–211, 214–216
rituals of, 211–214
safe methods, 197–198, 229–231
truth, 187, 189–191
understanding, 194–201
See also change
relationships
people unable to form, 271–274
See also couples; family history; genograms; parenting
remarriage and ex-spouse feuding, 63–65, 67–68
repairing multigenerational patterns, 281–284
researching family history. *See* family history
resolving feuds. *See* reconciliation
responsibility
blame differentiated from, 193–194
circularity of injuries, 192–194
and forgiveness, 205, 208–209
and guilt, 201–202
justice as an element of, 189–191
for our ancestors' actions, 217
rebuilding trust, 214–216
understanding as a key to, 194–202
See also authenticity; justice
restitution, 210–211, 214–216
rituals, 211–214
reunions. *See* family events
righteousness. *See* self-righteousness
rigid family role expectations, 140–142
risk-taking and well-being, 229
rituals
burial rituals, 213–214
contriteness rituals, 214

and forgiveness, 211–214
role reversal, 143–144
roles in the family. *See* family roles
role strain, 142–143

sacrifice (distinguished from forgiveness),
    205
safety in the family, 2–3, 153–155
    blame and, 185
    fear as an ally, 230
    rebuilding trust, 209–211, 214–216
    and reconciliation, 197–198, 229–231
    sociopaths in the family, 272–273
    See also abuse; enmeshment; sexual
        molestation and family dynamics;
        triangulation
scripts. *See* family roles
secrets, 109–126
    problems of, 113–116
    about traumas, 110–111, 124–125
    adoption, 120
    alcoholism, 121–122
    and denial, 114
    homosexuality, 122–123
    money, 123–124
    myths differentiated from, 109–110,
        121–122
    as protective devices, 110–112, 124–125
    purposes of, 110–112
    and reconciliation, 261–263
    sexual molestation, 91, 116–118, 227–228,
        239
    trauma, 91, 110–111, 124–125
    trust broken by, 114–116
    See also myths
self-blame, 177–179
self-forgiveness, 214–216, 219
self-limitations, 283–284
self-protection through secrets, 111–112
self-righteousness
    blame as, 180–181
    as a reconciliation deterrent, 155
self-understanding, 96, 194–198
service to society, 282–283
sexual molestation and family dynamics,
        89–94, 227–228
    case histories, 227–228, 239, 265–267
    denial, 93, 227, 239, 266–267
    mate selection, 92
    as a secret, 116–118
    in stepfamilies, 117
siblings
    age differences between, 147
    multigenerational history's effect on,
        19–21

sibling conflict patterns, 52–53
    and triangulation, 48–53, 128–131
    See also birth order
sisters. *See* siblings
society
    history of feuds in, 4–5
    influences on families, 137–138
    secrets for gaining approval of, 112
    serving, 282–283
spiritual dimensions of feuds, 12
spousal abuse, 192–193
spousal relationships. *See* couples
stepfamilies, 63–69
    child-stepparent feuding, 65–66, 136
    and ex-spouse feuding, 63–65, 67–68
    grandparent triangles, 68–69
    perfect stepparent triangulation, 66–67
    sexual abuse within, 117
stories as family links, 95–97
    See also myths
structural issues in multigenerational family
        history, 170
subjects to discuss when contacting family
        members, 236–237
substance abuse
    family myths and, 103–104
    as triangulation, 43–44, 75
success at reconciliation, 244–245
success and wealth myths, 104–107
suffering as a source of compassion, 283
suicide
    case histories, 14, 81–84
    impact on family, 14, 80–84
    rage linked to, 29
    sexual molestation linked to, 227–228
support in parenting, 281–282
symbols for genograms, 158–159

talking to family members. *See* contacting
        family members
teaching lessons with family myths, 96
telephone calls between family members,
        231–232, 240, 267
tension
    in feuds, 12–14
    from withheld information, 20–21
    See also emotional intensity
therapy
    for children, 2, 153–155
    for families, 3–4
third parties in relationships. *See*
        triangulation
threat
    blame as, 185–186
    healthy relationships as, 244–245

time element
    in change, 238–239, 242, 258–259, 284
    in forgiveness, 206, 210–211
timing for confrontations, 240–241,
        260–264
tragic events. *See* trauma
traps, emotional, 255
trauma, 77–94
    anniversaries of, 14, 78–80, 85–89
    and birth order, 87–88
    denial, 93
    and family role-playing, 131
    and gender expectations, 86–87
    holiday seasons and, 85–86
    honoring pain, 194–201
    loss experienced in, 77–78
    and mate selection, 92
    multigenerational influence, 80–84
    myths and, 101–102
    secrets about, 91, 110–111, 124–125
    trigger events for traumatic memories,
        78–80, 84–89
    See also abuse; grief; sexual molestation
triangulation, 43–75
    addiction as, 43–44, 74–75
    alcohol and drug abuse as, 43–44, 75
    as avoidance, 44
    and confrontation fallout, 243–244
    extramarital affair triangles, 69–73
    in-law triangles, 54–57, 65
    and multigenerational family history, 51
    parent-child triangulation, 44–53, 57–63
    rage as the root of, 53
    sexual abuse as, 117–118
    and sibling relationships, 48–53, 128–131
    in stepfamilies, 63–69
    work as, 73–74
trust
    broken by secrets, 114–118
    rebuilding, 209–211, 214–216
truth
    authenticity in confrontations, 245–248
    commitment to, 189–191
    distorted by blame, 182–184, 186–187
    and fantasy families, 279–281
    integrity, 259–260

reconciliation effected by, 187
    See also authenticity in confrontations;
        justice

uncles and aunts as family history sources,
        172–173
understanding
    definition, 199–200
    emotional understanding, 198–201
    and guilt, 201–202
    rational understanding, 197–198
    and reconciliation, 176–177
    self-understanding, 96, 194–198
    See also forgiveness
unresolved conflicts, 12–13

victim role
    blame as a reinforcer, 181, 184–185, 189
    and fantasy families, 279–281
    and forgiveness, 212
    healing through service to society,
        282–283
    victim/perpetrator distinctions, 192–194,
        199–200
    See also family roles; sexual molestation

wealth and success myths, 104–107
weddings. *See* family events
withdrawing from family relationships, 5–6,
        33–35, 36–37
    See also contacting family members
withholding information, 20–21
women's roles. *See* family roles; gender
        expectations
work
    family influence on, 105–107, 132
    as triangulation, 73–74
worst-case scenarios for confrontations,
        242–243
    letter writing, 232–236

youngest children, 148
    "baby of the family" role, 129–131,
        149–150
    See also birth order; siblings